1978

THE REVERSIBLE WORLD

Symbolic Inversion in Art and Society

SYMBOL, MYTH, AND RITUAL SERIES
General Editor: Victor Turner

Barbara A. Babcock, ed., *The Reversible World: Symbolic Inversion in Art and Society*

Shlomo Deshen and Moshe Shokeid, *The Predicament of Homecoming: Cultural and Social Life of North African Immigrants in Israel*

Mircea Eliade, *Australian Religions: An Introduction*

Frederick Karl Errington, *Karavar: Masks and Power in a Melanesian Ritual*

Raymond Firth, *Symbols: Public and Private**

Ronald L. Grimes, *Symbol and Conquest: Public Ritual and Drama in Santa Fe, New Mexico*

Alf Hiltebeitel, *The Ritual of Battle: Krishna in the* Mahābhārata

Eva Hunt, *The Transformation of the Hummingbird: Cultural Roots of a Zinacantecan Mythical Poem*

Bennetta Jules-Rosette, *African Apostles: Ritual and Conversion in the Church of John Maranke*

Frank E. Manning, *Black Clubs in Bermuda: Ethnography of a Play World*

Sally Falk Moore and Barbara G. Myerhoff, eds., *Symbol and Politics in Communal Ideology: Cases and Questions**

Nancy D. Munn, *Walbiri Iconography: Graphic Representation and Cultural Symbolism in a Central Australian Society*

Barbara G. Myerhoff, *Peyote Hunt: The Sacred Journey of the Huichol Indians**

Victor Turner, *Dramas, Fields, and Metaphors: Symbolic Action in Human Society**

Victor Turner, *Revelation and Divination in Ndembu Ritual**

Victor Turner, *The Ritual Process: Structure and Anti-Structure*†

* Also available in a Cornell Paperbacks edition.
† Available from Cornell University Press only in a Cornell Paperbacks edition.

THE REVERSIBLE WORLD

Symbolic Inversion in
Art and Society

Edited and with an Introduction by

BARBARA A. BABCOCK

Cornell University Press

ITHACA AND LONDON

First published 1978 by Cornell University Press.
Published in the United Kingdom by Cornell University Press Ltd., 2-4 Brook Street, London W1Y 1AA.

International Standard Book Number 0-8014-1112-2
Library of Congress Catalog Card Number 77-3113
Printed in the United States of America by Vail-Ballou Press, Inc.
Librarians: Library of Congress cataloging information appears on the last page of the book.

Let's have the giddy world turn'd the heeles upward
And sing a rare blacke *Sanctus,* on his head,
Of all things out of order.

Ben Jonson, *Time Vindicated*

Foreword

Recently both the research and theoretical concerns of many anthropologists have once again been directed toward the role of symbols—religious, mythic, aesthetic, political, and even economic—in social and cultural processes. Whether this revival is a belated response to developments in other disciplines (psychology, ethology, philosophy, linguistics, to name only a few), or whether it reflects a return to a central concern after a period of neglect, is difficult to say. In recent field studies, anthropologists have been collecting myths and rituals in the context of social action, and improvements in anthropological field technique have produced data that are richer and more refined than heretofore; these new data have probably challenged theoreticians to provide more adequate explanatory frames. Whatever may have been the causes, there is no denying a renewed curiosity about the nature of the connections between culture, cognition, and perception, as these connections are revealed in symbolic forms.

Although excellent individual monographs and articles in symbolic anthropology and comparative symbology have recently appeared, a common focus or forum that can be provided by a topically organized series of books has not been available. The present series is intended to fill this lacuna. It is designed to include not only field monographs and theoretical and comparative studies by anthropologists, but also work by scholars in other disciplines, both scientific and humanistic. The appearance of studies in such a forum encourages emulation, and emulation can produce fruitful new theories. It is therefore our hope that the series will serve as a house of many mansions, providing hospitality for the practitioners of any discipline that has a serious and creative concern with comparative symbology. Too often, disciplines are sealed off, in sterile pedantry, from significant intellectual influences. Nevertheless, our primary aim is to bring to public attention works on ritual and myth written by anthropologists, and our readers will find a variety of strictly anthropological approaches ranging from formal analyses of systems of symbols to empathetic accounts of divinatory and initiatory rituals.

VICTOR TURNER

University of Virginia

Acknowledgments

I am profoundly indebted to Victor Turner, without whose encouragement in person and in print this volume would not have come to be. He is in many respects its *magister ludi*. I am also indebted to Raymond Firth, who taught me much about symbols and encouraged my penchant for negation; to Clifford Geertz, who has urged us all to attend directly to "counteractive patterns of culture"; and to James Boon, whose comments and criticisms were invaluable in revising and reorganizing this collection of essays. I am especially grateful both to the contributors to this volume and to the other participants in the Forms of Symbolic Inversion Symposium held at the 1972 meetings of the American Anthropological Association, whose papers are not included here, for having turned a vague notion into a useful term of art. Among the latter, the papers by Brian Sutton-Smith, "Games of Order and Disorder," and Edward Norbeck, "Rites of Reversal in Cross-cultural View," were particularly important; I regret not being able to include them.

Many colleagues in the Departments of English and Anthropology at the University of Texas provided constant advice and stimulus. I am grateful to Richard N. Adams, Richard Bauman, and Dina and Joel Sherzer for their contributions within and without the symposium, and to Joseph Doherty, Anthony Hilfer, R. J. Kaufmann, Paul Schmidt, Warwick Wadlington, and Susan Wittig, who have participated in fact if not in deed in helping me pervert good sense. My greatest thanks go to Roger Abrahams, who helped immeasurably to coordinate both the symposium and this volume, and pushed me on when the difficulties of celebrating the negative seemed insurmountable.

The preparation of this manuscript was made possible by a grant from the University Research Institute of the University of Texas. I am very grateful to the Institute, the typing pool of the Department of English, and Frances Terry for giving me considerable assistance.

BARBARA A. BABCOCK

Austin, Texas

Contents

12   Contents

Introduction

BARBARA A. BABCOCK

The things of this world can be truly perceived only by looking at them backwards.

Balthasar Gracian, *El Criticon* [1]

The study of culture is predicated upon the distinctive trait of man that he is a creator and user of symbols, that he has "speech . . . to express his excellencie of mind over other creatures."[2] As Kenneth Burke reminds us, however, "the study of man as the specifically word-using animal requires special attention to this distinctive marvel, the negative" (1968:419). Not only is "this ingenious addition to the universe solely a product of human symbol systems" (p. 10), but symbol-using itself "demands a feeling for the negative (beginning in the Korzybskian admonition that the word for the thing is *not* the thing). A specifically symbol-using animal will necessarily introduce a symbolic ingredient into every experience. Hence, every experience will be imbued with negativity" (p. 469). And, since metaphor itself is a special kind of negation—"One uses metaphor without madness insofar as one spontaneously knows that the literal implication of the figure is *not* true" (p. 462)—it is profoundly ironic that studies of the social and artistic uses of metaphor have but

[1] Written in 1651 by a Spanish Jesuit, this epigraph is taken from a novel in which Proteus is the minister to a king who reigns over an inverted city where nothing is as it seems to be. The statement refers to Proteus, who so dissimulates that he can be seen only if one turns one's back and uses a mirror. The epigraph is quoted both by Rousset in his discussion of the baroque motif of *le monde renversé* (1954:24) and by Genette in his discussion of the principles of baroque poetry (1966:19).

[2] This statement was made by Ben Jonson in his *Discoveries*, and is quoted by Donaldson in his superb study of the comic uses of inversion (1970:64).

rarely examined directly this "distinctive marvel," the ability to negate. Studies of symbolic processes, whether by social scientists, philosophers, or literary critics, tend rather to obscure the centrality of negation to the systems of signification by which we live and communicate (including their own enterprise), and to ignore such outstanding questions as "what is the relation between the self-eliminating generation of metaphor and concepts of negative form?" (Derrida 1974:9).[3]

This lack of attention is understandable. There are certain dangers inherent in celebrating the negative, and in focusing on the negative we run counter to some of the strongest psychological habits of our culture and to the still tenacious positivist emphasis of social science. Even so, disregard is not excusable, and it is our intention in this book to attend directly, if not exclusively, to "counteractive patterns of culture," that is, to those "elements of a culture's own negation which in an ordinary, quite un-Hegelian fashion are included within it" (Geertz 1966:65). As an organizing concept for these diverse perspectives on cultural negation, I have used the term "symbolic inversion." This concept and the purposes of the Forms of Symbolic Inversion Symposium, at which many of these papers were presented, were described as follows:

"Symbolic inversion" may be broadly defined as any act of expressive behavior which inverts, contradicts, abrogates, or in some fashion presents an alternative to commonly held cultural codes, values, and norms be they linguistic, literary or artistic, religious, or social and political. Although, perhaps because, inversion is so basic to symbolic processes, so crucial to expressive behavior, it has not, until recently, been analytically isolated except in its obvious and overt forms such as "rituals of rebellion," role reversal, and institutionalized clowning. Precisely because it is such a widely observed form of symbolic action and because the nature of symbols and of expressive behavior has become a focus of anthropological

[3] In the same essay in which he raises this question, Derrida implies a universal negative character or sense of devaluation in metaphor by arguing that such words as *ab-solute*, *in-finite*, and *not-being* (in Hegel) reveal the negative character of the abstractions of metaphysics.

concern, symbolic inversion merits specific discussion. Recent considerations and re-considerations of forms of inversion have both
criticized and offered alternative explanations to the now-classic anthropological and psychological explanations of such phenomena;
have focused attention on inversions other than those specific to a
formal ritual context; and have begun to relate various levels and
types of inversion. The purpose of this symposium is to bring
together anthropologists, folklorists, historians, psychologists,
linguists, and literary critics who by their writing and research
have demonstrated an express concern with the forms and functions of symbolic inversion. [Babcock 1972, unpublished abstract,
American Anthropological Association]

I recognize that the term is somewhat redundant; in its
cultural uses, inversion is always symbolic. The modifying
term has been added to articulate both to authors and audience a desire that inversion be regarded as a dimension of deliberate, self-conscious, patterned behavior. Because of this
initial synthetic definition, none of the contributors, even
those concerned with more complex literary symbolic phenomena, have spent much time considering the term, but
have used the concept as a springboard to discuss their
unique inverted data. By way of introduction to these essays,
however, I would like to consider the semantics and etymo-
logy of "symbolic inversion."

As the term is used in this volume, symbolic inversion
derives from and conflates several existing discipline-specific
uses as well as past and present uses of inversion and analogous concepts. Since the early Renaissance at least, the word
"inversion" has been used to mean "a turning upside down"
and "a reversal of position, order, sequence, or relation"
(OED: 1477). More specifically, it was used as a synonym for
the rhetorical and grammatical figures of metaphor, *anastrophe*
(the reversal of the order of words), and *antistrophe* (the turning of an opponent's argument against itself). It is in the last
sense that T. Wilson used the word in his *Logike* of 1567:

"You may confute the same by inversion, that is to saie, tournyng his taile cleane contrary" (ibid.).

The concept, however, is even older than the word; the topos of the world upside down, *mundus inversus*, which grows out of stringing together *impossibilia*, is as old as Greek parody of the Homeric journey to Hades.[4] This topos, as David Kunzle's essay and the plates he has chosen for this volume illustrate, is "an ancient and widespread one, found very extensively in popular art and literature throughout Europe from classical times" (Donaldson 1970:21–22). And, as Rosalie Colie has pointed out, " 'the world upside down,' a more or less familiar environment arranged to contrast with the way the world is commonly experienced," is one of the simplest of a host of paradoxical commonplaces which demonstrate that what is "not" can be discussed, though in the strictest logical sense it cannot. Colie goes on to note that "similar inversion, or at least reversal, informs a major convention of paradox, nominally an 'impossible,' the utopia" (pp. 13–14).[5]

Symbolic inversion is central to the literary notions of irony, parody, and paradox. Verbal irony is a figure of speech in which the actual intent is expressed in words that carry the opposite meaning. As Kierkegaard demonstrates, there is a gap between saying and meaning in which the ironist is *negatively* free: he is not bound, in meaning, to what he says.[6] Paradox similarly operates at the limits of discourse: "Redirecting thoughtful attention to the faulty or limited structures of thought, paradoxes play back and forth

[4] In addition to David Kunzle's comprehensive discussion of this topos in this book, see Curtis (1963:94–98) for a brief survey of its history, and Donaldson (1970:22–23) for a discussion of the categories of images in these illustrations and a listing of collections of such illustrations.

[5] For further discussion of the relationship between utopia and verbal and imaginative play, see Michael Holquist, "How to Play Utopia" (Ehrmann 1968:106–123).

[6] I am indebted to my student Daniel Bidwell for insights into Kierkegaard's concept of irony and into the *negative* freedom of irony. For irony as "infinite absolute negativity," see Kierkegaard 1968:238, 276.

across terminal and categorical boundaries—that is, they play (*serio ludere*) with human understanding, that most serious of all human activities. . . . The most famous document in paradoxical anti-rationalism is surely the *Parmenides*, the dialogue in which opposites, contradictory opinions, and self-contradictions are exploited almost past bearing. . . . All paradoxes share with that mystifying dialogue respect and concern for the techniques they question or defy" (Colie 1966:7–8). Moreover, the paradox is always involved in dialectic: "Challenging some orthodoxy, the paradox is an oblique criticism of absolute judgment or absolute convention" (p. 10). And, like all forms of symbolic inversion, paradox is at once self-critical and creative, "at once its own subject and its own object, turning endlessly in and upon itself," one inversion leading to the making of another, into the infinite regress of self-regard. Parody, which involves the burlesquing or imitating in a literary work of another piece of literature, is of course the uniquely literary form of such creative self-criticism.[7]

More generally, the word inversion is used in literary studies to describe a central and ancient principle of comedy. This principle, as enunciated in Henri Bergson's "Le rire," significantly coincides with the rhetorical use of the term. The comic principle of inversion involves "a sudden, comic switching of expected *roles:* prisoner reprimands judge, child rebukes parent, wife rules husband, pupil instructs teacher, master obeys servant" (Donaldson 1970:5–6). For Bergson as for Freud (1960), the essence of such laughter-producing "topsyturvydom" is an attack on control, on closed systems, on, that is, "the irreversibility of the order of phenomena, the perfect individuality of a perfectly self-contained series" (Bergson 1956:118).

---

[7] I thank a fellow inverted contributor, Natalie Davis, for calling my attention to Colie's classic work on paradox. For discussion of irony as a similarly self-regarding and self-commenting trope, i.e., as "metatropological," see White 1973:37.

In "The Idea of 'Nothing' " (1913), Bergson also discusses the serious side of negation. He points out that there are no negatives in nature, and it is from this observation that Kenneth Burke develops his thesis on the negative as a function peculiar to symbol systems. Following Hegel and Nietzsche, Burke argues that religion is perhaps the most explicitly negativistic of all symbol systems. The very definition of man as a "moral being" centers in the primal negative of command, "thou shalt not" (Burke 1968:12–13).[8] Religions, moreover, are very often built in *antithesis* to other persuasions. And most importantly, religion is generally characterized by a *via negationis*, or what has become known as "negative theology":[9] God is generally defined in terms of what he is not. For, as Colie reminds us, "unavailable to human experience and to human speculation, the transcendent deity deals in *impossibilia*, is itself an *impossibilium:* the appropriate way to express transcendent deity is by tautology (e.g., God's own self-referential comment to Moses, I am that I am) *or* by negative affirmations which are by definition paradoxical (e.g., God is incomprehensible, or infinite)" (1966:24). So, in the mere "idea" of a transcendent realm we have a "positive-seeming word for what is *really* the function of the negative" (Burke 1968:437); or, as Hegel proclaimed in *The Phenomenology of Mind,* "Pure Being" is indistinguishable

[8] Like Burke, who centers the origin of language as well as "moral being" in the primal negative of command, Eco (1973) locates the genesis of both the linguistic system and the aesthetic use of language in the hortatory negative "Do not eat of the apple," which introduces a creative contradiction into Adam and Eve's simple semantic universe.

[9] For discussion of negative theology, see Burke 1961, 1968. While this notion was once confined to mysticism and the hermetic tradition, it is now a widespread topic of discussion in radical (or the new) theology. In this regard see Cox's discussion of radical theology, the "theology of creative negation" (1970), in which he criticizes radical theologians for their failure to see the playful and festive aspects of negation. His "proposed theology of juxtaposition" shares much with Burke's notion of "aesthetic negation" and with the concept of symbolic inversion. Similarly, in discussing his own "radically reductive philosophy," Merleau-Ponty remarks: *"One cannot make a direct ontology.* My 'indirect' method . . . is alone conformed with being—'negative philosophy' like 'negative theology' " (1968:179).

from "nothing." Moreover, it is from the *Phenomenology* that we learn that the principle of negativity is *the* characteristic of existence—or perhaps we learned it earlier from Heraclitus' theory of opposites, or later from the adaptation of Hegel's notion of the negative in the Marxist dialectic.[10]

In contrast, however, to the theological negative, what we define and describe in this volume as symbolic inversion is a negation of a negative, or what Burke calls a kind of "aesthetic negative," "whereby any moralistic thou-shalt-not provides material for our entertainment, as we pay to follow imaginary accounts of 'deviants' who in all sorts of ingenious ways are represented as violating these very Dont's" (1968:13). In his discussion of the generation of aesthetic messages, Umberto Eco similarly sees the poetic use of language as the result of the playful manipulation of the contradiction which God's apple interdiction introduces into Adam and Eve's semantic universe. Moreover, Eco asserts that only when he violates the system does Adam come to understand its structure (1973:173): "Adam has arrived at a comprehension of the system at the very moment in which he is calling the system into question and therefore destroying it. Just as he comes to understand the rigid generative law of the code which had governed him, so he realizes that there is technically nothing to stop him from proposing a new code. . . . While bent on destroying the system, he comprehends its full range of possibilities and discovers that he is master of it."

One of the best recent studies of the aesthetic negative and of the role of creative discontinuity is Morse Peckham's *Man's Rage for Chaos*. Peckham begins with the observation that "there is something seriously wrong with the current and

[10] The *Phenomenology of Mind* also contains Hegel's classic statement on the reversal or inversion of the master-servant relationship, the process of self-enfranchisement, and the resultant genesis of the "unhappy consciousness." For further discussion of this inversion see my essay on the picaresque in this volume.

dominant conception of art. I believe that that serious
wrongness lies exactly in the ancient effort to find order in a
situation which offers us the opportunity to experience disorder. After so many centuries of praising order, I think it is
time to praise disorder a little" (1967:40). Why, Peckham
asks, should man, who creates societies, builds cultures, and
otherwise seems to strive for order, also elaborate forms of
symbolic inversion and repeatedly seek experiences of disorder? He contends, as does Brian Sutton-Smith in "Games of
Order and Disorder" (1972) and several subsequent discussions of children's play (1973, 1975, 1976), that framed disorder in the form of the aesthetic negative is "variability
training," "rehearsal for those real situations in which it is
vital for our survival to endure cognitive tensions," and "reinforcement of the capacity to endure cognitive disorientation
so that a real and significant problem may emerge" (Peckham
1967:314).

The concept of symbolic inversion or aesthetic negation is
also closely related to Freud's theory of negation. In "Die
Verneinung," he states quite explicitly that negation is central and indispensable to intellectual function:

By the help of the symbol of negation, the thinking-process frees itself from the limitations of repression and enriches itself with the
subject-matter without which it could not work efficiently. . . .
The achievement of the function of judgement only becomes feasi-
ble . . . after the symbol of negation has endowed thought with a
first degree of independence from the results of repression and at
the same time from the sway of the pleasure principle.

This view of negation harmonizes very well with the fact that in
analysis we never discover a "No" in the unconscious, and that a
recognition of the unconscious on the part of the ego is expressed in
a negative formula. [1950a:182–185]

We could also—as the essays in this volume do—translate
this psychological view of negation into cultural terms and
say that it is through various forms of symbolic inversion

that culture frees itself from the limitations of "thou shalt not's," enriches itself with the subject-matter without which it could not work efficiently, and enables itself to speak about itself. And it is generally—though not always—with this meaning that anthropologists use the term inversion.

I cannot say with certainty exactly when or how the term inversion began to be used in anthropological studies. The development of the concept of inversion or reversal can be traced back to the *Année sociologique* school and the writings of Durkheim, Mauss and Hertz on classification and of van Gennep on rites of passage. Perhaps its earliest use in English is to be found in A. M. Hocart's *Social Origins*, where he remarks: "Fasting thus seems to be merely a case of *inversion*, that is, a form of ritual specially associated with death, in which everything is done with wrong way round" (1954:120). More recently, in "Two Essays concerning the Symbolic Representation of Time" (1953), Edmund Leach argues, following van Gennep, that "symbolic reversals" are associated with funerals, *rites de passage* (i.e., symbolic funerals) and year ends. And in his *Lugbara Religion* (1960), John Middleton uses the term in much the same sense we use it here when he describes as "inverted beings" various mythical personages who existed before the formation of Lugbara society, and who "behaved in ways which are the opposite of the ways expected of normal socialized persons in Lugbara society today." He notes that "the concept of 'inversion' represents the presocial period . . . before there was an ordered society, when there was, instead, a world of social disorder or chaos" (in Needham 1973:372). In his introduction (1963) to Durkheim and Mauss's *Primitive Classification*, Rodney Needham also uses the term "symbolic reversal" in the same sense in which we use "symbolic inversion" to describe the universal ways in which people "turn their classifications upside down or disintegrate them entirely" (xl). And most recently, James Fox uses exactly the same term in his essay,

"On Bad Death and the Left Hand: A Study of Rotinese Symbolic Inversions" (in Needham 1973:342–368).

Inversion, however, has also been used in the sense of perversion—notably by Evans-Pritchard in "Sexual Inversion among the Azande," which describes approved and disapproved male and female homosexuality. Among psychologists as well inversion usually denotes homosexuality. Evans-Pritchard notwithstanding, anthropologists generally use the term to describe ritualized "role reversals" and *not* actual sexual practices. It is in the sense of role and category reversal that the term is used in conjunction with those seasonal rituals and festivals (saturnalia) that have been termed "rites of rebellion" and "rites of reversal" by Gluckman and Norbeck respectively.

Following Heinrich Schurtz, anthropologists have long explained such reversals or inversions as means of letting off steam, *Ventilsitten.* [11] In his now classic formulation of rites of rebellion in "Rituals of Rebellion in South East Africa" (1963) and in *Custom and Conflict* (1965), Max Gluckman has retained this functionalist steam-valve explanation. He maintains that while such "rites of reversal obviously include a protest against the established order, . . . they are intended to preserve and strengthen the established order" (1965:109). Further, he asserts that such rebellious ritual occurs *only* within an established and unchallenged social order and is "effective so long as there is no querying of the order within which the ritual of protest is set" (p. 130). In developing this argument, Gluckman seems to be following later Marxist writers such as Trotsky who regarded seasonal folk rebellions as steam valves preserving the established order and thereby hindering the emergence of a revolutionary consciousness. Marx, however, regarded ritual rebellion positively, as a sig-

[11] I wish to thank Edward Norbeck for telling me of Heinrich Schurtz's early discussion of role reversal as *Ventilsitten* in *Alterklassen und Männerbunde* (Berlin: G. Reimer, 1902).

nificant step in the development of a revolutionary class consciousness. The occurrence of many actual rebellions, especially in the slave communities of the New World, during the Christmas and carnival seasons would seem to confirm Marx's insight and challenge Gluckman's thesis.

Indeed, Gluckman's theory of ritual rebellion has been much criticized and questioned—notably by Beidelman (1966), Rigby (1968a), Norbeck (1963), and Ortiz (1972). In their studies of Swazi and Gogo rituals, both Beidelman and Rigby regard "cathartic rebellion" as a very limited explanation and criticize the teleological functionalism of Gluckman's argument. Rigby asserts that "in fact, it is *not* necessary to postulate equilibrium and social cohesion as the functional roots of social structures when attempting to find structural explanation for role reversal rituals" (p. 170). Norbeck similarly questions Gluckman's functionalist assumptions and his contention that ritual reversal involves no dispute about the system itself. He also criticizes Gluckman's use of the word "rebellion" and his limiting of ritual reversal to seasonal rituals. In discussing seasonal rites of reversal among the Pueblo, Ortiz also points out the flaws in "group catharsis" reasoning and notes that this kind of "unicausal sociological and/or psychological reductionism . . . leaves many important questions unanswered" (p. 152). And, as the essays in this book attest, he argues that no *one* factor "can stand by itself to explain numinous phenomena like these" (p. 153). Most importantly, both Ortiz and Hieb (1972) argue against the traditional assessment of Zuni ritual clowning as a regression to an infantile and archaic level of behavior—an assessment that assures that such rites can have no "serious" social and political consequences.

In his discussion of *naven*—a Iatmul form of ritual reversal involving both male and female transvestism—Gregory Bateson offers an important alternative explanation which predates Gluckman's work. *Naven* was "written with a rigorous taboo on teleological explanation: the end could never be invoked as an explanation of the process" (1958:288). Using the model of systems theory and cybernetics, he explains this particular form of symbolic inversion as a form of "negative feedback," as one of the means by which the cultural system corrects itself.

These studies of ritual as well as those by Victor Turner and other contributors to this volume have modified Gluckman's concept of ritual reversal in at least three respects: (1) by demonstrating that such inverse ritual behavior is not confined to seasonal rituals and that, in fact, it is a central component of the liminal period of rites of passage (see Turner 1967, 1969); (2) by showing that "rebellious ritual" does not occur *only* within an established and unchallenged social order (see especially the essays by Peacock, Davis, and Babcock in this volume); and (3) by pointing out that ritualized role reversal is confined neither to "primitive" cultures nor to ritual proper (see Turner 1969 and 1974, Leach 1961, and the majority of essays in this volume). Turner's formulation of "liminality" and "anti-structure" as "the Nay to all positive structural assertions, but as in some sense the source of them all, and more than that, as a realm of pure possibility . . . involving the analysis of culture into factors and their free recombination in any and every possible pattern, however weird" (1967:106, 1974:255), and his application of these concepts to sociocultural phenomena other than specific rituals are especially important to the present concept of symbolic inversion. And, in his comments and conclusions to this volume, he significantly describes the points of commonality and difference between the symbolic inversions of small-scale agrarian societies and those of complex industrial systems.

Another alternative to the functional interpretation of reversal is the view advanced by some child psychologists, linguists, literary critics, and anthropologists who regard inversions of norms and basic categories both as a fundamental form of "play" and as a means of inducing "play"—that is, the freeing of focused energies within a restrictive or artificial environment in which social threat can paradoxically be expressed without threatening. In addition to its developing creativity and imaginativeness, Brian Sutton-Smith suggests that children's play has "the evolutionary biological function of *adaptive potentiation* through changing the habitual relations between means and goals, the psychological function of introducing *adaptive reversals,* and the epistemological function of abstracting and comprehending cultural crises by casting them in the form of ludic antitheses" (1973:5–10). And if, as Edward Norbeck suggests in his 1970 discussion of rites of reversal, we regard such "upside-downings" as forms of adult play, what is its function? Erik Erikson and others suggest that its function is much the same—by allowing us to engage in "reversible operations,"[12] symbolic inversions create *Spielraum,* a space in which to take chances with new roles and ideas. Or as Erikson says, it permits us to infuse reality with actuality. He defines these two terms and their relationship as follows: "If reality is the structure of facts consensually agreed upon in a given stage of knowledge, actuality is the leeway created by new forms of interplay. Without actuality, reality becomes a prison of stereotypy, while actuality must always resist reality to remain truly playful. . . . In adulthood an individual gains leeway for himself, as he creates it for others: here is the soul of adult play" (1972:165). An important form of such adult play rarely considered by students of ritual reversal is linguistic and literary gaming. The essays included here by Babcock, Christian, and Sherzer are important examples of recent literary and linguistic analyses of this form of symbolic inversion.[13]

[12] The notion of "reversible operations" is Piaget's. For discussion of this logical manipulation, its relationship to play, and its central importance in cognitive development see Piaget 1962:229ff.

[13] For further discussion of verbal play, see the classic studies by Huizinga (1950), Piaget (1962), Caillois (1958), and Ehrmann (1968). In addition see Michel Beaujour,

One of the most notable applications of play theory to inversive phenomena and a challenge to the traditional functionalist explanation is Clifford Geertz's recent essay, "Deep Play" (1972). In discussing illegal practices in Balinese cockfighting, Geertz points out that "any expressive form *works* (when it works) by disarranging semantic contexts in such a way that properties conventionally ascribed to certain things are unconventionally ascribed to others" (p. 26). The Balinese cockfight is set apart from the ordinary course of life and surrounded with an aura of enlarged importance, "*not*, as functionalist sociology would have it, [because] it reinforces status discriminations . . . but [because] it provides a metasocial commentary upon the whole matter of assorting human beings into fixed hierarchical ranks and then organizing the major part of collective existence around that assortment. Its function . . . is interpretive: it is a Balinese reading of Balinese experience; a story they tell themselves about themselves" (p. 926). As Geertz suggests, such forms of symbolic inversion manipulate—rendering discrete categories both indiscrete and indiscreet—and thereby question or dispute or at least comment upon the existing order of things.

As the preceding suggests, symbolic inversion, and negation in general, is closely related to the dynamics of classificatory systems which may be considered "the prime and fundamental concern of social anthropology" (Needham 1963:viii). Following the initial work of Durkheim and Mauss (1903), classification has been much discussed recently by Lévi-Strauss (1962), Leach (1964), Douglas (1966), Needham (1963, 1973), Fox (1973) and numerous others.[14] According

---

Le jeu de Rabelais (Paris: L'Herne, n.d.); Emile Benveniste, "Le jeu comme structure," *Deucalion* 2 (1947); Richard Lanham, *Tristram Shandy: The Games of Pleasure* (Berkeley: University of California Press, 1973); and most recently, Barbara Kirshenblatt-Gimblett and Joel Sherzer, eds., *Speech Play on Display* (Philadelphia: University of Pennsylvania Press, 1976). And there is also the enormous critical literature on nonsense that I won't go into.

[14] For more on discussions of classification, inversion, and ambiguity, see Babcock-Abrahams 1975b.

to this "structuralist" line of thought, the central categories of culture are dialectically defined by the positing of an opposite—that is, systems of classification are constructed according to the principle of binary opposition, which structuralists generally regard as an innate faculty of the human mind. Indeed, the very idea of transformation or inversion could not arise without the relation of opposition which is manipulated in order to express the reversal (cf. Needham 1973:307). Thus, as Needham points out, all forms of symbolic inversion "are for the social anthropologist problems in classification" (1963:xxxix). Because inversions involve relations between categories, "they are of outstanding importance, for if our first task as social anthropologists is to discern order and make it intelligible, our no less urgent duty is to make sense of those practically universal usages and beliefs by which people create disorder, i.e., turn their classifications upside down or disintegrate them entirely" (ibid.).

The world order of any culture is in great part determined not only by the things, events, or actions put into order, but by those acts, events, and anomalous things which exhibit disorderliness, chaos, and filth—which are, in Mary Douglas' term, "polluting." Similarly, the social interaction system involves both the conventional means of articulating orders and rules *and* the counteractive patterns by which those very conventions may be profitably and recognizably transformed.

An especially important form of symbolic inversion is "that used to mark a boundary, between peoples, between categories of persons, between life and death." For example, "hostile or suspect neighbours of the Lugbara are inverted; witches among the Kaguru dance upside down; in the Toraja land of the dead everything is the reverse of what it is in this world, to the extent that words even mean the opposite of their everyday connotations or are pronounced backwards" (Needham 1963:xxxix). This means that group membership is determined not only by what members share, but by what the members recognize that "significant others" do *not* share. Thus develop the notions of stereotyping and deviance: the definition of those outsiders "on the periphery" in terms of how they depart from insiders in the direction of nature or chaos (i.e., violation of the social order). This does not mean that the deviant is simply "a bit of debris spun out by faulty social machinery" (Erikson 1966:19). Rather, as Durkheim again pointed out regarding crime in *The Division of Labor in Society* (1960), deviant forms of behavior are a natural and necessary form of social life without which social organization would be impossible. We seem to need a "margin of mess," a category of "inverted beings" both to define and to question the orders by which we live (Abrahams, in press). It is perhaps for this reason, as Renato Rosaldo notes in his essay in this volume, that the Ilongots were never completely exterminated; and, as Bruce Jackson says in his, deviance may be regarded as "success."

With regard to the relationship between symbolic inversions and classificatory systems, Peacock's discussion in this volume of the difference between "classificatory" and "instrumental" world views is especially important. In explaining the reformist purges of the clowns and transvestites of Javanese popular drama he concludes that "the classificatory world view, which emphasizes the subsuming of symbols within a frame, nourishes and is nourished by symbols of reversal; the instrumental world view, which emphasizes the sequential harnessing of means to an end, threatens and is threatened by such symbols. The instrumental world view would reduce all forms to mere means toward the ultimate end, but symbols of reversal call forth enchantment with the form and veneration of the cosmic categories it embodies, a fixation dangerous to the forward movement, the struggle, the *perdjuangan*." The distinction between the classificatory and the instrumental world views is similar to that made by David Kunzle between the World Upside Down prints, which recognize and express social contradiction and conflict, and proverb collections, which express the conservative, repressive philosophy of popular moral authority. These two world views may also be related to "metaphoric" (substitutional, reversible) and "metonymic" (sequential, irreversible) patterns of linguistic arrangement, between which a competition is "manifest in any symbolic process, either interpersonal or social" (Jakobson 1963, 1973). And, as Jakobson significantly points out, the symbolic inversions of verbal play emphasize and exploit the tensions and interactions between these two modes of arrangement.[15] Similarly, structural analyses of narrative make a distinction between "paradigmatic" and "syntagmatic" organization of narrative. In this respect, it is not surprising that Lévi-Strauss in his *Mythologiques* (1964–1971) emphasizes the paradigmatic patterns of narrative, for he deals with myth which concerns the origins of culture, and the origin of culture involves contradiction.

All symbolic inversions define a culture's lineaments at the same time as they question the usefulness and the absoluteness of this ordering. Clown or trickster or transvestite never demands that we reject totally the orders of our sociocultural worlds; but neither do these figures simply provide us with a cautionary note as to what would happen should the "real" world turn into a perpetual circus or festival (Babcock-Abrahams 1975a). Rather, they remind us of the arbitrary condition of imposing an order on our environment and experience, even while they enable us to see certain features of that order more clearly simply because they have turned insight out. For, as Nietzsche has epigrammatically reminded us: "Objections, digressions, gay mistrust, the delight in mockery are signs of health: everything unconditional belongs in pathology" (1966:90).

The following ten digressions on mockery are organized

---

[15] For discussion of the dialogue between these two modes of arrangement in ritual and in narrative, see Babcock-Abrahams 1974.

into two parts: "Inversion in Image" and "Inversion in Action." The division was made according to the primary focus of the essays, but like all categories, these are arbitrary and imperfect. The five essays of the first part deal primarily with processes of inversion particular to Western art and literature, that is, to framed, staged, and written performances. In the main, they are less concerned with the specifically social uses and consequences of inversion than with the techniques through which writers and artists take domains of order—whether of social life or of other forms of literature or language itself—and upend them for expressive purposes. This, of course, involves double play or a play with play since it means symbolically manipulating material that is already operating primarily on the symbolic level of interpretation. Dina Sherzer discusses Beckett's inversions and other de-constructions of accepted linguistic behavior for comic purposes. Diane Christian is concerned with Blake's startling verbal and visual inversions of the erotic tradition. David Kunzle deals with the popular art forms of World Upside Down broadsheets and proverb collections and their relation to the social order of things, while I discuss picaresque narrative and its relationship to romance as comparable to the relationship of the rite of reversal to the rite of passage. Natalie Davis's essay deals with the historical and political consequences as well as the festive and artistic uses of the image of the disorderly woman, and in that sense it mediates between the two categories of discussion.

The five essays in part II focus on reversals in action, that is, on the ritual and social uses of inverted images. While they also deal with processes of play and performance in which inverse behavior is stylized, foregrounded, and licensed, they are more explicitly concerned with the sociocultural uses and consequences of this manipulation, with understanding how inversions may operate as a means of social control, of social protest, of social change, and of social deviance. Roger Abrahams and Richard Bauman describe the commonalities and contrasts between carnival in the West Indies and belsnickling in Nova Scotia and demonstrate the inadequacies of the steam-valve model in describing and explaining festive behavior. James Peacock discusses two prominent symbols of reversal in Indonesian culture, the clown and the transvestite, and the attempts of reformist Muslim regimes to purge them. His essay raises interesting questions regarding the antagonism between instrumental and classificatory world views and the different role of inversion in "primitive" and "modern" societies. Barbara Myerhoff tellingly describes the critical role of rituals of opposition and reversal in the peyote hunt of the Huichol Indians. Her description of elaborate speech reversals and verbal play is especially interesting in relation to Sherzer's discussion of Beckett's linguistic de-construction. Renato Rosaldo deals with the social and political consequences of stereotyping or the uses of inversion as a rhetoric of control for the Ilongots. Bruce Jackson also deals with stereotyping and stigmatized roles, in this case in contemporary American society. His essay is particularly valuable in elucidating the relationship of the "other" to its stigmatized role and the "double inversion" of (1) assuming a deviant role, and (2) regarding it as acceptable or successful.

Throughout, these essays share a common concern with the ways in which symbolic forms, especially inverted ones, affect the ways we perceive, group ourselves, and interact with others. These diverse discussions all pursue the ways and means and purposes for manipulating and upending sociocultural orders. If there is a given in these discussions it is that man both orders and disorders his environment and his experience. "Classification is a pre-requisite of the intelligible ordering of experience, but if conceptual categories are reified, they become obstacles rather than means to the understanding and control of both physical and social reality"

(Hamnett 1967:387). Such "creative negations" remind us of the need to reinvest the clean with the filthy, the rational with the animalistic, the ceremonial with the carnivalesque in order to maintain cultural vitality. And they confirm the endless potentiality of dirt and the pure possibility of liminality. The *mundus inversus* does more than simply mock our desire to live according to our usual orders and norms; it reinvests life with a vigor and a *Spielraum* attainable (it would seem) in no other way. The process of symbolic inversion, far from being a residual category of experience, is its very opposite. What is socially peripheral is often symbolically central, and if we ignore or minimize inversion and other forms of cultural negation we often fail to understand the dynamics of symbolic processes generally. On that note, "let us pervert good sense and make thought play outside the ordered category of resemblances" (Foucault 1970:898).

References

Abrahams, Roger D. In press. "Man as Animal: The Stereotype in Culture." In Bruce Jackson and Diane Christian, eds., *Hard Language*. Baltimore: Johns Hopkins University Press.

Babcock-Abrahams, Barbara. 1974. "The Novel and the Carnival World." *Modern Languages Notes* 89:911–937.

———. 1975a. "A Tolerated Margin of Mess: The Trickster and His Tales Reconsidered." *Journal of the Folklore Institute* 11:147–186.

———. 1975b. "Why Frogs Are Good to Think and Dirt Is Good to Reflect On." *Soundings* 58:167–180.

Bachelard, Gaston. 1968. *The Philosophy of No*. Trans. G. C. Waterston. New York: Orion.

Bann, Stephen, and John E. Bowlt, eds. 1973. *Russian Formalism: A Collection of Articles and Texts in Translation*. Edinburgh: Scottish Academic Press.

Barber, C. L. 1959. *Shakespeare's Festive Comedy: A Study of Dramatic Form and Its Relation to Social Custom*. Princeton: Princeton University Press.

Bateson, Gregory. 1958. *Naven: A Survey of the Problems Suggested by a Composite Picture of the Culture of a New Guinea Tribe drawn from Three Points of View*. 2d ed. Stanford: Stanford University Press.

——. 1972. "A Theory of Play and Fantasy." In *Steps to an Ecology of Mind*. San Francisco: Chandler. Pp. 177–193.

Beidelman, T. O. 1966. "Swazi Royal Ritual." *Africa* 36:373–405.

Bergson, Henri. 1911. "The Idea of 'Nothing.' " In *Creative Evolution*. Trans. Arthur Mitchell. New York: Holt, Rinehart & Winston.

——. 1956. "Le rire." In Wylie Sypher, ed., *Comedy*. New York: Doubleday. Pp. 61–190.

Burke, Kenneth. 1961. *The Rhetoric of Religion: Studies in Logology*. Berkeley: University of California Press.

——. 1968. "A Dramatistic View of the Origins of Language and Postscripts on the Negative." In *Language as Symbolic Action: Essays on Life, Literature, and Method*. Berkeley: University of California Press.

Caillois, Roger. 1958. *Les jeux et les hommes*. Paris: Gallimard.

Colie, Rosalie Little. 1966. *Paradoxia Epidemica: The Renaissance Tradition of Paradox*. Princeton: Princeton University Press.

Cox, Harvey. 1970. *The Feast of Fools: A Theological Essay on Festivity and Fantasy*. New York: Harper & Row.

Crumrine, N. Ross. 1969. "Capakoba, the Mayo Easter Ceremonial Impersonator: Explanations of Ritual Clowning." *Journal for the Scientific Study of Religion* 8:1–22.

Curtius, Ernst Robert. 1963. *European Literature and the Latin Middle Ages*. Trans. Willard R. Trask. New York: Harper & Row. Pp. 94–98.

Da Matta, Roberto. 1974. "Constraint and License: A Preliminary Study of Two Brazilian National Rituals." Paper prepared for Burg Wartenstein Symposium no. 64: Secular Rituals.

Derrida, Jacques. 1967. *L'écriture et la différence*. Paris: Editions du Seuil.

——. 1970. "Structure, Sign, and Play in the Discourse of the Human Sciences." In Richard Macksey and Eugenio Donato, eds., *The Languages of Criticism and the Sciences of Man*. Baltimore: Johns Hopkins University Press. Pp: 247–272.

——. 1974. "White Mythology: Metaphor in the Text of Philosophy." *New Literary History* 6:5–74.

Donaldson, Ian. 1970. *The World Upside Down: Comedy from Jonson to Fielding*. Oxford: Oxford University Press.

Douglas, Mary. 1966. *Purity and Danger: An Analysis of Concepts of Pollution and Taboo*. London: Penguin.

——. 1968. "The Social Control of Cognition: Some Factors in Joke Perception." *Man* 3:361–376.

Durkheim, Emile. 1960. *The Division of Labor in Society*. Trans. George Simpson. Glencoe, Ill.: The Free Press.

Durkheim, Emile, and Marcel Mauss. 1963. *Primitive Classification*. Trans., ed. Rodney Needham. London: Cohen & West.

Eco, Umberto. 1973. "Is There a Way of Generating Aesthetic Messages in an Edenic Language?" In Bann and Bowlt, pp. 162–176.

Ehrmann, Jacques, ed. 1968. "Game, Play, Literature." *Yale French Studies*, no. 41.

Erikson, Erik H. 1972. "Play and Actuality." In Maria W. Piers, ed., *Play and Development*. New York: Norton. Pp. 127–167.

Erikson, Kai T. 1966. *Wayward Puritans: A Study in the Sociology of Deviance*. New York: Wiley.

Evans-Pritchard, E. E. 1929. "Some Collective Expressions of Obscenity in Africa." *Journal of the Royal Anthropological Institute* 59:190–194.

——. 1970. "Sexual Inversion among the Azande." *American Anthropologist* 72:1428–1434.

Foucault, Michel. 1970. "Theatrum Philosophicum." *Critique* 282:885–908.

Fox, James L. 1973. "On Bad Death and the Left Hand: A Study of Rotinese Symbolic Inversions." In Needham, pp. 342–368.

Freud, Sigmund. 1950a. "Negation." In *Collected Papers*, ed. James Strachey, trans. Joan Riviere. London: Hogarth. Vol. 5, pp. 181–185. Originally published as "Die Verneinung," *Imago* 11 (1925).

——. 1950b. *Totem and Taboo*. Trans. James Strachey. London: Routledge & Kegan Paul.

——. 1960. *Jokes and Their Relation to the Unconscious*. Trans., ed. James Strachey. London: Hogarth.

Geertz, Clifford. 1966. *Person, Time, and Conduct in Bali: An Essay in Cultural Analysis*. Cultural Report no. 14, Southeast Asia Studies. New Haven: Yale University Press.

——. 1972. "Deep Play: Notes on a Balinese Cockfight." *Daedalus* 101:1–38.

Genette, Gérard. 1966. "L'univers réversible." In *Figures*. Paris: Editions du Seuil.

Gluckman, Max. 1962. *Essays on the Ritual of Social Relations*. Manchester: Manchester University Press.

——. 1963. *Order and Rebellion in Tribal Africa*. New York: Free Press of Glencoe.

——. 1965. *Custom and Conflict in Africa*. Glencoe, Ill.: Free Press.

Hamnett, Ian. 1967. "Ambiguity, Classification, and Change: The Function of Riddles." *Man* 2:379–392.

Hegel, G. W. F. 1964. *The Phenomenology of Mind*. Translated, with an introduction and notes, by J. B. Baillie. New York: Humanities Press.

Hieb, Louis A. 1972. "Meaning and Mismeaning: Toward an Understanding of the Ritual Clown." In Alfonso Ortiz, ed., *New Perspectives on the Pueblo*. Albuquerque: University of New Mexico Press. Pp. 163–196.

Hocart, A. M. 1954. *Social Origins*. London: Watts.

Huizinga, Johan. 1950. *Homo Ludens: A Study of the Play-element in Culture*. Boston: Beacon.

Kierkegaard, Søren. 1968. *The Concept of Irony*. Trans. Lee M. Capel. Bloomington: Indiana University Press.

Kolakowski, Leszek. 1962. "The Priest and the Jester." *Dissent* 9:215–235.

Kristeva, Julia. 1969. "Poésie et négativité." In *Sēmiōtikē: Recherches pour une sémanalyse*. Paris: Editions du Seuil. Pp. 246–277.

Leach, Edmund. 1961. "Two Essays concerning the Symbolic Representation of Time." In *Rethinking Anthropology*. New York: Humanities Press. Pp. 124–136.

——. 1964. "Anthropological Aspects of Language: Animal Categories and Verbal Abuse." In Eric H. Lenneberg, ed., *New Directions in the Study of Language*. Cambridge: M.I.T. Press. Pp. 23–63.

Leach, Edmund, ed. 1968. *Dialectic in Practical Religion*. Cambridge: Cambridge University Press.

Lévi-Strauss, Claude. 1962. *La pensée sauvage*. Paris: Plon.

——. 1963. *Structural Anthropology*. Trans. Claire Jacobson. New York: Doubleday.

——. 1964–1971. *Mythologiques*. Vols. 1–4. Paris: Plon.

——. 1969. *The Elementary Structures of Kinship*. Trans. James Harte Bell and John Richard von Sturmer. Boston: Beacon.

Maranda, Pierre, and Elli Köngäs Maranda, eds. 1971. *Structural Analysis of Oral Tradition*. Philadelphia: University of Pennsylvania Press.

Marcuse, Herbert. 1968. *Negations: Essays in Critical Theory*. Boston: Beacon.

Marmor, Judd, ed. 1965. *Sexual Inversion: The Multiple Roots of Homosexuality*. New York: Basic Books.

Merleau-Ponty, Maurice. 1968. *The Visible and the Invisible*. Trans. Alphonso Lingis. Evanston, Ill.: Northwestern University Press.

Middleton, John. 1960. *Lugbara Religion*. Oxford: Oxford University Press.

——. 1967. *Gods and Rituals: Readings in Religious Beliefs and Practices*. New York: Natural History Press.

——. 1968. "Some Categories of Dual Classification among the Lugbara of Uganda." *History of Religions* 7:187–208. Reprinted in Needham 1973, pp. 369–390.

Munn, Nancy D. 1973. "Symbolism in a Ritual Context: Aspects of Symbolic Action." In John J. Honigmann, ed., *Handbook of Social and Cultural Anthropology*. Chicago: Rand McNally. Pp. 579–612.

Needham, Rodney. 1963. "Introduction." In Durkheim and Mauss, pp. vii–xlviii.

Needham, Rodney, ed. 1973. *Right and Left: Essays on Dual Symbolic Classification*. Chicago: University of Chicago Press.

Nietzsche, Friedrich. 1966. *Beyond Good and Evil*. Trans. Walter Kaufman. New York: Vintage.

Norbeck, Edward. 1963. "African Rituals of Conflict." *American Anthropologist* 65:1254–1279. Reprinted in Middleton 1967:197–226.

——. 1970. "Rites of Reversal." Paper presented at the annual meeting of the American Anthropological Association, San Diego.

——. 1971. "Man at Play." *Natural History Special Supplement* (Dec.): 48–53.

——. 1972. "Rites of Reversal in Crosscultural View." Paper presented in the Forms of Symbolic Inversion Symposium, American Anthropological Association, Toronto, Canada.

Ortiz, Alfonso. 1972. "Ritual Drama and Pueblo World View." In Ortiz, ed., *New Perspectives on the Pueblo*. Albuquerque: University of New Mexico Press. Pp. 135–162.

Peckham, Morse. 1967. *Man's Rage for Chaos: Biology, Behavior, and the Arts*. New York: Schocken.

Piaget, Jean. 1962. *Play, Dreams, and Imitation in Childhood*. Trans. C. Gattegno and R. M. Hodgson. New York: Norton.

——. 1971. *Structuralism*. Trans. Chaninah Maschler. New York: Harper & Row.

Rigby, Peter. 1968a. "Some Gogo Rituals of Purification: An Essay on Social and Moral Categories." In Leach 1968, pp. 153–178.

——. 1968b. "Joking Relationships, Kin Categories, and Clanship among the Gogo." *Africa* 38:133–154.

Rousset, Jean. 1954. *La littérature de l'Age baroque en France: Circé et le paon*. Paris: J. Corti.

Sutton-Smith, Brian. 1972. "Games of Order and Disorder." Paper presented at the Forms of Symbolic Inversion Symposium, American Anthropological Association meetings, Toronto.

——. 1973. "Play as Adaptive Potentiation." Paper presented at the 1st Annual Symposium on Play and Exploratory Behavior, Georgia State University, Atlanta.

——. 1975. "Play as Variability Training and, as the Useless Made Useful." *School Review* 83:197–214.

——. 1976. "Current Research and Theory on Play, Games, and Sports." In T. T. Craig, ed., *Humanistic and Mental Health Aspects of Sports, Exercise, and Recreation*. Chicago: American Medical Association. Pp. 1–5.

Turner, Victor. 1967. "Betwixt and Between: The Liminal Period in *Rites de Passage*." In *The Forest of Symbols*. Ithaca, N.Y.: Cornell University Press. Pp. 93–111.

——. 1969. *The Ritual Process: Structure and Anti-Structure*. Chicago: Aldine (cloth). Ithaca, N.Y.: Cornell University Press (paper).

——. 1974. "Passages, Margins, and Poverty: Religious Symbols of Communitas." In *Dramas, Fields, and Metaphors*. Ithaca, N.Y.: Cornell University Press. Pp. 231–271.

van Gennep, Arnold. 1960. *The Rites of Passage*. Trans. Monika B. Vizedom and Gabrielle L. Caffee. Chicago: University of Chicago Press.

White, Hayden. 1973. *Metahistory: The Historical Imagination in Nineteenth-Century Europe*. Baltimore: Johns Hopkins University Press.

PART ONE

INVERSION
IN IMAGE

CHAPTER 1

World Upside Down:
The Iconography of a
European Broadsheet Type

DAVID KUNZLE

With its themes remaining unchanged over centuries, its frequent reuse of the same old woodblock over generations, its disregard for changes in styles of art or in currents of thinking, and a clientele presumed to be essentially rural, "popular imagery" presents an essentially static, conservative, archaic, or socially neutral view of the world. Its apparent denial of historical space, together with its international character and the primitiveness of its workmanship, have endeared it to the twentieth century, which sees in it a welcome alternative to, and respite from, a tradition in "high art" that seems narrowly bound to particular times, locales, and naturalistic modes of representation. But there are levels of popular imagery which, as the phenomenon generally engages wider scholarly attention, may well prove richer, more elusive, and more contradictory than the romanticized overview normally allows.

The broadsheet theme of the World Upside Down (WUD) is one that stands apart, not only for a longevity and geographical distribution exceptional even in a phenomenon marked by such characteristics, but also for the image it conjures up of a world the very opposite of static: one capable of total reversal in all its components. Unlike most themes of popular imagery, WUD lent itself historically to a variety of interpretations, and was capable of fulfilling diverse and even contrary social and psychological needs.[1]

Although the concept of WUD was familiar in ancient and medieval times, it was not until the modern era, which has been marked by chronic challenges to constituted power, that WUD became systematized and available to the mass of people. It is my contention that, while certain broadsheet and literary genres traditionally regarded as socially neutral, such as proverb illustration and collection, served the interests of a newly entrenched bourgeoisie by suggesting the immutability of the social structure, WUD was capable of a very different kind of appeal: to discontented, lower-class elements who sought or fantasized about the subversion of the existing order.

There is no evidence that WUD, as a class of popular imagery, appealed primarily to rural audiences; it may indeed have found its chief clientele in the towns and reflected the unrest endemic to their expansion. With its strong social content, it constitutes a bridge to another, clearly town-generated class of popular imagery that is popular in a different sense. This is the topical broadsheet, which concerned itself directly with the flux of history: war, natural disasters, miracles, crimes, peace celebration, the ebb and tide of individual and collective fortunes. The ever-expanding urban audience observed and participated in this process of history, which they tended to call the "play of fortune" in their failure to comprehend or control it. WUD stills the hand of For-

[1] I would like to acknowledge the helpful criticism of an early draft of this article by Barbara G. Myerhoff and Deena Metzger. My thanks also go to Helen Grant, for enlightening conversation on the topic in general, and in particular for bringing to my attention several Spanish WUD broadsheets hitherto unknown to me. Mr. Wilbur Smith, former Head of Special Collections at the Research Library, University of California at Los Angeles, was kind enough to help me locate the English chapbooks. Assistance was also provided by Michael Evans of the Warburg Institute, London; Michel Melot of the Bibliothèque nationale, Paris; J. P. Filedt Kok of the Rijksmuseum, Amsterdam; and Svetlana Alpers.

tuna turning her wheel in that favorite topos of the Renaissance—after she has given it the ultimate and fatal twist.

This study is based on an examination of about sixty distinct broadsheets spanning three centuries, from seven different countries, nearly all of them carrying in the title the term World Upside Down, or its equivalent in other languages: Mundus Perversus, Mondo alla Rovescia, Monde à l'envers, Mundo al Revès, Verkehrte Welt, Verkeerde Wereld.[2] All are prints laid out on a regular grid pattern, with the exception of the earliest, the sixteenth-century Italian engravings, and six English eighteenth- and nineteenth-century versions, which come in the form of tiny chapbooks with a single design on each page.

The motifs comprised in these prints vary in number between a maximum of 48 and a minimum of 12. About 15 motifs are common to well over half the versions; about 30 occur on five or more of the versions. The inversions are basically of seven types, affecting seven types of hierarchical relationships which permute human, animal, object, and element. Of these groups, only the first four are basic to our study: (1) human to human (e.g., husband to wife, master to servant); (2) human to animal (e.g., hunter to hare, peasant to ox); (3) animal to animal (e.g., cock to hen, cat to mouse); (4) animal to element (actually, element to element via animal—fish in air, beasts in water); (5) animal to object (e.g., horse to cart—rare); (6) object to object (e.g., tower to bell—rare); (7) human to object (e.g., smith to anvil—rare).

To the above may be added a final, heterogeneous group which, being composed of noninversive, nonhierarchical elements (usually animals in incongruous human activity) does not properly belong to the WUD broadsheet at all, but is often added to "fill up" or for humorous effect.

The principle of inversion is that there are two parties, the

[2] See bibliographical note at end of chapter.

one dominant, the other dominated, whose roles, in some action typifying their relationship, are simply reversed. In all these groups the inversion is hierarchical, involving a power relationship, except in the fourth, where elements, usually air and water, are treated as "opposite but equal" and switched around in respect to the creatures normally associated with them. The last three groups, which are the least important numerically, belong essentially to a tradition not under primary consideration here, that of pure nonsense and fantasy. Groups 3 and 4 tend to fuse, insofar as the hierarchical principle is often added to the element reversal, so that the fish in the air catches the bird in the sea. The only kind of element reversal not involving animals is a cosmic one, which is appropriately present in the majority of WUD prints, and indeed acts as a kind of frontispiece or motto for the theme as a whole: earth and city above, sky and stars below. There are also a few insignificant topical reversals-within-inversions. Thus the city in the sky may itself appear upside down, as may the mill to which the ass drives the miller.

The Character and Range of the Motifs

In the first place (often literally so in the print) stands the most ubiquitous motif of all: the inversion of male-female roles. The primacy of this motif reflects its centrality within the spectrum of popular satirical literature generally and the satirical broadsheet in particular. Emphasis on the domestic hierarchy, which there was no (male) popular desire to change, may also have served to deflect attention from the potentially subversive character of the other social inversions of the WUD prints (master-servant, etc.), which were always within the realm of latent if not explicit desire. Many female readers, no doubt, harbored a desire to revenge themselves on tyrannical husbands, and found in the prints symbolic solace. The motif served primarily as a warning to weak and vicious husbands, who might thus be fittingly punished. Followed as it is by the equally undesirable inversion of the parent-child relationship, the male-female reversal testifies to the widespread sense that patriarchy is the bedrock of society.

There is little variation in the formulation of the motif: the husband sits, holding baby and/or distaff; the wife stands, holding a weapon (Figs. 1.1, 1.2). The reversal of costumes, when it occurs at all, is always incomplete, for in the tiny space available and with the limited skill of the engraver, it risks confusion of identities, when attributes and attitudes are already switched. In the early and altogether exceptional Italian engraving (Cocchiara 1963, fig. 20) where the motif is enlarged and centrally placed in a unifying landscape arrangement, a prominent beard or female breasts identify figures otherwise wholly female or male in appearance and deportment.

Despite a literary tradition, reflected in the broadsheet, of satirizing sexual exchange in dress, the only (and rare) costume reversal in WUD prints is strictly a formalistic and male one: the trousers and shoes are worn above, the doublet and hat below. It is curious that the popular broadsheet topos showing women wearing breeches as the archetypal sartorial male dominance symbol is lacking in the WUD prints. The literary misogyny of the medieval and Renaissance periods is reflected in various visual media by the image of women fighting for the breeches, which satirized at once women's quarrelsome competitiveness for men, and their desire to dominate men once they had caught them. Another broadsheet favorite, that of wife physically beating husband, is also, no less curiously, absent from our WUD group.[3] The explanation may be that marital beating (all evidence from the comic genres notwithstanding) was not considered a normative but rather a corrective practice. In WUD

[3] Present only in a Spanish print (see Grant 1972, 1973).

1.1. (facing page) *Il Mondo alla Riversa,* probably Venetian, 1560s. *Top row:* cart goes before horse, ass washes master's head, sheep shears shepherd, ladies follow servant, horse drives man. *Second row:* women make war, ships travel on land, husband spins and wife is armed, (mother helps) son beat(s) father, patient examines doctor, gypsy has fortune told by client. *Third row:* gentleman serves beasts at table, peasant orders master to hoe, inverted globe, peasant contradicts wise man, old men play with childish toys, child instructs elders. *Fourth row:* hunting of terrestrial beasts in the sea, sowing seed in the waters, airborne fish attack birds in the sea, fish on land and in trees, mouse chases cat, crow attacks falcon, hare attacks eagle, chicken attacks fox, goat attacks lion. *Bottom row:* Ox with lyre serenades ass, ass rides miller, donkey drives laden master, ox drives men at plough, ox slaughters butcher, peasant rides while king walks.

1.2. (following page) Woodcut of late sixteenth century published by Ewout Muller in Amsterdam. From Van Veen 1971. *Top row:* peasant rides while king walks, child teaches professors, wife goes to war and husband spins, tower is inside bell. *Second row:* servant arrests master, cripple carries healthy man, blind man guides seeing one, poor man gives to rich. *Third row:* birds eat man, ass drives master, child punishes father, child rocks father. *Fourth row:* sheep eat wolf, peasants drive men at plough, young ladies draw carriage bearing horses, sheep shears shepherd. *Fifth row:* cart pulls oxen, ox flays butcher, pig guts butcher, chickens eat fox. *Sixth row:* hen sits on cock, fish nest in trees, women storm building, parrot teaches caged man to talk. *Seventh row:* mice catch cat, child feeds mother, little birds eat big one, fish catch birds. *Bottom row:* wild animals chase hunter, world upside down, sick man inspects doctor's urine, ships travel over land.

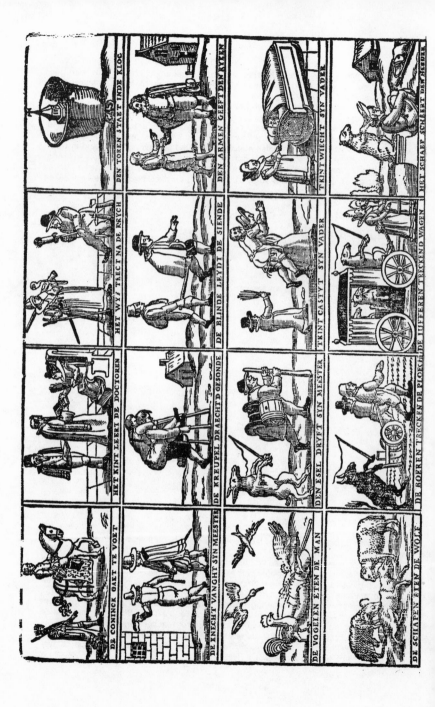

logic the normal beating situation was another: that of child-pupil and father-teacher, motifs of almost as high an incidence as, and usually immediately following, that of husband and wife.

Marital beating, if not strictly normal, was certainly customary, a rich field for comic inversions in many media and mined with frequency and gusto in the popular print, especially in Germany. The husband was commonly exhorted to beat the shrewish spouse before she got around to beating him. He might, on the other hand, deserve the humiliation through his own pusillanimous and dissolute behavior, and herein lies an ambivalence inherent in many popular representations of female dominance, WUD included. Among the most interesting prints on the male-female hierarchy are those which fantasize in narrative form[4] a legalized inversion of the kind incorporated into medieval folk custom (See Natalie Davis' essay in this volume), but by the seventeenth century presumably abeyant in practice. Like popular theater and other vehicles of comedy, the broadsheet preserves in symbolic form folk custom actually acted out in earlier times. With much pomp in the text, and some circumstance in the pictures, Lord Foeminarius is invested with all titles and honors, with the right to bear arms, control the family exchequer, and veto her husband's licentious habits. The very licentiousness of these habits gives us a clue to another level of meaning in the prints, which, although ostensibly satirizing the domineering woman, turn out to be as much a mockery of male depravity. They share this purpose with certain other broadsheets, whose primary intention is to use the fantasy of reversal to condemn the domineering, slothful, and lecherous husband who expects his wife to pander to all his vices.

The Dutch evolved a national variant on this essentially German mode, prints for children showing the husband

[4] Reproduced and analyzed in Kunzle 1973, pt. 2, ch. 8.

(often called Jan de Wasscher) succumbed to the national fetish of washing everything, as well as minding the baby, getting beaten, etc. Such figures were evidently stock figures of stage comedy.

Interdependent early Italian and Netherlandish WUD prints (cf. Figs. 1.1 and 1.2) add to the stereotype of the gun-bearing wife, relatively elaborate scenes of women going to war and besieging a city. There may be a reminiscence here of ancient legend about Amazons; but it is to be noted that the gun which the wife bears in the stereotypical scenes of WUD prints from the seventeenth century onward is usually for hunting, not war, perhaps because the lower and middle classes addressed by WUD prints tended to regard war as a dangerous and altogether less than ideal activity.

One WUD inversion from the animal realm is of a sexual nature, clearly referring symbolically to human affairs: the hen sitting atop the cock. Ribald broadsheets, like popular satire in all media, make much of the sexual symbolism of such creatures. An amusing Russian print from the eighteenth century, based on an old Indian fable, depicts the hens ganging up on and humiliating a wayward cock.[5]

The riding motif is a prominent symbol of dominance and humiliation in the WUD prints (horse or ass rides man, etc.), and adds spice to broadsheet satires on the wiles of women. The favorite topos here is the story of Aristotle and Phyllis (see Fig. 5.5). According to this irreverent medieval concoction, Aristotle reproached his pupil Alexander the Great for dalliance with the courtesan Phyllis. She, incensed at the interference, revenged herself by ensnaring the old philosopher with her charms, and making him carry her piggyback, on all fours, bitted and whipped, around the garden under the eyes of his pupil. Thus was the biter bitted, in what amounts to a triple reversal: male, old age, and wisdom subjected by female, youth, and folly.

[5] Reproduced in Kunzle 1973, fig. 8–31.

Ubiquitous motifs from the family hierarchy show the infant son beating his father and the infant daughter feeding the mother in a cot. Neither stands in an immediate relationship to broadsheet satire, although the irreverence of the young and the impotence of age are stock themes of comedy and proverb lore. Generational inversion is also expressed more farcically in the WUD prints, with the aged couple shown playing with childish toys, and the child shown as bigger than, and/or rocking the cradle of, the adult. WUD prints are lacking, however, in the sexual-economic application of generational inversion, otherwise so common in broadsheet satire, which shows a poor young girl caressing a rich old man, and, in the pendant (considered the more grotesque), a poor young man fondling a rich old hag. It may be the dependence of this motif upon space, and the technical prowess in the depiction of physiognomy, that excludes it from WUD.

In an analogue to the child-parent motifs, the pupil or apprentice beats his teacher or master with a birch; and, more benignly, the child lectures his elders and betters (there is some resemblance here to compositions showing the boy Jesus teaching the elders in the temple, in which painters often exaggerated the youth of the former and the wizened crabbiness of the latter). The birch was the standard emblem in medieval art of the schoolmaster; it was common belief, not dissipated until the twentieth century, that idleness had to be thrashed out and knowledge thrashed in. Pedagogic thrashing occurs not only in satires relating to education and ignorance, but also in broadsheet cartoons as a symbol of military defeat.

In the female sphere of WUD, the master-servant family relationship was depicted in scenes of ladies following their maids. This choice (very occasionally varied in early prints to show the servant ordering her mistress to work) reflects the ritual importance attached to the principle of precedence in the conduct of daily life, even among the middle classes.

The equivalent male motif appears invariably as an order to labor: the landlord digging or hoeing, while the peasant stands over him in a commanding attitude. The manner of going, as well as the matter of precedence, was replete with hierarchical significance, as we know from the highly developed symbolism of the ceremonial procession. So, in WUD, the subordinate (usually, peasant) rides on horseback, while the master (king) goes on foot. It is significant of the special role of the WUD print that while popular stage comedy often assumes a quasinatural superiority of intelligence on the part of the servant, in order to mock the folly of the master, and allows the master for purposes of intrigue to assume the guise of a servant, it stops short of conceiving an actual reversal of power.

The tendency of the rising bourgeoisie to confer rank and power upon intellectual and professional expertise, especially in the fields of law and medicine, met much popular hostility. The corrupt and greedy lawyer and the ignorant and mercenary physician were stock satirical butts in all popular media. In WUD, the client-defendant defends the lawyer, and the peasant judges the judge and teaches or refuses the advice of the learned. The sick man examines the physician (that is, his urine) and the thief (or poor man) takes the judge or policeman to jail. WUD inversions involving thieves and judges or policemen are close to the spirit of the proverb "the big thieves hang the little ones," illustrated by the story of the petty pirate who is brought before Alexander the Great and accuses the king of being the greatest robber of them all. Alexander, impressed by this audacity, hires him to rob legally, in his name.[6]

There are many other WUD motifs in the human hierar-

[6] Franck 1591:17.

chy that bear upon the extensive and much illustrated lore of proverb and folly, as also upon other vehicles and sources of moralizing art such as emblem books. To proverb, folly, and emblem illustration we may refer WUD motifs such as the lame man carrying the healthy, which adapts the topos of the blind man carrying the lame but seeing man, a symbol of mutual aid;[7] and the blind leading the seeing, which adapts Jesus' parable about the blind leading the blind, illustrated by Bruegel (see below). To this group we may add a motif appearing only in Italian and Italian-derived WUD prints—the gypsy having her fortune told by her client—as a further example of inversion about (in)sight.

Perhaps the most significant and potentially subversive of WUD motifs in the nonfamily hierarchy shows the poor man giving money to the rich man. This stood as more than the usual complaint against excessive taxation; it became indeed a protest against exploitation in its widest sense, as is testified by a caption on a German print from the period of the Thirty Years War, under an image which preserves the stereotype of money changing hands: "The poor man gives his sweat and blood to the rich."

Animal-Human Inversions

It may be taken for granted in WUD that, as in fable, proverb, and broadsheet satire generally, the human-animal and animal-animal hierarchy stands as a metaphor for human social relations. But, unlike the fable, WUD does not render the human satirical reference explicit. As we have already noted apropos Aristotle and Phyllis, broadsheet satire is replete with imagery of riding and driving as an expression of dominance; and it borrows from the fable the use of animals to convey basic human power relationships. Among high-incidence WUD motifs we find the ox driving the peasants at the plough (occasionally, as an additional subinversion, the

[7] Whitney 1586, no. 65.

ox driving gentlemen); the horse driving a carriage drawn by gentlemen (subinversion, ladies); and the ass riding the man or driving him, heavily laden, with a stick. One of the strongest political-satirical images of the peasant being ridden, as a symbol of his oppression, may be found in a German broadsheet of 1643 entitled *New Peasant Complaint against the merciless Peasant-riders* [i.e., mercenary soldiers] *of our time.*[8]

Rivaling the motif of the ass and his master in incidence, and possibly of greater symbolic and ritual significance, is the motif of the ox butchering the butcher (Fig. 1.3). Even in the primitive workmanship of the WUD prints this is a gruesome scene, with the human carcass suspended upside down, disembowelled, hands and feet cut off like the vilest criminal, quartered by the huge beast wielding a massive cleaver.[9] The ox is also cast in the role of the executioner in topical prints showing particularly barbaric punishments, or as the soldier in engravings of military atrocities.

Gruesome too are the motifs, again of high incidence although not found in Italian WUD prints, showing hogs slaughtering a man by sticking him in the neck and bleeding him slowly to death (in its normal form, this subject exists as a representation of the month of November in cycles of the seasons); and a huntsman or cook roasted on a spit turned by a hare, while the bird (goose and/or cock) bastes him. Already very common in medieval art, these themes were given narrative expansion in sixteenth-century woodcuts[10] and engravings based on a *Schwank* (comic poem) by Hans Sachs.

[8] Waescher 1955, vol. 1, p. 61.

[9] There is only one significant variation to this formula: Italian prints of the neoclassical period "dignify" it by adapting classical representations of sacrificial ritual—the man kneeling, the ox slamming him with a hammer.

[10] Design of c. 1535 attributed to Georg Pencz by Röttinger 1927, no. 3296. The *Schwank (Die Hasen fangen und braten den jeger)* is reprinted in Sachs 1893, vol. 1, p. 346, no. 128. A contemporary version of the reversal by Gilbert Shelton showing the chickens slaughtering Colonel Sanders in a dark Atlanta alley, reproduced in Estren 1974:147, is not so distant from the original WUD spirit of tyrannicide.

1.3. "An ox, no longer wishing to be an ox, became a butcher . . . ," Russian, mid-eighteenth century. Central section, from Rovinski 1881.

1.4. Theodor Galle, *Revenge of the Animals*. Engraving of ca. 1600.

This *Schwank* was illustrated by not only the roasting of the huntsman but also hanging of the dogs by the hares, the whole execution legitimated, in the manner of the fable, by scenes of deposition of evidence and sentencing (Fig. 1.4 represents a scene of this type).

The scene of the huntsman hunted brings us to a nexus of almost infinitely extendible inversions relating to hunting, whether of man by all and each of the creatures of land, sea, and air that constitute his normal prey, or of the animal predators by their natural animal prey. It is doubtful whether the human-animal inversions imply a protest against cruelty to animals as such, which is largely a product of nineteenth-century humanitarianism, except in two notable works by artists whose feeling for the plight of animals is inferable in the one case and explicit in the other. The earlier is a painting by the seventeenth-century Dutch artist Paul Potter, famed for his rendering of pacific landscapes with grazing cows and bulls. Imitating the strip layout of the broadsheet, and probably intended as a design for an engraving he was unable to finance, the painting (now in Leningrad)[11] shows in the border scenes the "normal" hunting of twelve different beasts, and in the middle the reversal and revenge, with the same persecuted animals sitting in judgment on their persecutors, roasting the huntsman and hanging his dogs, as in the Sachs illustration mentioned above.

The later work is by William Hogarth, the greatest pictorial satirist of his age. His narrative sequence called *Cruelty* (1751) is structured on the inversion principle. In the *First Stage of Cruelty*, Tom Nero and other small boys are shown torturing small animals (cocks, cats, and dogs); in the *Second Stage of Cruelty*, Nero, now a young coachman, cruelly beats a starved nag which has collapsed under the weight of his overloaded coach; in the background, a bull revenges itself on the men baiting it by tossing one in the air. In *Cruelty in Perfection*, Nero has graduated to murder of a human being, his mistress, for which, in the last print, *The Reward of Cruelty*, (Fig. 1.5), he is butchered with commensurate savagery by human executioners. He has been taken down from the gallows to be dissected in the surgeon's hall, and as he is disembowelled, a dog, the object of his childish cruelty, eats his heart. As so often in Hogarth's satire, there are many nuances of meaning and more than one layer of symbolism. The revenge of the dog is only one and in fact the lesser inversion, for this whole "judicial" act (public dissection to satisfy at once popular curiosity and medical science being a legally sanctioned form of posthumous indignity visited on the worst type of criminal) is a perversion in itself. The "judge" enthroned on high is the chief surgeon, presiding disdainfully and callously over the dissection. He is charac-

[11] Reproduced in Kunzle 1973, fig. 10–64.

1.5. William Hogarth, *The Reward of Cruelty* (*Cruelty* no. 4). Engraving of 1751.

terized as perverse, stupid, and cruel,[12] as are the "jury," the doctors and medical students he instructs. This is a satire on human justice: an individual criminal punished by a society of criminals, masquerading as scientists.

The realm of animal-to-animal inversions is extendible to any class of predator and prey; there is much repetition here, and the creatures in question are frequently only identifiable by the caption. Birds and mice chase cats; hens, doves, and ravens attack eagles, hawks, and foxes; fish catch birds, sheep attack wolves, etc. On occasion the theme is elevated by reference to bestiary and fable traditions, with the inclusion of a noble and exotic beast like the lion, who is shown chased by a goat or (in a moral rather than nature-based inversion) a goose.

A subgroup of human-animal inversions relate to nonlethal forms of exploitation of domesticated animals. Thus we have the sheep shearing the shepherd and (more rarely) the sheep guarding the human flock. (Aesop's wolf guarding the sheep appears only once.) When the normal situation is, as here, that of man caring for the animal, the inversion obviously acquires a different moral complexion and is less subject to radical satirical application. The common WUD motifs of horse grooming the groom and shoeing the farrier also fall into this class. The less common motif of beasts serving men at table is not a true inversion, although it clearly belongs to the ancient saturnalia tradition (otherwise absent from WUD) of master serving servant at table.

Onto such scenes of inverted human-to-animal relationships of the nonlethal or service kind, we find grafted humorous or fantastic combinations of animals engaged in human activities. The principle upon which these are based is that of maximum incongruity rather than inversion. Like

[12] Without suggesting that Hogarth was conscious at this moment of the WUD tradition, one is tempted to characterize his whole demeanor as one of *bovine* stupidity. He is the ox slaughtering the man, with professorial stick in lieu of cleaver.

the fable representations from which they derive, they are often of the greatest antiquity, especially in the case of the ass playing the lyre or lute, always a favorite topos for folly. Animal-in-human-activity is interpolated into early WUD prints, occupying a minor role which increases in the late eighteenth–early nineteenth century broadsheets and chapbooks, where we find a bizarre menagerie of oxen serenading asses, horses playing chess, elephants threshing corn, and pigs reading newspapers. The nonsense factor here passes from chapbook and nursery rhyme (where animals are also cast in incongruous activities) directly into the mainstream of the more sophisticated children's literature, such as that of Edward Lear and Lewis Carroll.[13] The association of the immortal Owl and the Pussycat, and of the Walrus and the Carpenter, is in the lineage of WUD fantasies.

Roots of WUD in Ancient Adynata and Medieval Drôlerie

Certain object-to-element relationships bring us to a primary historical source of the WUD inversion principle. Castles in the air, flying anvils, and floating millstones are reminiscent of the "adynata" or "impossibilia" employed by ancient writers for rhetorical effect. The adynaton (from the Greek *adúnatov*, meaning an impossible thing) is based on a familiar natural law which, when negated or reversed, pointed to the unnaturalness of some interpersonal or social anomaly. It was also used to imbue an oath with the elemental sanctity of a natural law, as in Euripides' "the stars will descend on earth, the earth will rise into the sky" (before a single word favorable to you passes my lips).[14] Plautus (*Asin-*

---

[13] It would be an amusing academic exercise to examine the work of this writer in light of the inversion principle. Some of his most inspired passages clearly depend upon a cunning logical inversion or reversal (of cause and effect, for instance, in screaming before one hurts oneself). The whole looking-glass concept is a device to facilitate a bewildering chain of inversions.

[14] *Electra*, II, 36. Cited by Cocchiara 1963:76.

aria) uses absurdities like "fishing in the air, hunting in the sea" which, like Euripides', passed into WUD imagery. Incongruities not involving a true reversal (ass playing lyre) are also classed as adynata.

Virgil's adynata are of a peculiar kind. They are more than rhetorical devices, being posited as the characteristics of a mythic Golden Age, that utopic world of universal peace and harmony, where now-impossible relationships were the norm: goats walked with wolves, lambs lay down with lions, eagles and doves lived in amity. This mythic reconciliation of natural contraries,[15] which had already been promised in the beautiful and famous passage from Isaiah (11:6–8), subsequently passed into fable lore, but remains, significantly, almost wholly absent from WUD iconography, which is basically nonconciliatory.

Adynata were also incorporated into apocalyptic imagery, as portents of the End of the World, at which time everything would be turned topsy-turvy. They were also held to characterize the rule of those tyrants who were hastening the advent of doomsday.

When we reach the high middle ages, the earliest period from which there survives an extensive body of *pictorial* adynata, proverb illustrations, and WUD motifs in various media (the ancient adynata were largely literary), it becomes necessary to distinguish between "pure WUD" and the commoner type of absurdities not involving hierarchical reversal.[16] The marginal or "drôlerie" illustrations to manuscripts of the thirteenth and fourteenth centuries abound in animal incongruities of all kinds, and include several true WUD in-

[15] For Mircea Eliade on the theme of *coincidentia oppositorum* as an eschatological symbol, see Myerhoff in this volume, p. 232.

[16] This distinction is not made by Cocchiara (1963), the only author who has studied the literature and iconography of WUD in any depth and to whom I am indebted for the preceding paragraphs. Nor is it made by writers who touch more briefly on the subject, such as, notably, Coupe (1966) and Curtius (1948). Pigler (1956:568) has a category called "Animals in Human Activities," of which *Verkehrte Welt* (WUD) appears as a subgroup or alternative title.

versions, such as mice hanging the cat from the gallows, geese capturing the fox (apparently derived from the *Roman de Renart*, source of so much fable illustration), an ass riding a man, and hares hunting men.[17]

It is significant for interpretation of WUD in the expanded, mass-distributed form it later took, that the kind of drôlerie fantasy which incorporated WUD motifs was, at first, generally condemned by clerical writers, who regarded them as foolish and profane intrusions into sacred contexts. By the fourteenth century, however, drôlerie had become more acceptable to orthodoxy, as long as the proper moral interpretation was attached, in the manner of fables. Drôlerie adynata may have fulfilled a role similar to that of entertaining exempla drawn from fable and romance, which were used by preachers to spice sermons and revive congregations bored by straightforward moral exposition. Adynata were tolerated as representations of the perverted way of the world as opposed to the Christian model depicted in the sacred texts and illustrations.

The Political Background to WUD:
Reformation and Peasants' Revolt

The antithesis between the material world and Christ's world was brought into the political arena by critics hostile to Rome, who perceived in the ever-increasing laxity of ecclesiastical mores a perversion of Christian principles on the part of the very classes who purported to represent and expound them. As the conflict between Rome and the reformers sharpened, the rhetorical device of antithesis was given polemical force. The contrast between the behavior of the Church and the principles of primitive Christiantiy, already adumbrated by Wyclif and Hus, was systematized, intensified and polarized by Martin Luther. The publication in 1521 of the *Passional Christi und Antichristi*, which identified

[17] Randall 1966, figs. 101, 191, 328, 355, 357, 358.

the so-called Vicar of Christ, the Pope, with Antichrist, marked the finality of Luther's split from Rome, and brought the conflict from the theological into the sociopolitical arena. With its simple German text (subsequently translated into other vernaculars) and stark woodcuts (subsequently translated into other media), the *Passional* was calculated to exert massive appeal to the lay middle classes. In a series of parallel images the character and activity of the Pope are revealed as inversions of that of Christ: the Pope is arrogant, corrupt, and greedy, lives in selfish luxury, and wages war. Jesus was humble, pure, and selfless, lived in poverty, and brought a message of peace. Christ was crowned with a crown of thorns, the Pope with a triple gold tiara. Christ washed his disciples' feet, the Pope's "disciples" kiss the Pope's foot. Christ protected his flock, the Pope attacks his by force of arms.

Other Lutheran images, which are both defamatory images in the medieval tradition and cartoons in the modern sense, employ various kinds of adynata—the Pope is likened to an ass playing the bagpipes, when he publishes bulls and "infallible" pronouncements; or to a *Papstesel*, a monster that is half ass, half naked woman, with elephant's hoof and eagle's claw, to signify papal ignorance, whorishness, and tyranny.

The violence and revolutionary appeal of Luther's language was fuel to the fire of a long-simmering unrest at the social base, which flared up periodically, especially in northern Europe, during the late middle ages, and culminated in the peasant revolt of 1525. Luther had legitimized resistance to the temporal authority of Rome; but it was one thing to show the peasant, satirically, defecating into the papal tiara (as a Lutheran cartoon did), and another for the peasant actually to assert his rights against his local lord.[18] So Luther

[18] My political bias is that of the (old) *Cambridge Modern History* (1907), vol. 2, ch. 6, the position of which is diametrically reversed by the *New Cambridge Modern*

joined the nobility in their call for a campaign to destroy peasants who tried to turn a revolution in religious thinking into a social reality, and to translate into action the hierarchical reversals for which Luther had provided the images and symbols.

The demands of the peasants were, in the first instance, of a limited and practical nature, relating to their land, their animals, and their labor, of which they were systematically robbed. The lords, who were supposed to protect them, had become predators upon them. The peasants were turned into beasts of burden, and hunted down like wild animals. They were deprived of their means of sustenance by being prohibited from hunting and fishing on land which was traditionally and rightfully theirs; they were not allowed to kill the game which destroyed their crops, so that (as they put it) the very animals which God had intended for their use became predators upon them. One of their leaders, when contemptuously challenged to define what "kind of animal" he represented, described it as "a beast that usually feeds on roots and wild herbs, but when driven by hunger, sometimes consumes priests, bishops and fat citizens."[19]

The peasant bands, supported by urban proletariats, roved freely over large areas of Germany, burning and looting monasteries and castles. For a few months, they seemed truly to have turned the world upside down. Peasant leader Jäcklein Rohrbach, after degrading and executing the cruel Count Helfenstein, had the Countess, a daughter of the Emperor, dressed like a beggar (that is, one of their own) and sent on her way in a dung cart. At this ceremony a peasant cried out: "You harnessed us like oxen to the yoke. You had

---

History (1958), vol. 2, ch. 2, which justifies the desire of the lords to assert their legal rights against the reactionary, arrogant peasants. To quote a proverb of Erasmus, as it appears in Richard Taverner's 1569 edition of Erasmus' *Adages* (p. 26): *Marx* [sic] *ultronea putet*.

[19] Adapted from Bax 1968:117. Cf. Bax's chief source, Zimmermann 1891:403–404.

my father's hands cut off, because he killed a hare on his own field."[20] Knights in rags were compelled to serve their vassals at table. The peasants dressed themselves in knightly raiment and mimicked knightly rituals.

Some peasant leaders quite seriously demanded that all ranks among men be abolished forever, that upper-class privilege—even that of riding on horseback—be eliminated, that wealth be abolished and men return to living in primitive communist communities. They wished to do away with the custom of the poor always giving to the rich by doing away with the rich. Thomas Münzer declared that property was theft, and that the peasant knew more of God than prince or priest. Broadsheets showed peasants disputing with learned theologians, ramming the Scriptures down the throat of priests, and pulling down the tyrant's castle.[21] Fortune, guided by the hand of God, turned her wheel in such a way as to tip the rich and grasping citizens who sought to clamber aboard over the city walls into the outstretched arms of the peasants gathered without.[22]

The peasants were propelled by Münzer's messianic message. The idea of an imminent and universal leveling to precede the Second Coming and the End of the World was particularly rife in the popular imagination at this time. The leveling idea was visualized in the increasingly popular themes of the Apocalypse (Dürer's, of 1499, was popularized in Lutheran versions) and the Dance of Death (Holbein's was executed in the 1520s though not published until 1538). Such imagery seemed to promise a final solution to intolerable oppression and disorder.

Bosch, Bruegel, Proverbs—Unrest in the Netherlands

The mental and spiritual confusion of the late middle ages and the eve of the Reformation, sharpened by the new con-

---

[20] Adapted from Bax 1968:127.   [21] Scheidig 1955, no. 282.
[22] By Georg Pencz, in Geisberg 1974, no. 1010.

sciousness of humanism, is nowhere more vividly conjured than in the paintings of Hieronymus Bosch. Although his work falls into the generation immediately preceding the outbreak of the Reformation (he died in 1516), it gained widespread social relevance only during the following age, when German Reformation cartoonists gave polemical force to his monsters, and Netherlandish engravers used his designs and ideas to reflect upon growing social disorder.

Philosophically, Bosch is concerned with the contradictions between flesh and spirit, and the manner in which all visible and tangible things become instruments of worldly perversion vis-à-vis the Christian ascetic ideal. Bosch's method is that of maximum formal incongruity, in which juxtaposition, opposition, interpenetration, and, to a degree, inversion of human and animal nature play a major role. The painter indicates that man's response to God having made him master of the animal kingdom is to behave himself no better or even worse than the animals. Bosch's beasts and bestial humans, of a type traditionally used in medieval art as guardians of hell and executioners of the damned, are rendered with such elaborate and ferocious specificity as to suggest that they permeate the here and now of this earthly existence; and they inflict upon their human victims such precise and particularized retribution that we seek to discover the exact nature of the crime through the nature of the punishment. We know from bestiary lore how beasts were associated with human vices and virtues, that the dog stood for envy and the deer for lasciviousness, etc. Thus we may interpret the motif of a man being attacked by dogs, or captured by deer, or most prominent of all, bound, bloody, by his feet to a hooked pole by a hare blowing a horn (Fig. 1.6) as the literal, dramatized visualizations of the verbal formula which describes a person as a "prey" to the vices of envy, lechery, or cowardice. But there is a profounder level of symbolic interpretation here, which may be derived from the

1.6. Hieronymus Bosch, Hare with hunter on pole. Detail from Hell wing of *Garden of Delights* triptych, Prado, Madrid.

tradition of adynata, especially in their apocalyptic thrust. The fantasy of Bosch is altogether of an apocalyptic nature, accumulating so many portents of divine wrath in an age which regarded the real-life monster as a sign from heaven (such as Luther's Pope-Ass and Monk-Calf, and Dürer's six-legged Saxon pig, which are based on real-life prodigies— Dürer's accurately, Luther's more fancifully so).

The human-animal, hunter-prey inversions in Bosch are of a particularly extreme kind, with particularly radical social implications, for it is not just the large and powerful animals like dogs and deer that capture and eat humans, but also, and perhaps typically, weak creatures like small birds and fish which, gigantically enlarged and weirdly armed, attack and gobble up people as greedily—and in this nightmare world,

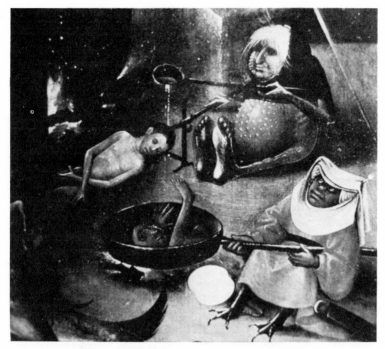

1.7. Hieronymus Bosch, Sinners fried and roasted by demons. Detail from central panel of *Last Judgment* altarpiece, Akademie, Vienna.

as casually—as people normally gobble up animal meat. Thus man is ingested (and excreted) by embodiments of his own lusts. Bosch inverts the whole cycle of zoophagic exploitation, from the hunting, capturing, cooking (Fig. 1.7), devouring, down to the excreting.[23]

Among the vexed symbolisms of Bosch there are many relating to the physical reversal of an object—for example, the funnel standing upside down on the head of the

[23] The major excreting figure is the bird-headed Satanic creature in the Hell wing of the *Garden of Delights*. The most "culinary" work by Bosch is perhaps the *Last Judgment*. The same triptych contains the typical WUD motif of a human being shod like a horse.

·GRANDIBVS EXIGVI SVNT PISCES PISCIBVS ESCA·
Siet fone dit hebbe tick zeer langhe ghiweten dat die groote viffen de clegne

1.8. Pieter Bruegel (after Bosch), *Big Fish Eat Little Fish* (proverb). Engraving of 1557.

"surgeon" in the *Stone Operation*, an incongruity as well as a reversal, signifying perhaps the ignorance and/or deceit he practices, and of which he is himself a victim. The chair on the head of the man representing Anger in the *Seven Deadly Sins* tabletop corresponds to the WUD nonsense reversal "chair sits on man"; recurs in the Goya *Capricho* (no. 26), which illustrates, in punning fashion, the phrase *Ya tienen asiento* ("they are seated all right"); and passes, not necessarily via Goya, into nineteenth-century Spanish WUD prints. In Bosch the reversal may have no other significance than to express the chaos and confusion caused by the sin of wrath. Perhaps the most frightening form of human-object inversion in the work of Bosch shows the passive instrument of human pleasure—a musical instrument, harp or hurdy-gurdy, for instance—turned into the active agent of punishment.

The most famous Bosch design to be published at this time was prepared for the engraver by the young Pieter Bruegel. It illustrates the popular proverb "big fish eat little fish," which comments on the inevitability, in any social conflict, of the weak getting swallowed up by the strong (Fig. 1.8).[24] A contemporaneous Italian WUD print, however, reverses the truism, which has also been most dramatically denied by revolutionary struggle in our own age (Fig. 1.9).[25]

Bruegel became addicted to proverbs independently of his model, Bosch, treating them several times, in different forms, both painted and engraved. The engraved set of *Twelve Proverbs* of 1568–1569 includes the blind leading the blind and both falling into the ditch, a subject illustrated independently in a famous Bruegel painting, and adapted by the WUD broadsheet into the blind leading the seeing; and the hay chasing the horse (Fig. 1.10), which is in its form pure WUD, although missing from the WUD broadsheets on a small scale. The Flemish caption translates: "For the hay to go after the horse, is perverted (*verkeert*), mark this, you girls who offer yourselves up so shamelessly. It is not proper for you to court the young men; but it is proper for the horse to go after the hay." In the background, a woman chases a fleeing man. The same idea was rendered, in the static manner typical of WUD prints, over the caption "the ladies court the gentlemen," and is subsumed, in a general way, under the more important motif of the wife dominating the husband.

[24] Compare that early proverb to: "The exactions of rings and monopolies, which bought in bulk, drove weaker competitors out of the field, 'as a great pike swallows up a lot of little fishes,' and plundered the consumer, were the commonplaces of the social reformer" (Tawney 1926:79).

[25] There is also a hint of a reversal, probably intended in the first place as an absurdity, in the Bosch-Bruegel engraving, which includes (lower right) a mussel shell astride a fish, as if the smaller creature were trying to devour the larger.

Hoehana (LNS)

1.9. Ken Sprague, *Little Fish Eat Big Fish*. Cartoon published to celebrate Victory of Vietnam over the United States in the *Guardian* (New York), 14 May 1975.

Bruegel's oeuvre contains adynata such as "the ass in school," the primary motif of a print satirizing scholastic ignorance; object-element reversals such as flying fish and a boat in the mountains (in *Big Fish Eat Little Fish*); and many Boschian hunter-hunted reversals, with particular accent on the concept of trapping (men caught in their own snares by the animals and fish they seek to catch).

Let us now turn to Bruegel's famous Proverb painting in Berlin. This was not engraved, but executed at a time (1559) when engraved compilations of proverbs, containing sometimes nearly one hundred items, were becoming very popu-

1.10. Pieter Bruegel, *The Hay Chasing the Horse* (proverb). Engraving of 1568/69.

lar.[26] Examination of the role of proverbs at this time provides a means of better determining the distinctive character of the WUD prints. Some of the later proverb engravings, dating from the seventeenth and eighteenth centuries, misleadingly include the term World Upside Down (Monde à l'envers, Verkeerde Wereld), as do later references to Bruegel's painting. Bruegel experts in our own time have retained what should be regarded as a misnomer, in the light of the true function of the WUD print properly so-called.[27] Its

[26] See Lebeer 1939:161–229.
[27] Among many other Bruegel experts, see Stridbeck 1956:171–206. See also David Kunzle, "Bruegel's Proverbs Painting and the World Upside Down," *Art Bulletin* 59 (June 1977), 197 n. 1.

loose application to proverb pictures testifies to the great popularity of the theme. The only WUD motif shared by the WUD prints on the one hand, and the proverb iconography of Bruegel, etc., on the other, is the inverted globe placed in first position, by way of frontispiece, in the WUD prints, and prominently displayed as a kind of house- or inn-sign in the proverb pictures (Fig. 1.11).

Paroemiology, or the study and collection of proverbs, is a morass into which one enters at one's peril. It is likely that certain proverbs based on antithetical or absurdist concepts, and seeming to contain within them an element of WUD, derive from a common source in adynata. There is moreover an evident verbal-structural similarity between WUD and a certain type of proverb, with a common accent on brevity, symmetry, and paradox. But there is relatively little direct duplication, and when a certain similarity does reveal itself, the difference is all the more significant.[28]

Yet it cannot be by accident that illustrated compilations of proverbs and of WUD emerge into popularity about the same time,[29] both north and south of the Alps, in prints of

[28] "Putting the cart before the horse" (*plaustrum bovem ducit*, our Figs. 1.1 and 1.2) is one of the few true WUD motifs that also exists in the same form as a proverb, but it is not one of those illustrated in the proverb pictures, nor is Erasmus' adynaton-proverb, also WUD, "fishing in the air, hunting in the sea," to which the humanist likens seeking a quiet life among the cares of public office (see Phillips 1954:34). The proverb "building castles in the air" appears in the caption to the WUD motif of buildings above, sky below, in the German print reproduced as our Figure 1.12. There are also a few proverbial motifs which appear in WUD prints but are extraneous, such as the Bruegelian adynaton "shearing the pig."

[29] On the dating of the earliest prints, see bibliographical note at end. Although most surviving prints from the second half of the sixteenth century appear to be Venetian, we must remember that there was a great deal of copying and importation, in both directions, between the Netherlands and Italy. A print entitled *Mondo alla Riversa* is listed in the catalogues of two Roman printsellers, Antonio Lafréry 1572, and Andrea and Michelangelo Vaccari 1614 (see Ehrle 1908:53). *Mondo alla Riversa* is no. 361 in the Lafréry list where it is immediately followed, significantly, by a print called *Proverbij*. Vaccari also lists both *Mondo alla Riversa* and *Proverbi*. An early French reference to the theme appears in an inventory of 1581 which mentions "Ung petit tapis princt sur thuille ou est figure ung Monde Renverse" (see Wildenstein 1951, vol. 2, p. 63, n. 52). The description indicates that the medium is a painting on canvas, which presumably derived from a print.

1.11 Pieter Bruegel, House- or inn-sign. Detail from *Netherlandish Proverbs* (1559), painting in Staatliche Museen, Gemäldegalerie, Berlin.

similar appearance (that is, before WUD became sectionalized into the standard grid pattern). But their purposes are different, perhaps even contrary or complementary, from the outset. The fact that the sixteenth-century Italian WUD prints are of a quality equal to that of the proverb illustrations should not blind us to the fact that they appeal to a different taste, a different cast of mind. The subsequent marked deterioration of quality in the WUD prints vis-à-vis proverb illustration, already very evident in the late sixteenth-century Netherlandish version (see Fig. 1.2), tends to confirm my hypothesis that, compared to the self-satisfied upper bourgeoisie who formed the clientele for proverb collections, the market for WUD prints included lower-class, dissident elements seeking a different kind of philosophy.

The proverb accepts the world "as it is," preaching worldly guile, cynicism, and Machiavellian morality. WUD, if it represents an existing world, defines it as perverse; if it imagines a fantasy or future world, it shows that the existing order is not permanent. The proverb accommodates to the hierarchy of the day; WUD mocks and challenges it. The "emblem" of the proverb is not, as has been surmised from its inclusion in the proverb pictures, so much the *inverted* globe as the *inclined* one, as it is also represented in the proverb illustrations, complete with a human figure stuck through it, WUD style, signifying the folly of trying to walk through the world totally upright, and the necessity of bending to its demands.[30] The individual who does walk upright, like the foolish Misanthrope of Bruegel's 1568/69 painting and engraving of that name, will only be cheated and robbed by the World, which doesn't.

The WUD print recognizes social contradiction and conflict that the proverb tries to mask. The proverb of the early capitalist era, like its late capitalist equivalent, the political and advertising slogan, presents readily understood, and often craftily formulated, moral and social catchphrases. In an extraordinary proliferation of printed collections,[31] the

---

[30] Lebeer 1939–1940, p. 202, no. 49; Marijnissen 1969, p. 79, no. 23.

[31] The most popular was that of Sebastian Franck, *Sprichwörter*, which went through innumerable editions in the second half of the sixteenth century, and was quarried by Netherlandish collections. It contains an extraordinary number of proverbs condoning selfishness and cynicism, and praising resignation and poverty. Just a few examples: "Hunger costs little, anger much" (1591:327); "Poverty is good for

proverb established itself over the second half of the sixteenth century as a major vehicle of popular moral authority
and a readily internalized means of social regulation. Long
since the object of veneration by humanists, poets, and peda-
gogues, who saw in the proverbs and adages of antiquity ornaments of learned discourse and mnemonic devices for the
teaching of foreign languages, they now became directed at
the masses from whom they were, in part, purported to
derive. Following the example of proverb-rich writing by
Luther and Erasmus, the sermons (and, one may assume, letters and conversations) of the bourgeoisie became larded with
proverbial wisdom and maxims, designed to bolster its new
moral and social power.

"Popular wisdom" as a social pacifier also underlies some
of Bruegel's best-known allegories, notably the *Battle of the
Strong Boxes and the Money Bags*, the *Tournament between Carnival and Lent*, and the pendants *Grasse et Maigre Cuisine*
(where the fat drive the thin out of their kitchen, and vice
versa), which illustrate, in typical humanist manner, the absurdity of conflict between social forces which are made to
appear balanced and equally reprehensible in their opposing
extremisms. Bruegel's view of social conflict is akin to that of
Erasmus, who in his commentary on the ancient
proverb/WUD/adynaton/fable "Scarabeus Aquilam quaerit"
(the beetle attacks the eagle)[32] condemns both the eagle,
symbol of the tyrant prince, and its enemy, the dung-beetle,
courageous and cunning but vile and filthy defender of the
hare, the eagle's natural prey: symbols both, beetle and hare,
of the people the tyrant oppresses. Erasmus sees beetle and
eagle as unequally armed yet somehow balanced opponents,
destined foolishly to fight forever.

---

many (or all) things" (repeated pp. 216, 267, 272); "Too much justice is injustice" (p.
267); "He who cannot lift a stone on his own, should leave it lying there" (p. 170);
and, epitomizing the whole collection, "Each should behave according to his rank"
(p. 161) and "God helps the strongest" (p. 6).

[32] Phillips 1954:229–263.

WUD and proverb print emerged in response to a moment in history particularly fraught with tensions and paradoxes. There was a great increase in material wealth, with gold flowing in from America, and great intellectual advance, as the Renaissance and humanism spread and solidified; but this happened at the price of chronic armed conflict, economic crises, and social dislocations. The wars of the Reformation in Germany spread north, causing protracted civil wars in France and the Netherlands. The redistribution of wealth and the social justice which the Reformation had seemed to promise did not come about. Protestantism became conservative, and retrenched as the Counterreformation gained momentum. Reactionary feudal princes recovered their power. The disparity between rich and poor, the irreconcilability of greed and need, became increasingly apparent. Peasant bands still threatened the towns, which were also full of discontented artisans squeezed by the monopolies; the peasants were sometimes joined by hordes of real and fake cripples and beggars, who were viewed as a veritable plague.

Even before Bruegel's death in 1569, the beetle had dared to challenge the eagle, and was destined to prevail. The rebellion against Spanish tyranny by the Dutch "beggars" and "geese," as they called themselves, started in 1566; as it gained momentum it was supported by numerous tracts and prints. Among the latter we find a group of four quite sophisticated and finely worked allegorical engravings datable to 1583, based upon WUD, proverb, and fable lore.[33] The first has verse starting "Hypocrite and Tyrant, hold the World upside down," which is illustrated by a globe lying on the ground against its surmounting cross, that is, as far as physically possible inverted; tied up in a rope to signify the

[33] The four prints are listed by Omodeo (1965, pp. 11–13, nos. 1–4), with a mistaken date of 1566 and many consequently mistaken assumptions about contemporary political allusions. Three of Antwerp's best draftsmen-engravers collaborated on the prints which, although numbered I–IIII, are not intended to be read as a chronological sequence.

oppression it suffers; and inscribed with the date 1576, the year of the terrible sack of Antwerp by Spanish troops. In the second print, the powerful lion, symbol of Netherlandish nationality, authority, and independence, is perversely asleep, while the patriotic geese are seized by the wolf. In the third plate, however, the weaker animals (fox and cat) force the wolf to disgorge the innocent creatures it has devoured. In the final print the wolf is permitted to shear the sheep, while the blind lead the blind. The wolf is of course Spain; the blind are the Netherlandish priests and princes who refused to join the rebellion or had defected from it, and in general the Southern provinces, which had failed to commit themselves as the Northern provinces had done. The confused and conflictive political situation has here given rise to allegories which mix natural and unnatural behavior, and show the rules of strong and weak as reversible. It is significant that the Dutch patriots see themselves both in the strong animal, the lion, behaving weakly, and in the weak animal, the goose, which is potentially strong.

Grimmelshausen: WUD between Nonsense and Protest

Germany, where there was a unique flowering of broadsheet art from the fifteenth to the seventeenth century, and where the link between broadsheet satire and popular literature was always particularly close, offers us a unique social context for the WUD print. It is small wonder that the German middle classes, living in prosperous (or once-prosperous) towns located within the "Empire"—that extraordinary agglomeration of petty states in a constant state of political flux which those classes could neither control nor understand—should have shown themselves particularly sensitive to concepts of social mutability and reversibility. The period of the Thirty Years War, the outset of which offered the spectacle of an elector of the Empire, Prince Palatinate and king of Bohemia, being suddenly reduced to poverty and the status of a common man, was very rich in broadsheets. These include two major WUD prints for which literary and social contexts were to be provided by the major novelist of the German baroque, Christoph von Grimmelshausen.

Grimmelshausen inherited from the sixteenth century a certain childish delight in verbal nonsense, repeating a Sachs ditty [34] which engages in a quite artless but charming verbal reversal. Since this device is of a type which occasionally infiltrates the WUD broadsheets, [35] and especially the English WUD chapbooks, and since it suggests one of the roots of much later children's nonsense verse, I offer the following translation of Sachs' text as it was adapted for a seventeenth-century broadsheet strip entitled *A new distaff print called the nonsensical world.* [36]

A village sat in a peasant, who liked to drink spoons with milk, together with a big bread-roll. His corner had four houses, he harnessed four carts to his horses, his kitchen stood in the middle of the hearth, his hay was full of barn. His courtyard lay in the straw, his stable stood in the horses, he pushed his oven into the bread. He made good milk from his cheese, his twill was made of jacket. He dug an earth in his hole and fields out of his turnips, he threshed his flails with sheaves of corn, and set his skittles on their points.

The ease with which such inversions roll off the tongue is in direct proportion to the difficulty of their pictorial representation. The German engraver did not shrink from the challenge (which could have been worse, for English chapbook illustrators were set quite impossible tasks, such as representing a man getting inside a quart bottle or jumping down his own throat). Nonsense verse of this kind, which found its true home, no doubt, in taverns, may have had no

[34] Sachs 1900, vol. 3, p. 78. Repeated by Grimmelshausen in *Teutscher Michel* (1673, ch. 8).
[35] E.g., tower inside bell, our Fig. 1, scene 4.
[36] Reproduced in Boesch 1900:72.

further immediate social significance than that of parodying rustic blunders of speech.

The literary origins of WUD in Germany may be traced back to the late medieval *Fastnachtspiel* (carnival play) and *Lügendichtung* (lie-poetry).[37] A mixture of adynata, WUD, and nonsense motifs seems to characterize a certain type of ballad about fantasy lands current through the seventeenth century. In one such ballad the narrator visits a strange land, where dumb men talk, blind men see in the dark, forests are treeless, cows walk on stilts, the cart goes before the horse, the geese go to church, the mouse captures the bear, the hedgehog plays the fiddle, the sheep attacks the wolf, birds swim, and fish fly, etc.[38] Human inversions, here in the minority, are predominant in the *Schulkomödie* (pedagogic play) of 1683 by Christian Weise called *Von der Verkehrten Welt*, which seems to be directly inspired by the broadsheets— miller carries ass, child rocks grandfather in cradle, pupils master their teacher, the patient drugs the doctor, etc. At a climactic moment the local judge, Alamode, appears in inverted costume, and makes everyone stand on their head until they believe his inverted "wisdom."

The currency of WUD iconography in Germany by the later sixteenth century is attested by Johannes Fischart, who in *Flohaz* (1573) marvels at the "strange combats our artists represent these days. For they bring into battle the cats against the rats, mice and rats [against the cats]. Who hasn't seen the hares turning the hunters on the spit."[39]

Christoph von Grimmelshausen drew inspiration at the profoundest level from the theme of WUD, and pays explicit homage to a WUD print very close to that reproduced here (Fig. 1.12).[40] The passage, which is probably autobiograph-

---

[37] See Wendeler 1905, p. 163, no. 11.
[38] Uhland 1844, vol. 2, p. 46, no. 241.   [39] Cited by Röttinger 1927:14.
[40] Grimmelshausen 1960:314–315.

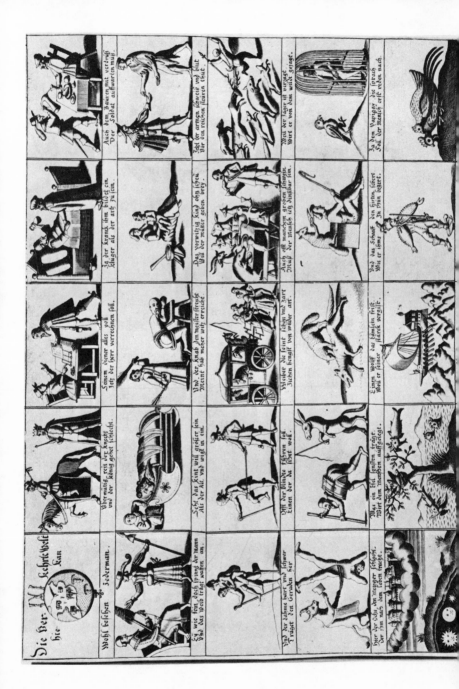

ical, is worth translating in full. When Simplicissimus was a seventeen-year-old soldier, he chanced upon a spinning parlor (*Kunckelstuben*, where women gathered together to spin).

I found on the distaff of the most delightful girl a broadsheet engraving [*Kupfer auf einem Bogen Papier*] with which I became as infatuated as with the charming spinner herself. And since I had never seen such an example, it seemed to me all the more curious; and after I had taken it down [from the distaff] with the owner's consent, I sat down behind her and caressed her distaff-print instead of the lovely spinner, and marvelled at the clever invention of the author. I considered that the World Upside Down could not be depicted better, more pungently and ingeniously, than on this print. My imagination was so struck by it that I also dreamed of it: I saw how the ox slaughtered the butcher, the deer felled the hunter, the fish ate the angler, the ass rode the man, the layman preached to the priest, the horse exercised the rider, the poor man gave to the rich man, the peasant made war and the soldier ploughed.

Simplicissimus (i.e., Grimmelshausen) thereupon resolves to use the WUD principle as an instrument of social interpretation.

Grimmelshausen's use of WUD is apparent throughout his major satirical novel, *Simplicissimus* (1669), a partly autobiographical narrative of the horrors and absurdities of the Thirty Years War. Grimmelshausen had himself been a soldier, and also a tax gatherer among the peasantry; he had seen civilians literally butchered like animals, and peasants

1.12. *Die Verkehrte Welt*, German, first half of seventeenth century. Engraving, Staatliche Galerie Moritzburg, Halle. *Top row:* peasant rides while king walks, master shows accounts to servant, sick man thinks he is wiser than physician, "even the soldier angrily has to serve the peasant." *Second row:* husband spins and wife bears arms, child rocks old man, boy beats master, child gives pap to mother, "now the poor man pays sweat and blood to the rich one." *Third row:* lame man carries healthy, blind man guides the seeing, young ladies pull carriage bearing horses, gentleman serves wild beasts, beasts hunt the hunter. *Fourth row:* ox slaughters butcher, ass drives laden man, lamb eats wolf, sheep shears shepherd, parrot teaches caged man to talk. *Bottom row:* "building castles in the air," fish attack birds, ships travel over mountains and valleys, upside-down costume, "now the hen would be the cock, that is the experience of many men."

take up arms against their military oppressor. The motif of the peasant overpowering the soldier, which is included among the motifs of the "distaff-print" and (uniquely) in the German print reproduced, climaxes the famous series of Callot etchings likewise based on the Thirty Years War, *Les Misères et les Malheurs de la Guerre* (1633), and features prominently in the frontispiece to a Simplicissimus continuation, *The Topsy-Turvy World of the Adventurous Simplicissimus.*[41] The title page verse describes the content of the frontispiece: "The stag lays low the bold hunter, the ox may kill the butcher, the poor man carries taxes to the rich, the soldier bestirs himself to labor, the peasant takes up arms. Such things the world may bring about."

Desperation did indeed drive the peasantry to take up arms during the Thirty Years War, as it had in 1525, and as it would do again.

World Upside Down and Reactionary Ideology: English Chapbooks

The essential ambivalence of WUD permits, according to circumstances, those satisfied with the existing or traditional social order to see the theme as a mockery of the idea of changing that order around, and at the same time, those dissatisfied with that order to see the theme as mocking it in its present, perverted state. But the discontented have yet another alternative: to see WUD as a promise of revenge and a vindication of just desires. In Grimmelshausen we see the mingling of these two functions, and it is evident that different groups in the WUD complex lend themselves to these different interpretive modes. Thus a dissident class might simultaneously identify on the one hand with the man slaughtered or burdened like an animal, that is the metaphoric rep-

---

[41] Grimmelshausen 1672. The frontispiece is reproduced in *Zeitschrift für Bücherfreunde* (1898, 2, p. 149). See also Scholte 1912, n.s. 4, fascicle 1 and 2; and Welzig 1959:424–430, 1960:133–140.

resentation of an actual oppressive condition; and on the other hand with the servant who has gained the upper hand over his master, which enacts, on a literal level, the fulfillment of a situation more or less consciously desired and more or less directly related to any existing potential for revolutionary change.

We have seen that the idea of "just revenge" for animals served, in the Reformation era, as a warning to tyrants; and we now come to a moment in history when that symbolic revenge was actualized and generalized into revolution and provoked its own reaction.

In England in the later eighteenth and early nineteenth century, fear of revolution generated some WUD chapbooks with more text and therefore more room for editorialization than the broadsheets had ever known, and a heavily rational, pedagogic, and political tendency, designed for the instruction rather than amusement of children. Their predecessors are relatively few: the earliest English print known to me that uses a self-contained group of WUD motifs is actually the frontispiece to a Royalist pamphlet of 1642.[42] A second print, of the early eighteenth century, is a broadsheet[43] on the standard grid pattern, probably dependent on continental prototypes, and outwardly apolitical, as is the earliest chapbook on the theme.[44] This chapbook is not intended (primarily) for children, as is shown by a certain bawdiness, but makes hesitant and inconsistent attempts to rationalize the in-

[42] John Taylor (the "Water Poet"), *Mad Fashions, Old Fashions, all of a Fashion, or the Emblemes of these distracted Times.* The woodcut purports to represent the "monstrous" and "transform'd" state of England at the beginning of the Civil War.

[43] *The Folly's Mankind Expos'd or the World Upside Down.* Printed for Bowles & Carver, London. 16 motifs. In British Museum, *Catalogue of Prints and Drawings in the British Museum*, Div. 1, *Political and Personal Satires* (compiled by F. G. Stephens), 4 vols., no. 1999. Part reproduced in Kunzle 1973, fig. 10–65.

[44] *The World Turned Upside Down or the Folly of Man exemplified in twelve comical relations upon Uncommon Subjects. Illustrated with Twelve curious cuts Truly adapted to each story. Printed and sold in London.* An edition printed by C. Dicey in Northhampton, preserved in the Harvard College Library, is datable to before 1712. Reprinted in Ashton 1882:265–272.

versions: the same ox who recovers ("as in times of yore") his right to rule the peasants who had maltreated him, later quite arbitrarily butchers the butcher who refused to give him a "two-legged calf" (i.e., fop) bespoken by another customer.

Later in the century the WUD chapbook enters the burgeoning children's market and begins to moralize in a more consistent and starkly reactionary fashion. There is an overt preaching of religious and social obedience. Several interpolations of motif and/or comment are directed against the behavior of the poor. In one example, the vicious gamekeeper to a virtuous, charitable landlord is shot by a deer; the gamekeeper was in the habit of poaching "for a penurious whim" (scene 12).[45] The "penurious" gamekeeper stands of course for the poor peasant, forbidden now (as in 1525, at the time of the German peasant revolts) to "poach" game on land which had once been common. An interpolated non-WUD motif, peculiar to English chapbooks of this period (scene 11) and relating an absurd story about a king who sent a man to steal the Monument, has this moral thrust upon it: "But 'tis in just degree / That peasants never shall be kings, / But know humility." Another interpolated non-WUD motif (scene 29) showing pickpockets in church, identifies them as the poor, ill-educated, ranting (perhaps Methodist) preachers. The interpretations often have an air of desperation about them, as if the writer had some vague sense of having to twist the inversions in a direction not provided by tradition: the peasants driven by the oxen are punished for having "consumed the wealth of others" (scene 20); and most revealing of all, the traditional motif of the poor man giving money to the rich becomes the *miser* giving alms (scene 21), with comment on the happy state of the indigent and starving

[45] *The World Turned Upside Down or the Comical Metamorphoses. A Work entirely calculated to excite laughter in grown persons and promote Morality in the Young Ones of both Sexes; decorated with 34 copper plates curiously drawn and elegantly engraved.* London, printed for Edward Ryland. About 1760(?).

classes, who are better off than the supposedly wicked, miserly rich.

In a chapbook of 1810,[46] at the high-tide of resistance to Napoleon, repressive ideology has become actively counter-revolutionary, and is expressed with some wit. Most of the non-WUD motifs, which constitute about half the whole, illustrate proverbial wisdom about the folly of trying to be different from, that is, better than, what nature has ordained. The verses to seven of the true WUD motifs reinforce the admonition with explicit allusions to the folly of revolutionary aspirations. They are political fables in miniature making little or no concession to the childish audience.

The first and third motifs illustrate revolutionary activity: the various animals which roast the cook are "patriots" who have made it a law to murder every cook they can catch; creatures of land and sea summon each other to seize the chance to win "freedom and glory": "To arms, brother hare . . . take courage, and man is your slave." But such aspirations are doomed to defeat: the fish who leave the sea, their natural habitat, with ambitions to fly in the air, will be quickly devoured by birds. The engraving here, following the verse, twists and reverses the traditional motif of fish flying unmolested or actually catching the birds from the air. The game, armed with guns (scene 21), gang up on the sportsman, but with the characteristic stupidity of revolutionary conspirators, forget to bring powder and shot. They are glad to return to being game, wisely reflecting "I very much doubt if we lawfully may / Revenge ourselves thus upon man." In *The Ass turned Miller* (Fig. 1.13a) the natural stupidity of the plotter is overlaid with the Orwellian theme of the new master assuming the vices as well as the power of the old one. A "frolicsome" ass, having overpowered, bitted,

[46] *Signor Topsy-Turvy's wonderful magic Lantern . . . or the World Turned Upside Down. By the author of "My Mother" and other poems* [i.e., Ann Gilbert]. *Illustrated with 24 engravings.* London, printed for Tabart & Co. by B. M'Millan, 1810.

1.13a. *The Ass turned Miller;* 1.13b. *The Hogs Council.* From Ann Gilbert, *Signor Topsy-Turvy's wonderful magic Lantern,* 1810.

and harnessed his master, foolishly surrenders the whip which hurts his now all-too-delicate paws. The miller thus recovers the whip hand. Moral: This is what happens to "silly brutes in their fetters" who "attempt to rule over their betters."

Most politically charged and highly developed of all is *The Hogs Council* (Fig. 1.13b). The hogs, having seized a man, debate the prevailing notion that man and pig were once brothers, but decide that these "idle, selfish gluttons, grovelling in mire" (i.e., man) cannot possibly be relations of theirs. " 'Say citizen pigs, can it ever be true, / Such wretches as these were related to you?' 'No, no . . . Long live the Republic!' " The hogs resolve to celebrate annually a national feast "On two or three fricasseed butchers at least. / The old hag in armour, with sword by his side, / As commander in chief undertook to provide, / And all the hot dishes serv'd up at the fete, / Were won by the prowess of Pig-Hog the Great." The satirical allusions to the politics of

France after the Revolution and under Napoleon are unmistakable.

Of the three other WUD chapbooks from the early nineteenth century known to me, none is at all politicized; they belong rather to another tradition in children's literature which emerges like an antidote to the excessively moralistic kind, that of the nonsense and nursery rhyme already briefly referred to above.

The English showed one way in which the subversive potential of WUD could be disarmed—by a species of cooptation. In other countries, at times of particularly severe political repression, censorship acted against WUD prints deemed to be carrying a covert political message. There are three instances of this known to me, but many more must have occurred at various times over the long period under review.

In 1797 a Dutch print [47] showing the war of the rats against the cat (a WUD motif with a distinct history in fable lore and the frequent, sole topic of separate broadsheets),[48] printed from a decrepit sixteenth-century wood block, caused the publisher to be arrested and jailed and all his stock—paper, prints, blocks—to be confiscated. Although clearly intended for children (*kinderprent*), it was condemned as "a revolutionary and seditious print, which is made to bear upon (*toepasselijk gemaakt*) the patriots." (Holland was at this time in an extremely unstable condition, owing to the resistance against the recent occupation by French revolutionary troops.)

The Russian authorities also faulted a print of the Cat and Rat theme, one which was enormously popular in the eigh-

[47] Van Veen 1976, p. 94, no. 16. A lengthy account of the arrest is contained in the MS note in Waller port. 5, "Volksprenten" (Rijksprentenkabinet, Amsterdam). I am grateful to Mr J. P. Filedt Kok for bringing this note to my attention.

[48] For instance, two seventeenth-century French prints reproduced by Jean Adhémar (1965, nos. 37, 38). Both prints are furnished with texts carrying political interpretations, the one condemning lower-class rebellion even against manifest oppression, the other warning the lower classes never to trust the blandishments of the great. This is also the moral of La Fontaine's fable of the cat and the rat.

teenth and nineteenth centuries, depicting the rats carrying their powerful enemy in a funeral procession.[49] The rats ("of Riazan, called Makares") have been identified as the persecuted Old Believers celebrating the death (in 1725) of Peter the Great, called, from his beardless, mustachioed face, the Cat of Kazan. The censorship demanded that a possible allusion to Peter be eliminated by turning the original sledge on which the rats dragged the cat into a wheeled carriage (Peter died in the snow-bound month of January). In 1842, officials seized the only known Russian WUD tabulation of its kind, an engraving dating from around mid-eighteenth century, with the peculiarity that the motif of the ox slaughtering a butcher is placed centrally, and rendered on a much larger scale than the surrounding scenes[50] (see Fig. 1.4). One wonders whether, under a policy of repression carried out by Nicholas I with "iron thoroughness and gigantic energy," this particular act of censorship was as wholly gratuitous as so many others, or whether the print actually represented one of those "remote allusions and innuendoes [which] kept alive the esprit frondeur";[51] and whether a scene of the servant beating his master really reflected on the numerous strikes of urban workers and revolts of the serfs during the 1840s.

The WUD broadsheet could, without basic changes in its form or content, be made to appeal at once to the political conservative, the dissident, and the lover of fantasy and nonsense. Herein lies one explanation for its exceptional longevity and geographical distribution. The theme also embodies distant memories of the great medieval peasant revolts, and of nonhierarchical communities destroyed in the feudal and feudal-bourgeois eras. The idea of social reversibility replaces, among a populace continuously shaken by social

[49] Duchartre 1961:14.   [50] Whole reproduced in Kunzle 1973, fig. 10–66.
[51] *Cambridge Modern History*, vol. 11, pp. 262–263.

unrest and civil war, the ancient but no longer—or less—functional myth of the Golden Age of harmony and equality. As this myth fades into the background, the dream of a World Upside Down moves into an arena of history where the most spectacular hierarchies of wealth and power are viewed as both intolerable and vulnerable. In order for such hierarchies to be abolished, they must first be reversed: in Marxian terms, a "dictatorship of the proletariat" is the necessary preparatory stage for the foundation of the truly communistic, egalitarian society—or a return of the Golden Age.

Within the rigid bars of its outward grid, the WUD broadsheet is an expansive and open-ended vehicle. The mixture of motifs tends to disguise the shift from the ominous to the absurd, from the apocalyptic to the nonsensical. The two extremes touch and inform each other. Revolution appears disarmed by playfulness, the playful bears the seed of revolution. "Pure" formal fantasy and subversive desire, far from being mutually exclusive, are two sides of the same coin. The formal confluence of motifs from the popular tradition of nonsense does not so much neutralize the social implications of WUD as it does preserve and enhance its primitive magical function: to exercise control. The imaginative capacity to reverse, conceptually, role relationships and create incongruities out of contrary forms, represents, when wielded by essentially powerless people, an ever-present threat to, and indeed a bid for power over, the real world "order," which is really the disorder of injustice. The truly impossible, the "purely playful" fantasies involving animals, objects, and elements, functions as a masking mechanism for the dangerous, vindictive, anarchic, "childish," but otherwise suppressed or unconscious desires which are embodied in the less-than-impossible human reversals.

The WUD broadsheet descended, like so much folk material in the nineteenth century, into the hands and minds of children. It had altogether expired, together with the broadsheet industry as a whole, by the beginning of the twentieth century. Today the theme, or motifs from the theme, survive of course in other forms; and certain nightmare elements have been added, such as the machine dominating the man, instead of the man dominating the machine. But as the social struggle continues and intensifies, WUD hovers still between fantasy and reality, in the endeavors of revolutionaries, surrealists, and other visionaries.

Bibliographical Note

The broadsheets listed below are "distinct" in the sense that they are printed from different wood blocks or copper plates, and show significant variations of design and motif. There is no space here to present an exhaustive bibliographical listing, but the following should give a rough idea of the distribution and offer leads for further research.

Italian: The earliest WUD prints are the following four from the third quarter of the sixteenth century. (1) Reproduced by Cocchiara 1963, fig. 20. Cocchiara's book is the fullest international handling of the theme in all media, iconographic and literary, and is particularly strong in ancient and medieval periods. Also in Lebeer 1939–1940:213. In Cabinet des estampes of Bibliothéque nationale (BN), Paris, folio Te 90, with monogram of Karterus; copy in reverse, in Arsenal Library, Paris, signed I. Honervogt (engraver of Cologne, traceable from 1608 in Paris) with Spanish title. (I owe these last two references to Helen Grant.) Unified landscape setting. (2) Reproduced as fig. 3 (p. 201) in Kunzle 1977 (see note 27 above), in five partly continuous strips, signed S. D. F. (3) Francesco Salviati, *Il Mondo Rovesciato or World Turned Upside Down. In twenty eight plates from the elegant designs of Giuseppe Salviati in the collection of the late A. Champernowne Esq. Under whose Direction and Patronage they were engraved, by F. C. Lewis . . ., London, published by John and Arthur Arch, Cornhill; R. Griphook, Old Bond Street; and F. C. Lewis,* 1822. Giuseppe Porta, known as Salviati (1535–1585) was a Venetian painter and designer of woodcuts for the book trade. The drawings, referred to in Lewis' book as a "jeu d'esprit" and "freaks of the pencil," were presumably for a broadsheet not known to have survived. (4) Reproduced in Bertarelli 1929:37 with an attribution to (based on a copy signed by?) Ferrante Bertelli of Venice ca. 1560. There is a discussion of the "satirical intentions" of the print in Omodeo 1965, p. 13, fig. 2, no. 5. This is our Figure 1. (5) Derived from no. 4. In the Bertarelli Collection, Castello Sforzesco, Milan, ca. 1600, with three additional non-WUD motifs.

Netherlandish: Eight prints, from the late sixteenth century to the nineteenth century, are reproduced in facsimile by Van Veen 1971, pls. 36–42, 68. Another, eighteenth-century, version is in Van Veen 1976, no. 173. Other reproductions are in van Heurck and Boekenoogen 1910:114–116, 343, 384; and de Meyer 1962.

German: Two seventeenth-century (1620s-1650s) versions, *Verkehrte Welt* and *Widerwärtige Welt* in Staatliche Galerie Moritzburg, Halle. See Wendeler 1905, p. 163, no. 151. Another seventeenth-century version, with title in Latin and German, and close to the Italian print no. 5 above, is reproduced in Lebeer 1939–1940:217 and in Cocchiara 1963, fig. 27. An eighteenth-century print is in Paris, BN Te 90, and has German and Italian titles. A facsimile of an 1835 version is in Zaepernick 1972, no. 8.

French: Two eighteenth-century versions are in Cocchiara 1963, figs. 29, 33. Eight others are in Paris, BN Te 90: three of ca. 1800, including one with French and German captions; one dated 1836; one with *dépot légal* date 1847; one with *dépot légal* date 1869, and a motif, unique of its kind, showing Robert Macaire, a satirical figure popularized on stage and in print (by Daumier, etc.), arresting the police; a print dated 1873; and a final one with *dépot légal* date 1879.

Spanish: There is an eighteenth-century version, according to Cocchiara 1963:253 (with reproduction), probably copied from an Italian model published by Remondini, possibly published by Remondini for the Spanish market, and clearly related (via a common prototype?) to the English print cited in n. 43. Grant 1972, 1973 contains an exhaustive discussion, with literary parallels and philosophic implications, of six broadsheets and two fan prints, and also a useful international bibliography. She makes important observations on the extent to which the Copernican and Galilean theories concerning the movement of the earth about the sun, which were condemned by the Inquisition for most of the period under review, contributed to uncertainty about the proper order of things, and provided a scientific justification for popular feelings about the topsy-turviness of existing social arrangements.

Russian: First published by Rovinski 1881, pl. 176; also in Kunzle 1973, fig. 10–66.

English: There are six chapbooks from the eighteenth and early nineteenth centuries; one early eighteenth-century print (see n. 43); and one later eighteenth-century print, in an unusual irregular arrangement, reproduced in *Catchpenny Prints: 163 Popular Engravings of the Eighteenth Century Originally Published by Bowles and Carver* (New York: Dover, 1970), p. 107.

References

Adhémar, Jean. 1965. *L'imagerie populaire française.* Paris: Electa.

Ashton, John. 1882. *Chapbooks of the Eighteenth Century.* London: Chatto and Windus.

Bax, E. Belfort. 1968. *The Peasants War in Germany, 1525–1526* [1899]. New York.

Bertarelli, Achille. 1929. *Imagerie populaire italienne*. Paris: Duchartre et Buggenhoudt.

Boesch, Hans. 1900. *Kinderleben in der deutschen Vergangenheit*. Leipzig: Eugen Diederichs.

Bonser, Wilfred, and T. A. Stephens. 1930. *Proverb Literature: A Bibliography*. London: Glaisher.

Cocchiara, Giuseppe. 1963. *Il mondo alla rovescia*. Turin.

Coupe, William A. 1966. *The German Illustrated Broadsheet in the Seventeenth Century: Historical and Iconographical Studies*. 2 vols. Baden-Baden: Heitz.

Curtius, Ernst Robert. 1948. *Europäische Literatur und lateinisches Mittelalter*. Bern: Francke.

Duchartre, Pierre-Louis. 1961. *L'imagerie populaire russe et les livrets gravés*. Paris: Gründ.

Ehrle, Francesco. 1908. *Roma prima di Sisto V . . . la pianta di Roma du Pérac-Lafréry*. Rome: Danesi.

Estren, Mark. 1974. *A History of Underground Comics*. San Francisco: Straight Arrow Books.

Franck, Sebastian. 1591. *Sprichwörter*. Frankfort on the Main: Egenolff.

Frank, Grace, and Dorothy Miner. 1937. *Proverbes en rimes: Text and Illustrations of the 15th Century from a French Manuscript in the Walters Art Gallery, Baltimore*. Baltimore.

Geisberg, Max. 1974. *The German Single-leaf Woodcut, 1500–1550*. New York.

Grand-Carteret, John. 1927. *L'histoire, la vie, les moeurs par l'image, le pamphlet, et le document*. Paris.

Grant, Helen. 1972. "El mundo al revés." In *Hispanic Studies in Honour of Joseph Manson*. Pp. 119–137.

——. 1973. "The World Upside Down." In R. O. Jones, ed., *Studies in Spanish Literature of the Golden Age, Presented to Edward M. Wilson*. London: Tamesis Books. Pp. 103–155.

von Grimmelshausen, Christoph. 1672. *Des abenteurlichen Simplicissimi Verkehrte Welt*. Berlin.

——. 1960. *Werke*, ausgewählt und eingeleitet von Siegfried Streller. Vol. 4, *Des abenteurlichen Simplicissimi Ewigwährender Calender*. Weimar.

van Heurck, Emile, and G. J. Boekenoogen. 1910. *Histoire de l'imagerie flamande et de ses rapports avec les imageries étrangères*. Brussels: van Oest.

Jackson, Mason. 1969. *The Pictorial Press: Its Origin and Progress* [1885]. London: Hurst and Blackett.

Kunzle, David. 1973. *The Early Comic Strip*. Berkeley: University of California Press.

Lebeer, Louis. 1939–1940. "De Blauwe Huyck." *In Gentsche Bijdragen tot de Kunstgeschiedenis*. Antwerp. Vol. 6, pp. 161–229.

Marijnissen, R. H. 1969. *Bruegel le vieux*. Brussels: Arcade.

de Meyer, Maurits. 1962. *De Volks- en Kinderprent in de Nederlanden, 1400–1900*. Amsterdam: Standaard.

Mitelli, Giuseppe Maria. 1967. *Proverbi Figurati* [1678]. Facsimile with introduction by Alfredo Petrucci. Rome: Edizioni dell'elefante.

Omodeo, Anna. 1965. *Mostra di stampe popolari venete del '500*. Gabinetto disegni e stampe degli Uffizi. Vol. 20. Florence.

Phillips, Margaret Mann. 1954. *The Adages of Erasmus: A Study with Translations*. Cambridge: Cambridge University Press.

Pigler, Andor. 1956. *Barockthemen*. Vol. 2. Budapest, Berlin: Akadémiai Kiadó.

Randall, Margaret. 1966. *Images in the Margins of Gothic Manuscripts*. Berkeley: University of California Press.

Röttinger, Heinrich. 1925. *Erhard Schön und Niklaus Stör der Pseudo-Schön*. Studien zur deutschen Kunstgeschichte, no. 229. Strassburg: Heitz.

———. 1927. *Die Bilderbogen des Hans Sachs*. Studien zur deutschen Kunstgeschichte, no. 247. Strassburg: Heitz.

Rovinski, Dmitrii. 1881. *Russkie Narodnie Kartinki*. 5 vols. St. Petersburg.

Sachs, Hans. 1893. *Sämtliche Fabeln und Schwänke*. Vol. 1. Halle: Niemeyer.

———. 1900. *Sämtliche Fabeln und Schwänke*. Vol. 3. Halle: Niemeyer.

Sanpere, Agustin Duranl 1971. *Grabados populares españoles*. Barcelona: Gustavo Gili.

Scheidig, Walter. 1955. *Die Holzschnitte des "Petrarcameisters" zu Petrarca's Werk "Von der Artzney bayder Gluck . . ."* [Augsburg 1532]. Berlin: Henschelverlag.

Scholte, J. H. 1912. *Christoph von Grimmelshausen und die Illustrationen seiner Werke*. Leipzig: Drugulin.

Stridbeck, Carl. 1956. *Bruegelstudien*. Stockholm: Almqvist and Wiksell. Pp. 171–206.

Tawney, Richard H. 1926. *Religion and the Rise of Capitalism*. New York: Harcourt, Brace.

Toschi, Paolo. 1964. *Stampe popolari italiane*. Milan: Electa.

Uhland, Ludwig. 1844. *Alte hoch- und niederdeutsche Volkslieder*. Vol. 2. Stuttgart, Berlin: Cotta.

Van Veen, C. F. 1971. *Dutch Catchpenny Prints: Three Centuries of Pictorial Broadsides for Children*. The Hague: Van Hoeve.

———. 1976. *Centsprenten, Catchpenny Prints: Exhibition Catalogue*. Amsterdam: Rijksmuseum.

Varrini, Giulio. 1642. *Scuola del Volgo*. Verona: presso Francesco Rossi.

Waescher, Hermann. 1955. *Das deutsche illustrierte Flugblatt*. Dresden: Verlager Kunst.

Weigert, Roger-Armand. 1973. *Inventaire du fonds français: Graveurs du XVIIe siècle*. Vol. 6. Paris: Bibliothèque nationale.

Welzig, Werner. 1959. "Ordo und verkehrte Welt bei Grimmelshausen." *Zeitschrift für deutsche Philologie* 78:424–430.

——. 1960. "Ordo und verkehrte Welt bei Grimmelshausen," *Zeitschrift für deutsche Philologie* 79:133–140.

Wendeler, Camillus. 1905. "Bildergedichte des 17ten Jahrhunderts." In *Zeitschrift des Vereins für Volkskunde in Berlin.* Fascicle 1. Berlin.

Whitney, Geoffrey. 1586. *Choice of Emblemes.* Leyden: Plantyn.

Wildenstein, Georges. 1951. "Le goût pour la peinture dans la bourgeoisie parisienne entre 1550 et 1610." *Gazette des Beaux-Arts*, vol. 38, no. 2.

Zaepernick, Gertraud. 1972. *Neuruppiner Bilderbogen der Firma Gustav Kuhn, mit einem Beitrag von Wilhelm Fraenger.* Leipzig: Verlag der Kunst.

CHAPTER 2

"Liberty's a Whore": Inversions, Marginalia, and Picaresque Narrative[1]

BARBARA A. BABCOCK

In one of the most recent picaresque fictions, my colleague Zulfikar Ghose's *The Incredible Brazilian*, his picaro-narrator informs his reader in the prologue:

I am aware of the danger of fantasies, of adding spice to situations which were no more memorable than a frugal meal of rice and beans. I am aware, too, that since the reader is inevitably going to consider some aspects of my narrative as unbelievably impossible, I have the temptation before me of straining incredibility still further by making incredibility a kind of literary convention, by suggesting, say, that the reader can only believe in my story if he first accepts the proposition that everything I say is unbelievable. This is an interesting notion, no doubt. But let me say it categorically once and for all: what ensues may seem incredible, but there is not one word of untruth in it. [1972:10]

This is precisely the problem faced by the writer of picaresque narrative that defines itself through dramatic inversions of social, moral, and literary orders: how to speak the truth about society, but from an ironic, inverse perspective. The writer wants to amaze and yet be believed at the same time, and so rather than talking of truths he must speak in double negatives of not untruths. This "not not" is the mainspring of

[1] I am indebted to my colleagues Avrom Fleishman, Anthony Hilfer, Gordon Mills, Warwick Wadlington, and Susan Wittig, all of whom read an earlier version of this paper and made extensive and valuable criticisms and suggestions. And to Roger Abrahams, I owe thanks for criticism, encouragement, and moral support.

the rogue's hit-and-run style; he maintains his position of constant mobility, his half-outsider stance, by being able to say to the reader-listener when asked "Is it *true?*", "Well, it's not *un*true, is it?"

The picaro-narrator establishes this perspective by playing with the conventions of the travel book and the confessional, both of which rely upon the trustworthiness of the narrator. But we can seldom attribute this trait to the picaro, the unwitting traveler, the rogue and trickster who is forced onto the road. Thus his confessions have the ring of the lurid, the voyeuristic, and they can never be regarded as illustrating the moral insights of a reformed individual, despite his claims to that effect. To the contrary, it is precisely the amoral tone which marks the genre and provides it with its sense of the fantastical, or at best, ambiguous. The force of this ostracism may be lost on us today, for we have come to idealize gypsying as a symbolic means of asserting our freedom from social constraints. But we haven't completely lost the sense of existence in a disapproved moral vacuum which is attendant upon such declassifying or dismembering moves; even Peter Fonda, who participated in the picaresque film of the 1960s, *Easy Rider*, noted that "my movie is about the lack of freedom, not about freedom. My heroes are not right, they're wrong" (Hardin and Schossberg 1969:28). But to us they are *both*, and it is how picaresque narrative creates this ambiguity, this "nondisjunction" of values, by inversions on various levels that I will examine in this essay.

The term *pícaro* was first documented in 1525 with the meaning of "kitchen boy" and the connotation of "evil living." In the first dictionary of the Spanish Academy of 1726, *pícaro* is defined as an adjective meaning "low, vicious, deceitful, dishonourable and shameless" (Parker 1967:4). By way of literary definition, it could be said that the *pícaro* is one of the first "low" characters in written narrative who is not just a supernumerary, but is a hero or antihero. The first protagonist of a novel to whom the word is applied in the novel itself is the title character of *Guzmán de Alfarache* (1599–1604). Since then *pícaro* has generally been translated as "rogue" or "delinquent," notably by A. A. Parker in his monograph on the picaresque novel, *Literature and the Delinquent*. The word, however, was first used in reference to a real social type rather than a literary one, and while it usually designates one who violates social and human norms, picaro always has the connotation of "prankster," and does not mean "criminal" in the serious sense in which we use that term.

The word "picaresque" was first used in English in 1810. It has since described a type of satirical novel, originating in Spain in the sixteenth century, whose hero is an amusing vagabond or rogue who tells of his life and adventures in a loose, episodic fashion. The "picaresque novel" is at best a problematic literary concept. In its narrowest sense the term refers only to certain novels of the Spanish Golden Age (ca. 1550–1650); in its broadest sense it is used to describe any first-person, episodic, on-the-road novel, and at times is erroneously used as a synonym for plotless, formless, or structureless.[2] In the hope of mediating these extremes, I will use the term to refer to a basic narrative form or pattern, that is, "an essential situation or significant structure derived from the novels themselves" (Guillén 1971:71), which can account both for a specific kind of literary narrative and for a general narrative pattern characteristic of a variety of expressive forms. I think this shift of focus toward viewing the picaresque synchronically as a particular narrative pattern is essential to any description of the distinctive features of the form and to an initial outline of generic distinctions.[3]

[2] For discussions of the uses and abuses of the concept of the picaresque see especially Frohock 1967:43–52, Dooley 1957–1958:363–377, Wicks 1972:153–216, and Guillén 1971:71–106. The last two essays are especially important efforts to redefine picaresque and to restore its usefulness as a critical concept.

[3] My concept of the picaresque as a synchronic narrative pattern is closely related to Guillén's concept of "picaresque myth" and Wicks' notion of "picaresque mode"

When performances define themselves primarily in terms of the inversion of social and moral order *and* of the form and content of accepted literary genres, the very act of inversion creates such confusion that these enactments are generally accused of being formless. This is, of course, the charge often leveled at the picaresque.[4] Yet on closer examination, this formlessness seems more apparent than real, more an initial impression created by somehow turning the world upside down than the actual embodiment of chaos.

In the first place, there is an order, almost a hierarchy, to the norms and institutions which are upended and thereby satirized—that is, to the masters the picaro serves or the collective conditions he observes. The order of inversions generally corresponds to (1) the relative importance of the norms and institutions in a given society, (2) the degree of "reality" or necessity of such social fictions in contrast to their artifice, and (3) the chronological development of the protagonist. And since the picaro is generally a social climber, this sequence also corresponds to his vertical movement through levels of society. Couple this with his horizontal movement through space and away from home, and you can also predict, as Guillén has pointed out, that his adventures will become increasingly cosmopolitan. Second, such unifying devices as recurrent images, thematic contrast sets, circular patterns, and a "dance pattern" of reappearing secondary characters superimpose an order on the picaro's seemingly random episodic adventures.[5] Third, episodes are frequently

(derived from Scholes' modal perspective) as developed in the essays cited above. Wicks' essay appeared when I was in the final stages of revision, and I have indicated those places in which we seem to agree on the description of the genre.

[4] See, for example, Chandler 1899 from which succeeding similar criticisms of formlessness largely derive. The low regard for episodic narrative generally derives from Aristotle, who remarked in the *Poetics* that "of all plots and actions the episodic [i.e., without probable or necessary sequence] are the worst."

[5] The concept of the dance pattern is developed by Miller 1967:13–20. This structuring has ideological significance with regard to the quality of the picaro's social relationships, especially his relations with women, which I will discuss later in this essay.

related through the structural mirroring or interior duplication of stories-within-the-story which reflect, duplicate, invert, and otherwise comment upon the episode within which they are told. Fourth, as the preceding implies, there are frequently causal or logical connections among two or more episodes even though the overall structure of the narrative may not be causal or developmental. Fifth, the antisocieties of rogues with whom the picaro associates are, contrary to assumptions about the motley state of the underworld, often more highly structured than the dominant society.

Underlying the episodic and antidevelopmental narrative of the picaresque is yet another important pattern of organization: the structure of the narrative genre (or genres) being parodied. While numerous critics have discussed the picaresque as "antiromance," as a "countergenre" that develops dialectically as an inversion of the pattern of chivalric romance, few have realized that it embodies the structures or the romance at the same time as it inverts them. The code which is being broken is always implicitly there, for the very act of deconstructing reconstructs and reaffirms the structure of romance. This formal, generic nondisjunction is central to the picaresque's problematic ambiguity: the pattern of expectation created by the inverted form (i.e. the picaresque) competes with the still somewhat operant, formal constraints of the genre or genres that have been inverted. In other words, the reader receives at least two sets of competing formal metacode signals: "this is a romance"; "this is a picaresque antiromance."[6] As a consequence, even a reader familiar with the tradition is somewhat confused and frustrated, and the narrative "message" has an initial appearance of chaos. These

---

[6] The term "metacode" is derived from Roman Jakobson's six-element model of a speech act, which he sees as consisting of: sender, receiver, message, code, channel, and context (1960). What literary critics term a "generic pattern of expectation" may be defined in Jakobson's terms as the "code" of a given type of narrative. A metacode signal is a statement which explicitly refers to the code or generic pattern(s) being used and manipulated, e.g., "This incredible story is a true confession."

conflicting systems of formal constraints or inherent expectations create some specific problems with regard to the picaresque (especially its ending) which I will discuss later.

As both Wicks and Guillén have pointed out, parody of
other fictional types (notably, romance, pastoral, travel book,
and confession) and of the picarseque tradition itself is a distinctive feature of the genre. In addition to explicit inversions
of accepted social norms and institutions, judgement and satire of a society is implicitly made through a critical lampoon-
ing of some of its favorite literature. The impulse to parody
is fundamental to the satiric mode, for nothing comments so
fully on hypertrophied and banal formalism as the overimita-
tion of the form. The "as-if" quality of all our necessary
social fictions is repeatedly expressed in the critical parody of
our accepted literary ones. While we tend to dissociate criticism and satire, defining the former as literary critique and
the latter as social critique, it is interesting to note with
regard to the picaresque that Roman satire (*satura*), from
which picaresque narrative ultimately derives, was the traditional vehicle for literary criticism. The *satura* or "plate of
mixed fruit" consisted, like the picaresque, of an admixture
of genres and their reciprocals.

Historically, the picareseque dialectically develops and dis-
tinguishes itself as an inversion of the patterns of the chivalric romance and the pastoral.[7] The base transformation of
the romance is the substitution of a lowlife delinquent for a
princely hero. This initial inversion is developed by a mocking perversion of the hero's career pattern. The romance hero
is born into a firm place in society, usually noble. He is then

[7] For reasons of time and space, I have limited the discussion that follows to the
picaresque's inversions of the romance. For an historical discussion of the picaresque's emergence in counterdistinction to the romance *and* the pastoral, see Guillén
1971:135–158. His concept of "countergenre"—and his statement that these negative
impacts or *influences à rebours*, through which a norm is dialectically surpassed (and
assimilated) by another, or a genre by a countergenre, constitute one of the main
ways in which a literary model acts upon a writer (pp. 146–147)—is especially relevant to the present discussion.

forced because of circumstance (often the loss or questioning of patrimony—patrimony operating here as a symbol of social place) into a physical and spiritual exile, in which he faces at least two tasks (usually the defense of a lady and the killing of a beast) that he must and does complete through his courage, intelligence, and hard work. Thus endowed with special power, he returns from the wilderness to society and reachieves social status through marriage to a noble's daughter or some other ceremonial conferral of renewed status.[8]

This exile-and-return pattern emphasizes the necessity for the hero to go beyond the margins of society and there undergo a liminal experience to find his sense of self and thus realize (often with the aid of mediating figures) symbolic power through victory in his tasks. This attainment of power makes possible the status change which is realized upon his reentry into society. The parallel between the hero's career pattern and the pattern of status change in rites of passage as described by Arnold van Gennep and Victor Turner is patent. But it is precisely this serious pattern of status passage which is perverted in the total extension and elaboration of liminality into a rhythm of "continuous disintegration" characteristic of picaresque narrative. Liminality with all its "betwixt and between" aspects is perhaps the most important distinctive feature of this countergenre.[9]

The picaro's parentage, in contrast to the hero's, is low and "marginal" (e.g., Don Pablos' father in the classic *El Buscón* is a thief, his mother a witch)—if it is specified at all. If the picaro is not orphaned through the agency of jail or execution, he orphans himself by disowning his parents (or

[8] For a discussion of the exile-and-return, quest-and-test pattern of romance, see Rank 1914 and Lord Raglan 1936.

[9] If, as Victor Turner suggests in his commentary in this volume, we reserve the use of the terms "liminal" and "liminality" for *ritual* proper and use the term "liminoid" for nontribal, modern industrial leisure-time genres, then the perpetual betwixt-and-between situation of the picaresque would more properly be defined as an extended liminoid state.

parent) at an early age. In so rendering himself fatherless and statusless, he inverts the hero's pattern of loss of patrimony through the agency of society—what Wicks calls the "ejection motif." This symbolic social suicide is comically exemplified in *Huckleberry Finn* when Huck frees himself from father and society by faking his own murder. More recently, *Easy Rider* expresses an even more radical deracination: there is no mention of Captain America's or Billy's homes or families; all we know is that they "come from L.A." This canceling of connections is underlined by "a stranger" they meet who, when asked where he's from, replies "It's hard to say. . . . A city" (Hardin and Schlossberg 1969:72–73), and by the rejection and mockery of his All-American past by the drunken lawyer, George Hanson.

Once the picaro has been ejected or has ejected himself from society, he sets out to eliminate economic and status privation by ingratiating himself to a noble friend, continuing his formal education as a manservant (as in *El Buscón*), or by apprenticing himself to a series of "masters" and learning a "trade" to make his way in the world (as in *Lazarillo*), or by doing both. In any case, there is a mockery if not an explicit inversion of the educational system, the system of mentorship, the master-servant relationship,[10] and, I should add, of the benevolent mediating figures of romance.[11] In contrast

[10] This particular inversion has ideological implications that go beyond the scope of this essay, and yet are ultimately relevant thereto. Hegel's classic discussion (1964: 228–267) of the inversion of the master-servant relationship, the process of self-enfranchisement, and the resultant "unhappy consciousness" is especially pertinent to the situation in the picaresque.

[11] On the basis of her work with medieval romance, my colleague Susan Wittig has speculated that what we have in the hero-preceptor or hero-mediator dyad is a latent *avuncular* relationship. The fact that the hero usually marries his "uncle's" daughter implies a *cross-cousin* marriage, which medieval European culture explicitly denied but implicitly allowed. This suggests that in the picaresque the protagonist who refuses to marry, refuses to live within the community's kinship patterns and is outcast for his refusal. Thus this inversion of the educational system may imply a more profound inversion of kinship rules.

to the latter, the picaro's preceptors present an appearance of virtue and a reality of corruption (see Guedj 1968:83). Even if not a servant to many masters in recent renderings, the picaro encounters a number of collective conditions; through his naive and uncomprehending initial response he exposes basic hypocrisy and duplicity. He soon becomes accomplished in the art of deceit and deception, outwits his masters, and sets out on his own to "live by his wits." In contrast, however, to the marked urban-rural contrast in the exile of the romance, the picaro seems to hang on the fringes of the city, for when he goes "on the road" he encounters only a greater variety of marginal types. He attains only the special power of the art of deceit. The only status change attendant upon his return is the transition from deceived to deceiver. These changes occur *within* the city context (urban renewal, as it were); unlike the romance and the pastoral, the rural excursions of the picaresque are mere placebos, confirmations in roguery (Wadlington 1973).

This perversion of the hero's education is repeatedly illustrated in the satire of religion endemic to the picaresque. That religion is singled out is not surprising given its predominance as a cultural system and its control of education in early modern Europe. For instance, Lazarillo de Tormes' second master is a priest who "presented a living portrait of the utmost niggardliness" (Flores 1957:41). He hypocritically preaches temperance in eating and drinking and virtually starves Lazarillo to death. Lazarillo, in turn, begins to pray for people to die, for only at funeral feasts does he truly eat, or, as he says, "in nothing could I find relief except in death." From a tinker (who is traditionally a marginal, wandering figure endowed with dangerous powers, but is described by Lazarillo as an "angel sent by God"), the starving Lazarillo obtains a key to the priest's chest or *arca* (also meaning Holy Ark) in which are kept the loaves of communion bread. The ironies and inversions continue to multiply.[12] Finally the priest suspects mice and boards up the chest, but "necessity is a wondrous sharpener of wits" (Flores 1957:48), and what the priest does by day Lazarillo undoes by night and vice versa. One night the priest beats the "snake" to which he now attributes the desecration and discovers that the mouse/snake is Lazarillo, whom he turns out to suffer an even worse master, an impoverished hidalgo.

This first picaresque novel establishes a pattern of desacrementalization that virtually every narrative in the picaresque mode repeats. Even in one of the more recent renderings, *Easy Rider*, a meal in New Orleans during Mardi Gras becomes a mass; a church becomes a brothel; a whore, Mary; LSD, the sacred host; and a cemetary, the place of conversion—"turning on." And in addition to such inversions of the sacred and the profane, there is a transvaluation of the more general religious and moral categories of good and evil which I will discuss later.

Rather than inheriting a place in society, experiencing a temporary period of liminality and exile, and rejoining the social order in a new and improved status, the picaro is born into what Victor Turner calls a position of "structural inferiority" (1974:234). He declines to climb the social ladder through the formula of hard work and reward (inverting through trickery the customary work-play distinction), and opts for the truly marginal position of being a "half-outsider" who can neither join nor reject his fellow-men (Guillén 1971:80).[13] The marginal man is condemned and condemns himself "to live, at the same time, in two worlds and (is compelled to assume), in relation to the worlds in which he lives,

[12] For a brilliant discussion of the innumerable ironies and inversions generated by the controlling inversion of the meaning of life and death in *Lazarillo*, see Gilman 1966:149–166.

[13] In addition to Guillén, see Kolakowski 1962 on the jester's similar relationship to society and Cox's discussion of a "theology of opposition" and Christ as jester (1962:133–138).

the role of cosmopolitan and stranger" (Stonequist 1937:xvii). In short, he exploits and makes permanent the liminal state of being "betwixt and between all fixed points in a status sequence" (Turner 1974:232).

One of the major differences between the picaro and the hero, which is central to the former's maintenance of marginality, is his refusal or inability to reintegrate himself socially through marriage. He is either exposed in his attempt to marry (as in *El Buscón*) or his marriage (like Lazarillo's) is based on false premises and self-delusion. The picaro's behavior regarding marriage is indicative, moreover, of his general inability to form any abiding relationships, most especially with women, whom he uses and abuses. Despite his much touted sexuality the picaro ultimately fails to perform.[14] This experience of a number of missed connections is echoed structurally in the "dance pattern" of "meetings and remeetings, . . . one character quickly slipping from another" (Miller 1967:14,17). And as Allan Janik notes, "the very point of the 'dance' motif [is that] sex without love is a meaningless, mechanical ritual" (Janik and Toulmin 1973:64).

In yet another contrast to the idealized and spiritualized realm of romance, the picaresque stresses the material level of existence. The monsters of the picaro's world are all too real and all too human, and he uses his wits as well as his religion simply to survive—physically and immediately—rather than toward some greater end. Beyond the subsistence level, the picaro, unlike the hero of spiritual pursuit, is a lover and pursuer of things found only in this world—the immediate gratification of material things, physical comforts,

[14] This failure to perform sexually and to establish lasting, meaningful relationships with women together with the picaro's assumption of female roles and clothes among his many masks connotes both transvestism and homosexuality. In several novels, moreover, the protagonist is a *picara*. This creative androgyny characteristic of trickster types finds its fullest expression in Virginia Woolf's neopicaresque *Orlando*, in which the title character changes sex every century.

and delights of the flesh. The very processes of signifying in such narratives express both the extreme materiality and the lack of connectedness in the picaro's world: there is a proliferation of signifiers and a relative poverty of signification, of meaning (Guedj 1968:82–83).[15] This too contributes to the meaninglessness or the reversibility of meaning of his experience, for those things which he covets have meaning only within a system which he has rejected.

The oft-repeated phrase "he lives by his wits" expresses yet another paradox of the picaro's existence. In this sense, too, he lives outside the ordinary feelings of the community: the hypertrophy of his practical intelligence replaces a full emotional development. Ironically, he usually just "takes over available patterns of feelings, and these are most likely to be conventional or orthodox" (Heilman 1958:549). In both a positive and negative sense the picaresque experience is an exercise of mind, a reveling in the mind as conqueror, a relishing of power through purely mental rather than physical or political or social means. Although necessity gives birth to the picaro's trickery and sharpens his wits, there is a point in every picaresque narrative beyond which trickery is indulged in for trickery's sake. In *El Buscón*, for example, Don Pablos joins and enjoys the band of "gentlemen" thieves despite the inheritance in his pocket. But, as Robert Heilman has pointed out: "In all literature that deals with the wit-conducted life there is, ultimately, ambiguity. Perhaps only detective stories naively exploit the passion for the mind's control of existence. Tragedy and picaresque set this passion in play; yet . . . both are penetrated by a sense of failure of mind alone. Picaresque heroes, at their best almost infinitely clever, nonetheless fall prey to . . . the irrationalities of cir-

---

[15] In another essay, "The Novel and the Carnival World (1974), I have discussed the uses and effects of a "surplus of signifiers" in symbolic processes, notably as an inversion, a mockery of the mode of signification of serious discourse.

cumstance" (1958:557–558). This ambiguity both delights and threatens us, for we cannot escape the fact that the picaro's intellectual virtue is also his vice, that his "shallowness" is both a disadvantage and an advantage.

Just as the picaro as protagonist has been criticized by literary commentators for his "shallowness," "flatness," and lack of self-awareness, so too the picaro as narrator is criticized for his limited and distorted perspective. While this is usually pointed out as a flaw—another instance of the rudimentary nature of this type of narrative—this convention of limited or restricted perspective is actually one of the virtues of the genre and is essential to its total inverse effect. This particular limitation is both a distinctive feature and a source of the vitality of the narrative form. Were the narrator-protagonist aware of his defects, much of the humor, irony, and ambiguity would be diminished, contaminated by dull and explicit social criticism or the typical self-righteousness of the satirist. The picaro's defects create an equivocal perspective which functions as an unknown, unexpected source of vitality to constantly repair the solvent effects of a critical attitude within the narrative itself.

In this regard, it is no accident that almost every picaresque narrative presents itself as a first-person autobiographical reminiscence. This mode of narration underlines the picaro's isolation and estrangement as well as the narrative's questioning, if not rejection, of norms, of authority, of objective reality. As Guillén points out, the use of the first person is "more than a formal frame. It means that not only are the hero and his actions picaresque, but everything *else* in the story is colored with the sensibility, or filtered through the mind, of the picaro-narrator" (1971:81).

The first-person point of view, which is split between an experiencing "I" and a narrating "I," calls our attention to the radical estrangement between inner and outer man and inserts the tale into "a double perspective of self-concealment and self-revelation" (Guillén 1971:82).[16] This difference between narrative attitude and events narrated is the major structural irony of the genre: he (narrator) who tells the reader to trust the credibility of his tale then describes himself (protagonist) as the master of deception and deceit. The narrator's statement to the reader about his narrative and his seeming contradiction of it, like the metacommunicative statement, "this is play," "generates a paradox of the Russellian or Epimenides type—a negative statement containing an implicit negative metastatement" (Bateson 1972:179–180). The liar's assertion that "this is not an *un*true story" establishes a paradoxical frame comparable to Epimenides' "Liar" paradox: "All Cretans are liars. I am a Cretan" (Colie 1966:6). Like all paradoxes, the paradox of the picaresque is both a direct criticism of itself as narrative statement and an oblique criticism of absolute judgement or absolute convention in general. Ultimately, of course, the reader, like the picaro himself and his other victims, is taken in, caught in the vertigo of infinite reflection and the play with human understanding. The first-person prevarication of the picaresque is intimately connected with the charges of formlessness, for it is almost impossible not to confuse the paradoxical and "unreliable" mode of presentation with the events that are presented, and hence to regard them and their organization as improbable and illogical. How else, when language has become the instrument of dissimulation and irony (Guillén 1971:81)?

There is yet another irony in the double perspective of first-person reminiscence if we think of "remembered" in the literal sense of the presumptuous autobiographical re-membering of something which is basically dismembered and disjointed. For, as Oskar Seidlin has pointed out, there is an ironic discrepancy between the lowly, marginal picaro and

---

[16] See also Wicks 1974:244–245.

the effrontery with which he dares to say "I," to reconstruct his life and adventures, and to offer them to the public with high moral seriousness (Seidlin 1951:191).

It is significant, therefore, that this public revelation may become even more self-conscious—the picaro finding his fullest expression of self as a performer-illusionist, either as one who identifies himself as a maker of illusions or as one who throws himself into a world of illusion in which misrule (or at least poetic license) is the rule. In *El Buscón* Don Pablos' career culminates in the profession of actor and playwright; in Thomas Mann's novel, Felix Krull is identified as an artist; and in *Easy Rider* the destination of Captain America and Billy is New Orleans' Mardi Gras. Mardi Gras is, of course, carnival, the period of license before Lent, and is defined in terms of masking, transformation, and inversion of norms and perceptions. The repeated identification of picaro and artist in modern expressions of the genre indicate that the preceding examples are not simply episodes or temporary professions in the life of the picaro, but synecdoches or base metaphors representing the entirety of the picaresque pattern in life and in art—fiction as a way of life.[17] That this lowlife delinquent is a master of many masks should not surprise us, for it is very likely that there is a positive correlation between marginality and fantasy. "Maybe groups and individuals who are cut out of the benefits of a given society are the ones who most often dream about another, and sometimes act to bring it about" (Cox 1970:64). We can at least say with certainty that in the picaresque, "fantasy thrives among the dissatisfied" (Cox 1970:64).[18]

[17] On the art of illusionism and manipulation as a vital part of the picaresque tradition, and the picaro as a man of imagination who "handles experience much the say an artist handles the materials of his art," and so on, see Alter 1965:126–132.

[18] The connection between fantasy and marginality is of course exemplified in the tales and myths of the Trickster, and the picaresque could be regarded as the written version of this in the modern Western world. For further discussion of the correlation between the marginal and the creative, see my " 'A Tolerated Margin of Mess': The Trickster and His Tales Reconsidered" (1975). This creativity is notably

Ultimately, the effect of such masking, transformation, and inversion as is characteristic of the picaresque is to render ambiguous or "nondisjunctive" (as Kristeva terms it) primary categories which are usually distinguished, such as good and evil, fidelity and treason, sacred and profane, life and death, and "high" and "low" style, and to negate these disjunctions as they are commonly maintained in the older genres of epic and romance.[19] When such basic discretions are inverted, the absolute separation of the discretion is called into question and, in terms of perception and behavior, a continuum of indistinction is created. Thus the utility, if not the validity, of such distinctions becomes a matter of debate. In *El Buscón*, for example, evil is initially equated with unreality and deception, and good with the real and the normal. But, as T. E. May points out, the "reality" that young Pablos confronts is so grotesque and deformed that he can only cope with this evil by assuming a role which is not a true one, by opting for "unreality" or inauthenticity (1950:322). Through this nondisjunction Quevedo raises the moral or metaphysical question, "What does it mean to choose unreality with one's eyes open?" Such transvaluations of values are characteristic of what happens when the hero of a novel must define his rebellion, his alienation from society, in terms which take their meaning from the very authorities he has come to reject (Poirier 1968:101). A reversibility of meaning is both the cause and the effect of a discontinuous world.

Nondisjunction both of meaning and of formal generic

---

expressed in the marginal's delight in the activity of disguise, his quick-change artistry denying the garment as a fixed symbol of class and the fixity of the social system (see Alter 1965:41–44).

[19] Kristeva (1970) sees just such nondisjunction of values and of generic patterns of expectation as essential to the development of complex prose fiction in the form of the realistic novel. With regard to the Spanish picaresque novel in particular, Whitbourne (1974:1–24) regards moral ambiguity as "one of its most essential and persistent characteristics, and which may account in some measure for its considerable popularity" (p. 16).

constraints—that is, the coexistence of two or more metacode signals and thus of several sets of expectations—also contributes to the "problematic" ending characteristic of the picaresque. Simply stated, the problem is this: If you don't have a developmental and an end-determined plot, if you parody the conventions and narrative structure of other literary forms, and if you deny the validity of all either-or categories, how *do* you conclude the picaro's life and adventures and yet maintain the novel's fundamental ambiguity? The narratives I have discussed here offer three alternatives:[20] (1) the picaro reenters society, sometimes through marriage, and is apparently reintegrated into the social structure; (2) the picaro is killed or punished; and (3) the picaro's adventures are "to be continued."

The first of these alternatives is the expected end of the romance or comic pattern. It is an unsatisfactory conclusion to the picaresque which has in other respects parodied and inverted the romance pattern. Unless the author has depicted a society which offers alternatives and the possibility of change, or evidence of an official culture that has an historical dignity, which the picaresque does *not*, reaggregation is not a viable or credible conclusion (Poirier 1968:101). When a picaresque narrative does end with reintegration, it is based upon false premises or self-delusion: for example, Lazarillo de Tormes marries the priest's whore and deludes himself regarding her fidelity as well as the importance of his social role as towncrier; Huck Finn is "reborn" in the form of Tom Sawyer and then uses the latter's literary lies to secure Jim's

[20] There are at least three other possible endings: (1) the wanderer reenters society but refuses to abandon his antisocial, antinormative behavior, in which case he is incarcerated in jail or the insane asylum—the modern version of banishment; (2) the deviant returns and remakes the society which expelled him—the pattern of idealistic, revolutionary narrative; and (3) the exile in his wanderings finds a society structured according to his own values, or returns home to find that the society he left has been transformed—the pattern of utopian literature. In all three cases there is a triumph of *one* set of values which reduces the ambiguous nondisjunction of social and antisocial values upon which the picaresque is predicated.

freedom. Such perversions of the romance ending result in little more than a deceptive and temporary restoration of equilibrium. It won't be long until Huck "lights out for the territories."

The second alternative expresses another vector of formal influence: the violation-punishment pattern of melodrama and tragedy in which the individual who violates social and human boundaries is punished, the social order preserved through "the sacrificial principle of victimage," and the victim elevated as martyr. Since picaresque narrative intermittently mocks this very pattern and is itself based on a violation of boundaries, this conclusion is also unsatisfactory if not gratuitous, as illustrated in the violent ending of *Easy Rider*.

Fonda's comments about his movie, its ending, and what he regards as the audience's misinterpretation, are illustrative of the problems of picaresque conclusions:

My movie is about the *lack* of freedom, not about freedom. My heroes are not right, they're wrong. The only thing I can end up doing is killing my character. I end up committing suicide; that's what I'm saying that America is doing. People go in and they think, "Look at those terrible rednecks, they killed those two free souls, who needed to love, blah, blah, blah." That's something we have to put up with.

We don't give out any information through dialogue. We have a very loose plot, nothing you can follow. You can't predict what's going to happen, and that puts everybody off. People want it predicted for them, they want violence to happen when they expect it to happen, so they can deal with it, they want sex to be a certain way and drugs to be a certain way and death to be a certain way. And it ain't. Neither is freedom. "Easy Rider" is a Southern term for a whore's old man, not a pimp, but the dude who lives with a chick. Because he's got the easy ride. Well, that's what happened to America, man. Liberty's become a whore, and we're all taking an easy ride.   [Hardin and Schlossberg 1969:28]

In terms of picaresque conventions, Fonda's interpretation,

the typical audience interpretation, and the ending are all in error in that they deny or cannot tolerate the fundamental ambiguity of the genre—they want things "to be a certain way"—which the movie *does* set up in its sympathetic and humorous treatment of antisocial characters and values. His movie is about *both* freedom *and* the lack of freedom; his heroes are *both* right *and* wrong, and we would have gotten that message had the film ended with that penultimate bit of dialogue, "We've done it" "No, we blew it," rather than motorized sacrifice.

This third alternative, the inconclusive conclusion exemplified in *El Buscón*'s "to be continued," is appropriate to the formal and ideological "openness" of picaresque narrative; it is also the logically probable ending of a first-person account of one's life and adventures.[21] In this sense, it doesn't really matter that Thomas Mann never finished *Felix Krull*. Further, I would suggest that "to be continued" is a conventional exit formula for any symbolic process or literary structure based on inversion and on formal and moral nondisjunction. The refusal to end maintains the ambiguity and the vitality of the form but, in most cases, is not meant to be taken literally. And yet, paradoxically, with the picaresque as with all "play" forms (see Bateson 1972) it doesn't work unless we do take the threat of inversion and the violation of boundaries seriously, seeing it in this case as a realistic reflection of the underlife of the group. As Frank Kermode has pointed out in *The Sense of an Ending*: "Men . . . make considerable imaginative investments in coherent patterns which, by the provision of an end, make possible a satisfying consonance with the origins and with the middle. . . . But they also, when awake and sane, feel the need to show a marked respect for things as they are; so that there is a recurring need for adjustments in the interests of reality as

---

[21] On the impossibility of ending a picaresque novel, see Alter 1965:33–34.

well as of control" (1967:17)—a need which the openness and infinite possibilities of picaresque structure fulfills. The absence of plot in Aristotle's sense is the result neither of carelessness nor of ineptitude, for there is, as Howell once said, "an art to not arriving."

To question why we continue to write and to read and to enjoy the picaresque pattern of inversion is tantamount to asking why are there always "social bandits"? Perhaps the old brigand had the last word when he said, "We are sad, it is true, but that is because we have always been persecuted. The gentry use the pen, we the gun" (Hobsbawm 1969:13). Or, as Vita Sackville-West said of Virginia Woolf when she called her gamekeeper's coat a poacher's, "The poacher would naturally be dearer to her mind than the gamekeeper" (Noble 1972:136). Such literary poachers remind us that even the gamekeeper's laws are man-made fictions.

References

Alter, Robert. 1965. *Rogue's Progress: Studies in the Picaresque Novel.* Cambridge: Harvard University Press.

Anon. 1554. *Lazarillo de Tormes* (trans.). In Flores, pp. 25–84.

Babcock-Abrahams, Barbara. 1974. "The Carnivalization of the Novel." *Modern Language Notes* 89:911–937.

———. 1975. " 'A Tolerated Margin of Mess': The Trickster and His Tales Reconsidered." *Journal of the Folklore Institute* 11:147–186.

Bataillon, M. 1931. *Le roman picaresque.* Paris: La Renaissance du livre.

Bateson, Gregory. 1972. "A Theory of Play and Fantasy." In *Steps to an Ecology of Mind.* San Francisco: Chandler. Pp. 177–200.

Chandler, F. W. 1899. *Romances of Roquery: An Episode in the History of the Novel.* Part I, *The Picaresque Novel in Spain.* New York: Macmillan.

Colie, Rosalie Little. 1966. *Paradoxia Epidemia: The Renaissance Tradition of Paradox.* Princeton: Princeton University Press.

Cox, Harvey. 1970. *The Feast of Fools: A Theological Essay on Festivity and Fantasy.* New York: Harper & Row.

Dooley, D. J. 1957–1958. "Some Uses and Mutations of the Picaresque." *Dalhousie Review* 37:363–377.

Flores, Angel, ed. 1957. *Masterpieces of the Spanish Golden Age.* New York: Holt, Rinehart & Winston.

Frohock, W. M. 1967. "The Idea of the Picaresque." *Yearbook of Comparative and General Literature* 16:43–52.

———. 1969. "The Falling Center: Recent Fiction and the Picaresque Tradition." *Novel* 3:62–69.

Ghose, Zulfikar. 1972. *The Incredible Brazilian.* New York: Holt, Rinehart & Winston.

Gilman, Stephen. 1966. "The Death of Lazarillo de Tormes." *PMLA* 81: 149–166.

Guedj, Aimé. 1968. "Structure du monde picaresque." *Linguistique et littérature.* La nouvelle critique, Numéro special, Colloque de Cluny, 16–17 April. Pp. 82–87.

Guillén, Claudio. 1971. *Literature as System: Essays toward a Theory of Literary History.* Princeton: Princeton University Press.

Hardin, Nancy, and Marilyn Schlossberg, eds. 1969. *Easy Rider: Original Screenplay by Peter Fonda, Dennis Hopper, Terry Southern.* New York: New American Library.

Hegel, G. W. F. 1964. *The Phenomenology of Mind.* Trans. James Baillie. New York: Humanities Press.

Heilman, Robert B. 1958. "Felix Krull: Variations on Picaresque." *Sewanee Review* 66:547–577.

Hobsbawm, Eric. 1969. *Bandits.* New York: Dell.

Jakobson, Roman. 1960. "Closing Statement: Linguistics and Poetics." In Thomas A. Sebeok, ed., *Style in Language.* Cambridge: M.I.T. Press.

Janik, Allan, and Stephen Toulmin. 1973. *Wittgenstein's Vienna.* New York: Simon and Schuster.

Kermode, Frank. 1967. *The Sense of an Ending: Studies in the Theory of Fiction.* New York: Oxford.

Kolakowski, Leszek. 1962. "The Priest and the Jester." *Dissent* 9:215–235.

Kristeva, Julia. 1970. *Le texte du roman: Approche sémiologique d'une structure discursive transformationnelle.* The Hague: Mouton.

Mann, Thomas, 1955. *Confessions of Felix Krull, Confidence Man: The Early Years.* New York: Vintage.

May, T. E. 1950. "Good and Evil in the Buscón: A Survey." *Modern Language Review* 45:319–335.

Miller, Stuart. 1967. *The Picaresque Novel.* Cleveland, London: Case Western Reserve University Press.

Noble, Joan Russell, ed. 1972. *Recollections of Virginia Woolf.* London: Owen.

Parker, A. A. 1967. *Literature and the Delinquent: The Picaresque Novel in Spain and Europe, 1599–1753.* Edinburgh: Edinburgh University Press.

Poirier, Richard. 1968. "Huck Finn and the Metaphors of Society." In Claude M. Simpson, ed., *Twentieth Century Interpretations of "The Adven-*

tures of Huckleberry Finn." Englewood Cliffs, N.J.: Prentice-Hall. Pp. 92–101.

de Quevedo, Francisco. 1626. *The Life and Adventures of Don Pablos the Sharper* (trans.). In Flores, pp. 85–234.

Raglan, Lord. 1936. *The Hero: A Study in Tradition, Myth, and Drama.* London: Methuen.

Rank, Otto. 1957. *The Myth of the Birth of the Hero.* Trans. F. Robbins and Smith Ely Jelliffe. New York: R. Brunner.

Seidlin, Oskar. 1951. "Picaresque Elements in Thomas Mann's Work." *Modern Language Quarterly* 12:183–200.

Stonequist, E. V. 1937. *The Marginal Man: A Study in Personality and Culture Conflict.* New York: Scribner's.

Turner, Victor. 1967. *The Forest of Symbols: Aspects of Ndembu Ritual.* Ithaca, N.Y.: Cornell University Press.

——. 1969. *The Ritual Process: Structure and Anti-Structure.* Chicago: Aldine.

——. 1974. "Passages, Margins, and Poverty: Religious Symbols of Communitas." In *Dramas, Fields, and Metaphors.* Ithaca, N.Y.: Cornell University Press. Pp. 231–271.

van Gennep, Arnold. 1960. *The Rites of Passage.* Chicago: University of Chicago Press.

Wadlington, Warwick P. 1973. Personal communication.

Weightman, John. 1969. "The Outsider Rides Again." *Encounter* 33:46–50.

Whitbourne, Christine J., ed. 1974. *Knaves and Swindlers: Essays on the Picaresque Novel in Europe.* London: Oxford University Press.

Wicks, Ulrich. 1972. "Picaro, Picaresque: The Picaresque in Literary Scholarship." *Genre* 5:153–216.

——. 1974. "The Nature of Picaresque Narrative: A Modal Approach." *PMLA* 89:240–249.

Woolf, Virginia. 1928. *Orlando: A Biography.* New York: Harcourt Brace Jovanovich.

CHAPTER 3

Inversion and the Erotic:
The Case of William Blake

DIANE CHRISTIAN

Inversion is familiar in literature. Satire and irony derive generic definition from the play of symbolic inversion, and tragedy and comedy employ reversals, transgressions, and partial inversions of order. My interest here is in a specific range of thematic inversions—those involved in the literary presentation of the erotic. The poet I choose is William Blake (1757–1827), a poet and painter whose composite art form itself invokes questions of verbal and visual inversion. Although Blake is an artist who tests the boundaries and paradoxes of conventional perception, my concern is not with this interesting formal problem but rather with Blake's startling inversions of the erotic tradition.

Blake's position on desire and the erotic challenges the religious and moral traditions he both springs from and continues. He rejects conventional Spenserian or Miltonic distrust of desire. The proverb from *The Marriage of Heaven and Hell* runs: "Sooner murder an infant in its cradle than nurse unacted desires" (10:67, E37).[1] Like Swift's "A Modest Proposal," this is to be read, of course, not as incitement to infanticide, but as admonition to effective desiring. The jaunty and energetic devil of Blake's satire is instructively outra-

---

[1] All Blake citations are from Blake 1970 except for letters. For works in illuminated printing the plate and line numbers are given (separated by a colon) and the Erdman text page is preceded by an "E." If there are no line numbers, only the plate number is given.

geous. Yet the closing admonition of the same text is more directly hortatory and more obviously problematic:

Let the Priests of the Raven of dawn, no longer in deadly black. with hoarse note curse the sons of joy. Nor his accepted brethren whom, tyrant, he calls free: lay the bound or build the roof. Nor pale religious letchery call that virginity, that wishes but acts not!
For every thing that lives is Holy.   [25, E44]

Blake rejects religious repression along with societal repression but seems at the same time to employ the diction of holiness to justify his counsel. Critics have more easily dealt with Blake's social passions and pronouncements than with those on pleasure. In condemning sexual repression and the virginal ideal, Blake questions Milton and centuries of orthodox Christian doctrine. He does so to establish an inversion which is meant, like so many ritual inversions, to reestablish a valued order.

In manuscript, Blake has several short poems dealing with desire. The most famous, perhaps, is the following:

What is it men in women do require
The lineaments of Gratified Desire
What is it women do in men require
The lineaments of Gratified Desire.   [E466]

Desire is said to be mutual, and the poem does not type women as differing from men. The poem also avoids moralizing. Whatever the "lineaments of Gratified Desire" are, all wish them, and such lineaments seem universally positive. Another poem in the same notebook repeats the phrase but articulates a distinction in female desire or role:

In a wife I would desire
What in whores is always found
The lineaments of Gratified desire.   [E465]

This poem emphasizes the frankly sexual nature of the lineaments and the desire of the persona for a sensual partner. The wife should emulate the wanton in desire. This is somewhat surprising in Blake as he attacked the virgin-whore split (which Freud would later label the most common form of degradation in erotic life; 1963:58–70). Blake argued that "Every Harlot was once a Virgin" and that brothels were built with bricks of religion.[2] He castigated cults of virginity for canonizing a state of enshrined enervation and, worse, for being passive-aggressive tactics of sexual domination. They enslave by negation, shame, and guilt, he would say. In *Jerusalem* Blake pointed to a deeper identity beneath the moralized dichotomies:

> What is a Wife & what is a Harlot? What is a Church? &
>   What
> Is a Theatre? are they Two & not One? can they Exist
>   Separate?
> Are not Religion & Politics the Same Thing?
>
>   [57:8–10, E205]

What Blake means to do in referring to wife and whore is not to reaffirm the good and bad moralizations of woman, but to praise sexual desire by a calculated reversal of moralized expectation.

One Blakean inversion, then, is the upset of conventional social usage. Erotic desire is affirmed, asceticism decried in this manuscript poem:

> Abstinence sows sand all over
> The ruddy limbs & flaming hair
> But Desire Gratified
> Plants fruits of life & beauty there.   [E465]

Blake rejoins the old psychomachia between reason and desire, taking the devil's part against conventional moral restraint. *The Marriage of Heaven and Hell*, which sets out to satirize the old diction, is full of appropriately shocking proverbs:

[2] *Jerusalem* 61:52, E210; *The Marriage of Heaven and Hell* 8:21, E36. The parallel continuation of "Every Harlot was once a Virgin" is "every Criminal an Infant Love!"

The road of excess leads to the palace of wisdom.   [7:3, E35]
Damn. braces: Bless relaxes.   [9:57, E37]
Prudence is a rich ugly old maid courted by Incapacity. [7:4, E35]
The head Sublime, the heart Pathos, the genitals Beauty.
                                                        [10:61, E37]

In *The Marriage of Heaven and Hell*, reason, not desire, is regarded as ruinous to man. Desire, on the contrary, is energy and life, and those who restrain it do so because theirs is weak enough to be restrained. In these people, Blake says, reason usurps desire's primary place, and desire becomes a passive shadow of itself. Blake wryly remarks that the history of this is written in *Paradise Lost*, where reason is called "Messiah" (5, E34). That critique of Milton, who sought to make reason as passionate as possible, is telling. It is also noteworthy because Milton was Blake's hero and model, the only poet in the English tradition who was republican and prophetic enough to suit him. Blake registered his disagreements, however, and argued at the beginning of his epic *Milton* that this poet, like Shakespeare, had been infected by false heroism, by "the silly Greek & Latin slaves of the Sword" (1, E94). In the epic, however, Milton returns to correct his errors, one of which is erotic puritanism. Blake attempted to reverse the reason-passion dialectic which Milton labored, seeing in its obsession with temptation and the flesh an implicit judgment against the body and women. The error of the moralist Lavater and his contemporaries, Blake wrote in an annotation to Lavater's aphorisms, was that they thought woman's love a sin (p. 227, E590). For Blake, hostility to the body and toward the feminine underlies antipassional diction, and mistakes the real battle of man. It is a self-division before it is a social one, and it is that personal self-division, according to Blake, which structures all war. The rejection is of one's own body. The first error to expunge, announces the persona of *The Marriage of Heaven and Hell*, is the notion that man has a body separate from his soul. The voice of the devil pronounces further historical judgment on the recurring error and its consequences:

All Bibles or sacred codes. have been the causes of the following Errors.
   1. That Man has two real existing principles Viz: a Body & a Soul.
   2. That Energy. calld Evil. is alone from the Body. & that Reason. calld Good. is alone from the Soul.
   3. That God will torment Man in Eternity for following his Energies.

He continues, to argue that

the following Contraries to these are True
   1 Man has no Body distinct from his Soul for that calld Body is a portion of Soul discernd by the five Senses, the chief inlets of Soul in this age
   2 Energy is the only life and is from the Body and Reason is the bound or outward circumference of Energy.
   3 Energy is Eternal Delight.   [4, E34]

Blake inverts the body-soul diction and rejects the religious distrust and contempt of desire and pleasure. He is not content, however, to be a romantic rebel or the dysangel Swinburne incorrectly envied. On the contrary, he retains and reshapes the diction of the holy, though he jettisons the temptation-versus-passion scenario of goodness. Desire is prescribed, not proscribed. In Blake's "A Vision of the Last Judgment," a commentary on his painting, he asserts that

Men are admitted into Heaven not because they have ⟨curbed &⟩ governd their Passions or have No Passions but because they have Cultivated their Understandings. The Treasures of Heaven are not Negations of Passion but Realities of Intellect from which All the Passions Emanate ⟨Uncurbed⟩ in their Eternal Glory The Fool shall not enter into Heaven let him be ever so Holy. Holiness is not The Price of Enterance into Heaven Those who are cast out Are All Those who having no Passions of their own because No Intellect. Have spent their lives in Curbing & Governing other Peoples by the Various arts of Poverty & Cruelty of all kinds.
                                         [p. 87, E553–554]

The inversion of the body-soul and reason-passion dichotomies serves to reexamine the conventional wisdom and
claims to serve it more correctly. Body is not to be blamed,
Blake argues; mind is the villain.[3] In his mythology, as in
"The Human Abstract" (in *Songs of Experience*, E27), Blake
pursues that insight. He views psychic disruption or fall as
the impoverishment of sensual life rather than a lapse into it.
The primal human error for him is not passionate sensual in-
dulgence, but mental murder. The first crime is abstraction,
*dis*incarnating reality. The tree of mystery and deceit and
human sacrifice grows not in nature but in the human brain.
Blake's inversion of erotic distrust does more than revalue
eroticism. It offers eroticism as a model of primary integration instead of primary dissolution. With this, Blake also
reintroduces the acceptability of psychic conflict and energy.
He names a contrary dialectic as necessary to human life:
"Without Contraries is no progression. Attraction and Repul-
sion, Reason and Energy, Love and Hate, are necessary to
Human existence."[4]

Yet Blake's contraries are not simple reversals. He reverses
mind-body priorities and excellence, and equates sensual energy with eternal delight. Heaven becomes the reward of
energy and is described as passionate life itself. But the conversion is not simply from Apollonian to Dionysian attitudes. Blake means by his inversions to redefine desire and
passion, not simply to indulge them.

In the classical understanding of erotic desire, the debate
to which Blake speaks, desire is usually analyzed in terms of

[3] Blake's reproof of reason and his praise here of intellect as the source of passion
is at first confusing. The paradox informs much of his dialectic, but a kind of resolu-
tion can be understood by noting that Blake redistributes the reason-passion terms
as purely mental conflict. He makes intellect or mental things the battleground
rather than the body.

[4] *The Marriage of Heaven and Hell* 3, E34. The rest of the passage is appropriate
also: "From these contraries spring what the religious call Good & Evil. Good is the
passive that obeys Reason[.] Evil is the active springing from Energy. Good is
Heaven. Evil is Hell."

theories of need. In Plato's *Symposium*, love or desire is said to come from lack. Poverty seduces Contrivance and births Eros.[5] Aristophanes offers a loftier view of need and asserts that love is a name for the desire and pursuit of the whole. He tells the myth of the original androgynes who are split by Zeus and eternally wander in search of their other halves. Love seeks to restore us to our former state and heal the wounds humanity has suffered. The final theory in the discussion is offered by Socrates, who shows love moving one up the Platonic ladder. Love transmutes erotic physical impulse into procreative spiritual love, into man's approximation of immortality. Desire in each case is linked to appetite and lack, and the grades of gratification range from simple pleasure to philosophic rapture.

Such generally Apollonian views can be balanced by darker and more violent Dionysian theories. It was also anciently argued that eros had strange relations with thanatos. Bataille, a modern theorist, has pressed the Dionysian insight and can represent the case well. He links eroticism and sensuality directly to death in his study *Death and Sensuality* (1962). He romanticizes erotic activity as a testing of the boundaries of continuity and discontinuity, attempting to dissolve the discontinuous and thus being mimetic of death. Eroticism, in his view, exorcises death by ritual sacrifice, by acting it out. Violation and transgression are tabooed because they are our true desire. Erotic activity does not so much transform as unmask the murder behind. The genitals are ugly and obscene, Bataille says, eroticizing them marks their true terror. The finest erotic object, he continues, is the beautiful woman, because violation is heightened by greater despoilation.

In both representative theories, then, the erotic sacrifice is

---

[5] Plato 1969:545. For this text the Walter Hamilton translation in the Penguin edition of *The Symposium* (p. 65) is better (ed. Betty Rodicet and Robert Baldick, Baltimore, 1967).

the body. In Plato, the physical is transcended; and it is not simply subordinated, but denigrated. In Bataille, it is ravished. What begins in the *Symposium* as a highly charged erotic encounter ends with Socrates resisting the beautiful Alcibiades and preaching against physical pleasures. He goes off to bathe. Reason wins as the philosopher takes his pleasure in transforming desire out of its object. That, in fact, is the very refining process of love which Socrates outlines. The process begins with attraction to one beautiful youth, then grows to find beauty in many, then turns to greater, moral beauty, and finally flies to the world of the ideal. Bataille, who is less attracted to metaphysics, is more erotically interesting, as are the Dionysians generally. But still the body is sacrificed to another appetite; it is ravished to serve the desire for death, for despoilation, for the dissolution of all boundary and individuality.

Bataille, unlike Plato, separates physical and emotional eroticism from the higher or religious eroticism. The former is sealed in its violent mimesis and depends on an object, on the chance of finding and sustaining relations with an other. But religious eroticism eliminates the object: "the divine is the essence of continuity" (p. 113). It is not dependent on discontinuous individual lovers. Like Platonic eroticism, it is ultimately dependent on man's will. And it turns from the tumults of physical passion to a self-contained and more serene passion. Religious mysticism in Bataille approximates philosophy for Plato: it is both learning death and rapture.

These erotic theories attempt to stabilize sexual volatility and terror by denial and by translation to a superior plane. Eroticism is linked to a theory of or appetite for immortality (and to the dualism structuring that problem). It may be a staying of death, as Bataille suggests, an assent *up to* the point of death, or an exorcism of it. Or it may be the escape from death that Plato makes it. But in some manner eroticism faces that violence of the body which looms as body's supreme and opposite spectre: death.

These views, which characterize the classical Apollonian and Dionysian positions, differ from Blake's. Plato works a paradox: he starts from physical eroticsim and shows its end to be physically anti-erotic and spiritual. Bataille works a dualism which collapses: he sees physical and emotional eroticism as mimetic of death and violence, and religious eroticism as free of that physical mimesis but still obedient to the same force. Mysticism becomes more subtle spiritual sensuality; the self-violence of ascesis satisfies the model of violation and transgression. Blake, in contrast, works an inversion which does not destroy physical eroticism. He first denies the dualism of body and soul which Apollonian and Dionysian extremes employ. And he inverts the traditional diction dependent on that body-soul split—giving energy, delight, and life to desire and the body, and the contraries to reason and mind. Body grows and rejoices; mind limits and denies. Abstinence sows sand but desire gratified plants seeds of life and beauty (ms. poem, E465). Idealist and Apollonian diction is denied and so also is the Dionysian, because desire and the erotic are not linked with death but with life. In Blake's system, desire is not the double of bodily convulsion or violence and death; it is the contrary. Man's psyche in Blake's schematization does have a double, a shadow part of him which is a murderous and killing rage, but it belongs not to man's body but to his reason. As Los says in *Jerusalem:*

> The Spectre is the Reasoning Power in Man; & when
>   separated
> From Imagination, and closing itself as in steel, in a Ratio
> Of the Things of Memory. It thence frames Laws &
>   Moralities
> To destroy Imagination! the Divine Body, by Martyrdoms
>   & Wars.   [74:10–13, E227]

Blake uses a triad to express psychic organization. There is a shadow double of the same sex and an emanation of the opposite sex. The male-female strife is not the central conflict; the real warfare is between the doubles. Self-murder is man's real menace and its consequences are social and sexual murder. Blake saw war as perverted sexual energy and read it further as a rejection of heterosexuality. His manuscript poem is a succinct statement:

> Twas the Greeks love of War
> turnd Love into a Boy
> And Woman into a Statue of Stone
> And away fled every Joy. [E470]

Blake's belief in the goodness and beneficent power of eros remains a central inversion of the tradition. It reverses the Platonic attitude toward the physical and denies the tragic fury of the Dionysian stance. The first is impressive because of the powerful religious and ethical strictures against the flesh, the second because it casts man's desires in a comic rather than a tragic perspective. Bataille's Dionysian insistence on the despoilation and transgression inherent in eros speaks to the sadistic overtones which mark treatment of the erotic as violation. Though Bataille maintains only an interest in de Sade's conclusion of that logic—namely the hold of murder over the senses—his view is shot through with that sense of perversion or criminality as intrinsic to desire. He writes, for example, "In essence the domain of eroticism is the domain of violence, of violation," and "this aura of death is what denotes passion" (Bataille 1962:10, 15).

Denis de Rougemont (1963) has tried to place the case against such a tragic view of eros in his study, *Love in the Western World*. He links it historically to the cult of courtly love and traces its origins to an heretical Christian contempt for the flesh. He finds the view radically antibody, antimarriage and antichild. Tristram's sword is his true desire, says de Rougemont, not the lady lying on the other side of it. For him, the tragic tradition of fated love has poisoned the Western world's view of eros. Though Blake is capable of charting astonishing psychic violences in his myths, he does not deny the positive fulfillment of eros. And he links that fulfillment to great art. He writes his artist friend Cumberland to "show the antique borers that domestic peace and plenty are the source of true art."[6] Unlike Freud, Blake sees eroticism and art as essentially unneurotic.

Plato finds the physical repulsive and Bataille says that man comes to the erotic through guilt and shame, for the sexual act is always—like murder—tabooed. But Blake identifies the genitals with beauty and the nakedness of woman with the work of God.[7] For Blake the sense of despoliation comes not from the body but from divorce from it, from sense deprivation, enervation, and impotence. Blake's sense of despoliation, in fact, comes from man's very romance with the spectre of death. For Blake, eroticism and sexual desire may mirror corporeal war, when they are perverted to serve power. They become the merchantry of the harlot or the passive-aggressiveness and cruelty of the virgin, the brutishness of the ravisher, or the pious repressions of the secret lechers. But desire and sexual love also mirror what Blake called mental war, the energetic exercise of art. Lovemaking for Blake is an active image of the forgiveness and inclusiveness possible to man, the reunion of division joyfully overcome.

One of Blake's engravings for Blair's *The Grave* is the reunion of the body and soul. It shows a lady swooping passionately into the embrace of a man climbing from the grave. The body-soul unity is the resurrection from death for Blake.

---

[6]*Letter to Cumberland* 6 (Dec. 1795), in Geoffrey Keynes, ed., *The Letters of William Blake* (New York: Macmillan, p. 30. The rest of the sentence is also appropriate: "& prove to the Abstract Philosophers that Enjoyment & not Abstinence is the food of Intellect."

[7]*The Marriage of Heaven and Hell* 10:61, E37; 8:25 E36.

That experience of ecstasy and joy is for Blake the continuity which Bataille attributes to death and which Plato seeks in freedom from the body. Thus Blake's inversions of the tradition serve not only to challenge its two central expressions, but to invert with an erotic literalness their anti-erotic conclusions.

References

Bataille, Georges. 1962. *Death and Sensuality: A Study of Eroticism and the Taboo*. New York: Ballantine.

Blake, William. 1970. *The Poetry and Prose of William Blake*, ed. David Erdman. Garden City, N.Y.: Doubleday.

Freud, Sigmund. 1963. "The Most Prevalent Form of Degradation in Erotic Life," trans. Joan Riviere. In Philip Rieff, ed., *Freud, Sexuality and the Psychology of Love*. New York: Collier.

Plato. 1969. *The Symposium*, trans. Michael Joyce. In Edith Hamilton and Huntington Cairns, eds., *The Collected Dialogues of Plato*. Princeton: Bollingen.

Rougemont, Denis de. 1963. *Love in the Western World*. New York: Fawcett.

CHAPTER 4

De-construction in
Waiting for Godot

DINA SHERZER

Waiting for Godot is a play stripped of action. Vladimir and Estragon, two puppets suffering in the middle of a no-man's-land, say they have an appointment with a man called Godot, and during the two acts of the play they wait for him. While they are waiting Pozzo and Lucky come by, stay for a while, and go away. To help pass time the characters talk. The play lacks a plot, development of characters, or suspense; action exists nevertheless, but at the level of language. More precisely, speech is the animating principle of *Waiting for Godot.* However, the characters do not attract attention because of their witty repartees or because of their lively dialogues, but by the way they play with language at several levels. I do not mean play in the ludic sense of playing for fun, but in the sense of manipulating elements of language, or rearranging them using different patterns of association. It is important to stress that this verbal activity is not a deviation from commonly held rules of language, but rather a manipulation of them which results in an exploitation of syntactic, semantic, phonic, and discourse possibilities.[1]

Beckett has been noted for saying that in his work he is preoccupied mainly with sounds and that he accepts respon-

[1] For the notion of deviation see Cohen 1966, Levin 1967, and Ohmann 1971. To say that an utterance is a deviation from a norm is a very limiting statement, however, since it is quite difficult to define what the norm is, and since a deviation used repeatedly creates its own norm. It is more fruitful to observe what is manipulated and see how rules and properties of language are exploited for particular effects.

sibility for nothing else (1958b). This claim has to be taken tongue in cheek. Beckett is indeed a writer who is preoccupied with sounds, but he is also interested in and plays with verbal behavior, so much so that in *Waiting for Godot* it is possible to establish a typology of the different ways in which rules of language and speech are manipulated: (1) the discourse of speech acts and events, that is, the communication established between characters in particular contexts, (2) the manipulation of the rules of semantic association, (3) the use of different registers of language, (4) the use of semantic paradigms and synonyms, (5) the use of common expressions and clichés, (6) the exploitation of the different meanings of a single word, and (7) the use of sounds and sequences of sounds.

The play was first written in French (published by Editions de Minuit), then translated into English by Samuel Beckett himself (published by Grove Press). I will quote examples from both texts, especially when certain effects of the French text have disappeared in the English version because of English grammar—for instance the opposition *tu/vous*, the singular or familiar (*tu*) versus the plural or formal (*vous*) forms of "you."

Play with the Rules of Discourse

In order to understand the ways Beckett manipulates rules of discourse it is necessary to view language in the context of its use. To do so I will make use of the components of the speech event described by Jakobson (1960) and elaborated by Hymes (1972): *participant* (addressor-addressee), *key* (the way the message is to be taken—seriously, mockingly, etc), and *topic of discourse.*

Manipulation of the relationship between participants and discourse. Pozzo is talking to Vladimir and Estragon and also to his servant Lucky: "Gentlemen, I am happy to have met you. Yes, yes, sincerely happy. *Closer! Stop!* Yes the road seems long when one journeys all along for . . . yes . . . yes, six hours. That's right six hours on end, and never a soul in sight. *Coat! Hold that! Coat!* Touch of autumn in the air this evening. *Whip!* Yes, gentlemen, I cannot go for long without the society of my likes even when the likeness is an imperfect one. *Stool!*" (p. 16). This speech has one addressor—Pozzo—and two sets of addressees—Vladimir and Estragon form one set and Lucky alone forms the other. To Vladimir and Estragon, Pozzo comments on his recent meeting with them, talks about his situation as a traveler, and makes remarks about the weather. He establishes contact by means of an ordinary, superficial conversation. On the other hand, when he addresses himself to Lucky he gives orders. Pozzo is thus involved in two speech events which are mingled and overlapped within a single discourse. The result is a verbal pattern analogous to juggling, and it recalls the technique of a clown.

Play with the key. Another interesting example of manipulation of the relationship between the participants and the discourse is provided in the scene where Vladimir and Estragon look at Lucky:

Vla: He's not bad looking.
Est: Would you say so?
Vla: A trifle effeminate.
Est: Look at the slobber

. . . . .

Vla: Perhaps he's a halfwit.
Est: A cretin. [p. 17]

Vladimir and Estragon talk about Lucky in his presence; they are very close to him and in fact are inspecting his neck. Furthermore, Vladimir and Estragon express their private thoughts about Lucky; they make remarks that ordinarily would not be uttered in front of the person that is talked about, unless done in a humorous way, in which case both the addressor and the addressee are aware of it. But the conversation about Lucky is carried on very seriously, and it can therefore be taken as a playing with what Hymes calls the key. In other words, the serious (rather than humorous) key used by Vladimir and Estragon is that appropriate to talk about children, animals, and other "nonpersons" in their presence.[2] This speech usage thus renders Lucky a nonperson. Another example of playing with the key occurs in the following remark by Vladimir who, looking at Estragon's leg after it has been kicked, says *triomphantly* (this is the stage direction given by Beckett): "There's the wound! Beginning to fester!" (p. 43). The content of the constatation is negative since it has to do with a wound that is becoming infected, but the assertion is pronounced as if it was a marvelous discovery.

Play with the rules of logical sequencing of discourse. Here is a verbal exchange between Vladimir and Estragon:

(1) Vla: The last moment . . . Hope deferred maketh the something sick, who said that?
Est: Why don't you help me?
Vla: Sometimes I feel it coming all the same. Then I go all queer. [p. 8]

Further in the play Pozzo and Estragon carry on in the same fashion:

(2) Est: Why doesn't he put down his bags?
Po: I too would be happy to meet him. The more people I meet the happier I become. . . . Even you . . . even you, who knows, will have added to my store.
Est: Why doesn't he put down his bags?
Po: But that would surprise me. [p. 20]

In (1) Estragon answers Vladimir's question by another question. It is quite possible in conversation to do so, but the question put forth as an answer usually has a logical link

---

[2] This notion is presented by Goffman 1959.

with the first one, as for instance in the interchange: "Would you close the window?" "Are you cold?" But Beckett manipulates this form of discourse (question answering) so that the two questions have nothing in common: Vladimir asks the name of the author of a biblical saying whereas Estragon asks Vladimir to help him take off his shoe. In (2) Estragon requests some information about Lucky, and Pozzo answers that he likes meeting people. The two sequences have nothing in common; each of the characters is involved in his own trend of thought and does not pay attention to what the other one is saying. Similar examples are quite frequent in the play. For instance, at one point Pozzo complains of having lost his pulverizer, and Estragon answers, or rather does not answer, since he complains of having a weak lung (p. 27). Here Beckett plays with the rules of sequencing. Instead of topics being dealt with successively, they are brought up simultaneously, and consequently no communication is established; it is just an exchange of sentences which does not bring the characters together or lead to an understanding, but results in mere coexistence.

Sometimes exchanges of this type can yield a meaning of metaphysical significance. For instance, when Estragon gives up trying to take off his boot, he says: "Nothing to be done," which can be understood as "it is impossible to take off my boot," but also can be interpreted as a general statement about life. Vladimir takes it as such since he says: "I'm beginning to come around to that opinion. All my life I've tried to put it from me, saying, Vladimir be reasonable, you haven't yet tried everything. And I resumed the struggle" (p. 7). This particular way of making sense, which is frequent in the verbal exchanges of Beckett's characters, is what Cavell calls "hidden literality." [3]

[3] Stanley Cavell (1969), studying *Endgame*, points out that it is erroneous to say that language is undergoing disintegration in Beckett's plays, that on the contrary language takes on a hidden literality which makes us aware of what language really says.

Play with ratifiers. The following examples also involve the manipulation of a rule of verbal exchange.

(1) Est: I had a dream.
Vla: Don't tell me!
Est: I dreamt that—   [p. 11]
(2) Est: You know the story of the Englishman in the brothel?
Vla: Yes.
Est: Tell it to me.
Vla: Ah stop it!
Est: An Englishman having drunk. . . .   [p. 11]

Estragon behaves as if he had been asked to continue his story, to go on talking, when in fact he has been told to stop. In other words, the order to stop is reacted to as if it was a request to go on. It would be plausible after hearing "don't tell me" for Estragon to proceed and tell his dream, had he said for instance, "listen, it's quite interesting"; in other words the addressor has to show a reason why he can go on. Here this link is missing and Beckett plays with what have been called conversational "ratifiers" (Ekmann and Friesen 1969).

Play with the topic. Vladimir and Estragon are always looking for things to do or say to make time go by, and at one point Estragon suggests, "What about hanging ourselves?" After the two characters have agreed to hang themselves, the following exchange takes place:

Vla: Go ahead.
Est: After you.
Vla: No, no, you first.   [p. 12]

Such formulas of politeness are quite common and can be heard in a bus or in front of a door: they refer to such insignificant actions as taking a seat or going through a door. But here this everyday ritual is used by characters talking about hanging themselves. It is not the structure of the interaction that is played with, but the relationship between the topic and the discourse. This distortion creates a comic and a disturbing effect at the same time, because a banal subject is re-placed by a serious one and because the characters can talk about hanging themselves in a very matter of fact fashion, as if it were a subject of no more importance than who goes through a door first. Here the verbal exchange draws on a perfectly normal use of the politeness formulas of everyday interaction and applies them to the serious act of hanging oneself.

Play with the relationship between the meaning of individual elements of an utterance and its total meaning. When Vladimir first sees Estragon at the beginning of the play he says to him: "So there you are again." And Estragon answers: "Am I?" (p. 7). Vladimir's utterance is a speech act of greeting and has to be understood as a whole; instead Estragon interprets it at a more superficial syntactic level and focuses on the literal meaning of the verb *to be*. Further in the play Vladimir, re-ferring to Godot, says to Pozzo: "Oh he's a . . . he's a kind of acquaintance." And Estragon adds: "Nothing of the kind, we hardly know him" (p. 16). The ambiguity is created by the word "acquaintance" which means "somebody one knows." Estragon things that Vladimir has not said the truth, and wants to correct him, because for him acquaint-ance means "somebody one knows well," when in fact Vladi-mir tells Pozzo they do not know Godot intimately.[4]

In this section of the play the manipulation of the rules of discourse has two results. First, the characters do not use language according to commonly held rules but rather in in-congruous ways. Second, language does not establish com-munication between the characters; thus these devices

[4] This is a frequent device exploited in comedies. In the French version of *Waiting for Godot* the following example occurs. Vladimir is surprised that Estragon has read the Bible because he attended "L'école sans Dieu" (school without God). Estragon answers, "Sais pas si elle était sans ou avec" (don't know whether it was without or with) (p. 13). In *La leçon* by Ionesco one finds this exchange: "Professeur: Prenez le mot front" (Professor: Take the word forehead). "L'élève: Avec quoi le prendre?" (Student: With what should I take it?). For a study of language in the plays by Ionesco see Revzine (1971).

present them as absurd.[5] At the linguistic level, Beckett shows an awareness of discourse structure. By his manipulations he creates not deviant structures but deflective ones (Halliday 1971) which always point back to the basic structure. Thus the reader and the spectator are able to understand how he is modifying this structure.

Play with the Logic of Semantic Association

In the following examples a certain semantic expectation is built up at the beginning of the sentence but by the end of the sentence what was expected logically is not said; instead the sentence changes direction.

Estragon asks Pozzo to sit down: "Come come, take a seat I beseech you, you'll get pneumonia" (p. 24). One expects that Pozzo should take a seat not to get tired or to rest; but instead Estragon says it is to avoid pneumonia.

Another pattern is created when Pozzo explains what he is going to do with Lucky: "But instead of driving him away as I might have done, I mean instead of simply kicking him out on his arse, in the goodness of my heart I am bringing him to the fair, where I hope to get a good price for him" (p. 21). In the beginning of the sentence we are led to think that Pozzo is going to accomplish a good deed, that is, help Lucky, but at the end of the sentence the situation is completely overturned to the advantage of Pozzo, since the goodness of his heart turns out to consist of selling Lucky to make money.[6] In the next example Beckett plays with a cliché. Vladimir is insulting Pozzo for wanting to get rid of Lucky: "After having sucked all the good out of him you chuck him away like a . . . like a banana skin" (p. 22). Because of the verb "suck" one expects that Lucky is thrown away like a bone, but in-

---

[5] Esslin (1961) defines the absurd as what is incongruous, unreasonable, illogical, or ridiculous (p. xix).

[6] In the French version the contrast is even more striking because Pozzo is bringing Lucky to a market called "Saint Sauveur," which reinforces the idea of charity and good will.

stead Vladimir compares him to a banana peel. In these examples what is striking is that the characters use language in a very idiosyncratic way. They have their own logic, one which contributes to rendering them absurd.

Play with Registers

Registers are the different types or styles of language used in different situations (language of sport, familiar language, formal language of lecture or conference, poetical language, child language, and so forth) (Halliday 1968). Pozzo, for instance, speaks in very lyrical terms of the night, of torrents of red and white lights, of the sky which looses its effulgence, of a veil of gentleness and peace; and then adds, "That's how it is on this bitch of an earth" (p. 25). In the same speech he switches from a lyrical, poetical mood to a vulgar one. This is a common device in Pozzo's speeches. Later on in the play he provides information about his watch: "A genuine half-hunter gentlemen, with deadbeat escapement," and to this he adds, "Twas my granpa gave it to me" (p. 30). Pozzo juxtaposes technical details and child talk. In the French text a similar type of discrepancy is achieved with the use of terms of address. Vladimir calls Pozzo *monsieur*, a formal term of address which connotes respect, then in the same sentence he switches to the second person singular of the pronoun which is the familiar form (*te*); in both cases Pozzo is the adressee: "Monsieur Pozzo! Reviens! On ne te fera pas de mal" (Mr. Pozzo! Come back! We won't hurt you) (p. 117). The juxtaposition of registers—lyrical/vulgar, technical/child talk, respect/familiarity—creates a comic effect in the play because the characters do not seem to understand the difference between the various levels of language.

Spiraling of Semantic Paradigms

A recurrent device employed by Beckett is the use of series of words that are related to each other in one way or the other. When these series appear in the text it seems that a spring is uncoiling. Pozzo has lost his pipe, and we hear:

What have I done with my *pipe?*
What can I have done with that *briar?*
He has lost his *dudeen.*
I have lost my *Kapp and Peterson.*   [p. 23, my italics]

The italicized words are all ways to refer to the same object, and they form a kind of paradigm. Pipe is the neutral, basic word, briar is a metonymy which insists on the quality and is slightly slang, dudeen is an Irish word for a type of pipe, and Kapp and Peterson is a brand name that would be used in a pipe store or by a specialist. Here a paradigm, namely the different ways to name a pipe, is exploited in order to create a verbal pattern.

In the following example Vladimir tells Estragon that Godot did not give any precise information about the time of his coming and that "he would see." This answer generates the following series:

Est: That he couldn't promise anything.
Vla: That he'd have to think it over.
Est: In the quiet of his home.
Vla: Consult his family.
Est: His friends.
Vla: His agents.
Est: His correspondents.
Vla: His books.
Est: His bank account.   [p. 13]

What is presented here is a juggling with relatively synonymous clichés; they could all be said to avoid giving a precise answer on the spot, and the characters really "return the ball to each other."

Sometimes the characters juggle with words whose meaning is slightly different. Vladimir says it would be an "occupation" to play with boots and Estragon answers:

Est: A relaxation.
Vla: A recreation.
Est: A relaxation.   [p. 44]

Obviously Beckett is also playing with sounds since he repeats the same one several times. In these two examples, all
the synonyms, all the extra words used to complement the
first one, do not add to the meaning or explain anything,
rather they are a kind of verbal skidding.[7]

In the examples cited above, the words in the series are
related by synonymy; they are also linked because they form
a semantic field. In another example, Vladimir and Estragon
talk about dead voices.

Vla: They make a noise like wings.
Est: Like leaves.
Vla: Like sand.
Est: Like leaves.

.   .   .   .   .

Vla: They make noise like feathers.
Est: Like Leaves.
Vla: Like ashes.
Est: Like leaves.   [p. 40]

The objects "wings," "leaves," and "feathers" have several elements in common. They are light, they can make a noise
like a whisper or a murmur, and they can rustle in space. But
this unity is disrupted by the two nouns "ashes" and "sand,"
which are like foreign bodies because they do not belong
semantically in the series. Thus again, when Vladimir and
Estragon exchange insults:

Vla: Moron!
Est: Vermin!

[7] The example par excellence of verbal skidding is Lucky's monologue, which is a
paratactic juxtaposition of stock expressions of formulas and fillers that occur in
demonstration and speeches: "it is established beyond doubt, namely, concurrently,
simultaneously, what is more, I resume, for reasons unknown . . ." The content of
the speech has disappeared and what remains is only its frame, its outer trappings.

Vla: Abortion!
Est: Morpion!
Vla: Sewer-rat!
Est: Curate!
Vla: Cretin!
Est: Crritic!   [p. 48]

One insult calls for another one, and again it is a verbal
juggling where juggling has to be taken literally, since the
characters face each other and throw words at each other.
The characters did decide to abuse each other, so all the
words of the series are intended as insults. Yet nouns that are
not necessarily considered insulting are used; they become
insulting terms by association with the others. Furthermore,
their presence is justified phonetically since the sounds in
these words answer each other: moron/abortion, sewer-
rat/curate, cretin/critic. Thus the words form both a semantic and a phonic set;[8] to call such a verbal pattern a mere
deviation would be to miss Beckett's ability to exploit the potentialities of language.

Play with Common Expressions and Clichés

Sometimes a particular word calls to mind a set expression
in which the word appears, and the characters use some element of this expression. Vladimir mentions that the tree they
see is a willow and the following development takes place:

Est: Where are the leaves?
Vla: It must be dead.
Est: No more weeping.   [p. 10]

The word "willow" suggests by association the expression
"weeping willow." In the French version a similar example
occurs:

[8] The concept of semantic and phonic set operates also in Lucky's monologue
when he enumerates rates different types of sports and when he suddenly talks
about "conating": ". . . the practice of sports such as tennis football running cycling
swimming flying floating riding gliding conating camogie skating . . ." (p. 29).

Est: Je me demande si on est liés.

      .   .   .   .   .

Vla: Comment liés?
Est: Pieds et poings.   [p. 27]

Est: I wonder if we are tied.

      .   .   .   .   .

Vla: Tied how?
Est: Feet and fists.   (My literal translation)

Estragon says "pieds et poings" because the word "liés" belongs to the expression "pieds et poings liés."

In his writings Beckett frequently uses proverbs or sayings which he transforms.[9] An example of such a manipulation is found in *Waiting for Godot*. Vladimir suggests they wait to see what Godot has to say, and Estragon, who had suggested that they hang themselves, answers: "on the other hand it might be better to strike the iron before it freezes" (p. 12), a humorous modification of to "strike the iron while it's hot."[10]

Play with the Various Meanings of a Single Word

The various meanings of a particular word as it shifts context are also exploited to create puns, as in this example which appears in the French version—"Vla: En effet nous sommes sur *un plateau*. Aucun doute nous sommes servis sur un *plateau*" (p. 104, my italics). During the whole play the characters give indications that this is in fact a play (Cohn 1962a), and the word plateau means first a stage. Then the characters say they are on a plateau from which they can look down in the valley, so plateau is the geographical term.

[9] See Sherzer 1976 for an analysis of the use of such expressions in Beckett's *Molloy* (1951).
[10] In *L'innommable* Beckett uses the same expression, "battre le fer pendant qu'il est chaud," but he modifies it differently; he speaks of "un moment de découragement à battre pendant qu'il est chaud" (a moment of discouragement to strike while it's hot—literal translation) (p. 51).

And finally, "être servi sur un plateau" means to be served, to have everything brought to you as you desire, on a tray. The characters do not have to disturb themselves since Pozzo and Lucky are coming right where Estragon and Vladimir are, that is as if they were being catered to.

Play with Sounds and Sequences of Sounds

On reading or on watching the play one cannot but notice that very careful attention has been paid to the sounds of words and that several types of phonic manipulation are deployed.

All through the play the sounds "o" and "i" reappear in the names of Godot, Gogo, and Pozzo, and Didi and Lucky. In addition the play is punctuated several times by the same exchange between Vladimir and Estragon:

Est: Let's go.
Vla: We can't.
Est: Why not?
Vla: We're waiting for Godot.

These four lines (which appear on pp. 10, 31, 44, 45, 50, 54) repeat the principal ideal of the play, that of waiting, and in each case the same words are in the same position so that the same phonic exchange takes place, similar to a refrain.

Another behavior which is striking is the characters' bouncing of the same words, leading to a repetition of sounds, as in the following examples:

Vla: Damn it haven't you already told us?
Po: I've already told you?
Est: He's already told us?   [p. 27]

Pozzo might have said "Have I?" Instead he repeats the whole question, in a sense conjugating it, and so does Estragon, with the result that the question generates a paradigm based on shifting the subject and object pronouns and holding the adverb and verb structure constant. In the next example the noun "hat," instead of being replaced by a pronoun after having been mentioned once, keeps being repeated:

Po: Give him his hat.
Vla: His hat?
Po: He can't think without his hat.
Vla: Give him his hat.   [p. 27]

The words *of-the-kind* are juggled in the following lines addressed as answers to Pozzo's question "Who is Godot?"

Vla: Oh he's a . . . he is *a kind of* acquaintance.
Est: Nothing *of the kind*, we hardly know him.
[p. 16, my italics][11]

Variations on proper names allow the characters to play with sounds also. The name Pozzo clicks off a series of other names with similar sounds: Pozzo, Bozzo, Gozzo. Pozzo, not remembering the name of the person Vladimir and Estragon are waiting for, suggests Godet, Godot, Godin (p. 19), then a little further he inverts the order: Godin, Godet, Godot (p. 24). Lucky fills silence with the piling up of Feckham, Peckham, Fulham, Clapham (p. 29).[12]

The repetition of sounds and expressions is a comic device because it confers a machinelike rigidity to the speech of the characters; but at the same time it attracts attention to the phonic properties of language.

The different types of manipulation of language that I have discussed have several consequences. The accumulation of synonyms, the repetition and bouncing of sounds, the juggling with words, expressions, or speech acts, and the misunderstanding of certain expressions are all comic devices. They function together with the play with hats, the

[11] In the French version the play with sounds was achieved by the noun "connaissance" and the verb "connaître": "Vla: Eh bien, c'est un . . . c'est une connaissance." "Est: Mais non, voyons, on le connaît à peine" (p. 30).

[12] One also senses here an obscene semantic field lurking behind the phonic and morphological structure.

pratfalls, the costumes, and the grotesque behavior of the grotesque characters. That is, various communicative systems converge to make the play a comedy.[13]

This comedy presents characters that are absurd, and the absurdity is not only conveyed in their helpless condition, that of tramps waiting for a character that might never come or wandering on empty roads, but it also insinuates itself in their language. One of the main devices at work in the play to convey the absurd through language is the principle of "similarity" rather than "contiguity" (Jakobson 1963). This principle is at work in the use of synonyms in the exchange of slightly different words, in the use of the same word in different registers, and in the repetition of the same sounds.[14] As a consequence of these devices, no new information is provided. In addition the characters use language incongruously and do not communicate. All of their stichomythic exchanges lead to an "insidious undermining of language as a means of communication" (Cohn 1962b), and this devaluation of language is a *destruction*.

On the other hand, paradoxically, while this destruction is taking place, it is accompanied by a *construction*. Referentially the play is rather stark, repetitive, and static, but in this empty plot the characters do not sink in despair. They create verbal games, they manipulate words and expressions and throw them, and they bounce and juggle words and sounds.[15] In this linguistic animation potentialities of lan-

---

[13] For a discussion of the polysemy of theatrical art see Bogatyrev 1971.

[14] The song that Vladimir sings at the opening of act two is also a juggled repetition of lines. The principle of similarity is also at work in the overall macrostructure of the play since it is a juxtaposition of two acts, the second one containing variations from the first one. For instance, Vladimir acts like Pozzo when he orders Estragon to show him his other leg: "the other, pig" (p. 43), or "the other, hog" (p. 44), copying Pozzo giving orders to Lucky. Thus the play is a static construct.

[15] One should notice that Estragon has a real flair for language; he is the one who takes advantage of and manipulates existing expressions, but in addition he is also playing with different ways of speaking. He uses trading French (pidgin) to explain to Vladimir that he should hang himself first: "Gogo light-bough not break-Gogo dead. Didi heavy-bough break-Didi alone" (p. 12); he imitates the pronunciation of

guage are used and exploited. When there is a choice between several possibilities, they are mingled and grouped
(several speech acts, several registers, several synonyms); we
are made aware how a word or an expression can generate
another word, another expression, another meaning; we are
reminded that language is not uniform but that it contains
several registers that can be put to use; we are made to feel
that language is not only meaning, but that it also has phonic
properties that can be manipulated.

We are thus in the presence of characters that create disorder and, while doing so, create a new order. In this play a
devaluation of language becomes a linguistic construction
which animates the play while expressing the absurd. To account for what Beckett is doing in *Waiting for Godot*, one has
to talk about *de-construction*, since there is a destruction of language to convey the absurd while at the same time another
type of construction is taking place.

References

Beckett, Samuel. 1951. *Molloy*. Paris: Editions de Minuit.
———. 1952. *En attendant Godot*. Paris: Editions de Minuit.
———. 1953. *L'innommable*. Paris: Editions de Minuit.
———. 1954. *Waiting for Godot*. New York: Grove.
———. 1958a. *Endgame*. New York: Grove.
———. 1958b. Fourteen letters, to Alan Schneider, *Village Voice*, New York,
March 19.
Bogatyrev, Petr. 1971. "Les signes du théâtre." *Poétique* 8:517–530.
Cavell, Stanley. 1969. "Ending the Waiting Game." In *Must We Mean
What We Say?* New York: Scribner's.
Cohen, Jean. 1966. *Structure du langage poétique*. Paris: Flammarion.
Cohn, Ruby. 1962a. "Plays and Players in the Plays of Samuel Beckett."
Yale French Studies 29:43–48.
———. 1962b. *Samuel Beckett: The Comic Gamut*. New Jersey: Rutgers Uni-
versity Press.

English: "Calm . . . calm . . . The English say cawm" (p. 11); he also imitates an
English-speaking person speaking French with a thick accent: "Oh tray bong, tray
tray tray bong" (p. 25).

Ekmann, Paul, and W. P. Friesen. 1969. "The Repertoire of Nonverbal Behavior: Categories, Origins, Usage, and Coding." *Semiotica* 1:49–98.

Esslin, Martin. 1961. *The Theater of the Absurd.* New York: Doubleday.

Goffman, Erving. 1959. *Presentation of Self in Everyday Life.* New York: Anchor.

Halliday, M. A. K. 1968. "The Uses and Users of Language." In Joshua Fishman, ed., *Readings in the Sociology of Language.* The Hague: Mouton.

——. 1971. "Linguistic Function and Literary Style." In Seymour Chatman, ed., *Literary Style.* London, New York: Oxford University Press. Pp. 330–368.

Ionesco, Eugene. 1958. *Four Plays.* New York: Grove.

Hymes, Dell. 1972. "Models of the Interaction of Language and Social Life." In John Gumperz and Dell Hymes, eds., *Directions in Sociolinguistics.* New York: Holt, Rinehart & Winston. Pp. 35–71.

Jakobson, Roman. 1960. "Linguistics and Poetics." In Thomas Sebeok, ed., *Style in Language.* Cambridge: MIT Press. Pp. 350–377.

——. 1963. "Deux aspects du langage et deux types d'aphasie." In Nicholas Ruwet, ed., *Essais de linguistique générale.* Paris: Éditions de Minuit. Pp. 43–67.

Levin, Samuel. 1967. "Poetry and Grammaticalness." In Seymour Chatman and Samuel Levin, eds., *Essays on the Language of Literature.* New York: Houghton Mifflin.

Ohmann, Richard. 1971. "Speech, Action, and Style." In Seymour Chatman, ed., *Literary Style.* London, New York: Oxford University Press.

Revzine, Olga and Isaak. 1971. "Expérimentation sémiotique chez Eugène Ionesco." *Semiotica* 3:240–262.

Sherzer, Dina. 1976. "Saying Is Inventing: Gnomic Expressions in *Molloy.*" In Barbara Kirshenblatt-Gimblett, ed., *Speech Play on Display.* Philadelphia: University of Pennsylvania Press.

CHAPTER 5

Women on Top: Symbolic Sexual Inversion and Political Disorder in Early Modern Europe*

NATALIE ZEMON DAVIS

The Image of the Disorderly Woman

The female sex was thought to be the disorderly one par excellence in early modern Europe. "Une beste imparfaicte," went one adage, "sans foy, sans loy, sans craincte, sans constance" (an imperfect animal, without faith, law, fear, constancy). Female disorderliness was first seen in the Garden of Eden, where Eve had been the first to yield to the serpent's temptation and incite Adam to disobey the Lord. To be sure, the men of the lower orders were also believed to be especially prone to riot and seditious unrest. But the defects of the males were thought to stem not so much from nature as from nurture: the ignorance with which they were reared, the brutish quality of life in the peasant's hut or artisan's shop, and their poverty, which led to envy.[1]

With the women the disorderliness was founded in physiology. As every physician knew in the sixteenth century, the female was composed of cold and wet humors (the male was hot and dry), and coldness and wetness meant a changeable, deceptive, and tricky temperament. Her womb was like a hungry animal; when not amply fed by sexual intercourse or

---

* Reprinted, with minor revisions, from *Society and Culture in Early Modern France: Eight Essays by Natalie Zemon Davis* with the permission of the publishers, Stanford University Press. © 1975 by Natalie Zemon Davis.

[1] Grosnet 1530–1531, f. F vii^r; de Rubys 1574:74; Hill 1966:298–324.

reproduction, it was likely to wander about her body, over-powering her speech and senses. If the Virgin Mary was free of such a weakness, it was because she was the blessed vessel of the Lord. But no other woman had been immaculately conceived, and even the well-born lady could fall victim to a fit of the "mother," as the uterus was called. The male might suffer from retained sexual juices too, but (as Doctor François Rabelais pointed out) he had the wit and will to control his fiery urges by work, wine, or study. The women just became hysterical. In the late seventeenth century, when more advanced physicians were abandoning humoral theories of personality in favor of more mechanistic notions of "animal spirits" and were beginning to remark that men suffered from emotional ills curiously like hysteria, they still maintained that the female's mind was more prone to be disordered by her fragile and unsteady temperament. Long before Europeans were asserting flatly that the "inferiority" of black Africans was innate, rather than due, say, to the effects of the climate, they were attributing female "inferiority" to nature.[2]

The lower ruled the higher within the woman, therefore, and if she were given her way, she likewise would want to rule over those above her. Her disorderliness led her into the evil arts of witchcraft, so ecclesiastical authorities claimed; and when she embarked on some behavior for which her allegedly weak intellect disqualified her, such as theological speculation or preaching, that was blamed on her disorderliness too.

What were the proposed remedies for female unruliness? Religious training that fashioned the reins of modesty and humility, selective education that showed a woman her moral

[2] Joubert 1578:161ff; Poullain de La Barre 1675:136ff, 156ff; Veith 1965; Screech 1958, ch. 6; Sydenham, in his important *Epistolary Dissertation to Dr. Cole* (1681) connects the delicate constitution of woman with the irregular motions of her "animal spirits" and hence explains her greater susceptibility to hysteria; Jordan 1968:11-20, 187-190.

duty without enflaming her undisciplined imagination or loosing her tongue for public talk, honest work to busy her hands, and laws and constraints that made her subject to her husband.[3]

In some ways, that subjection gradually deepened from the sixteenth to the eighteenth centuries, as the patriarchal family streamlined itself for more efficient property acquisition, social mobility, and preservation of the line, and as progress in state-building and the extension of commercial capitalism were achieved at a cost in human autonomy. By the eighteenth century married women in France and England had largely lost what independent legal personality they had had; they even had less legal right to make decisions about their own dowries and possessions. Propertied women were involved less and less in local and regional political assemblies. Working women in prosperous families were beginning to withdraw from productive labor and in poor families they increasingly filled the most ill-paid positions of wage labor. This is not to say that females had no informal access to power or made no continuing contribution to the economy, but the character of their political and economic role was in dispute.[4]

Which side of the conflict was helped by the image of the disorderly woman? Since it was so often used as an excuse for the subjection of women, it is not surprising that one strain in early feminist thought argued that women were *not* by nature more unruly, disobedient, and fickle than men. If anything it was the other way around. "By nature, women be sober," said the poet Christine de Pisan, "and those that be not, they go out of kind." Women are by nature more modest and shamefast than men, claimed a male feminist, and this is demonstrated by the fact that women's privy parts

[3] See, for instance, Vives 1524 and Fénelon 1966.
[4] Timbal 1963:38–39; Ourliac and de Malafosse 1968:145–52, 264–268; Abensour 1923, pt. 1, ch. 9; Clark 1968; LeRoy Ladurie 1966:271–280, app. 32, p. 859.

are totally covered with pubic hair and are not handled by women the way men's are when they urinate. Why then did some men maintain that women were disorderly by nature? Because they were misogynists—vindictive, envious, or themselves dissolute.[5]

These claims and counterclaims about sexual temperament raise questions not merely about the actual character of male and female behavior in pre-industrial Europe, but also about the varied uses of sexual symbolism. Sexual symbolism is, of course, always available for use in making statements about social experience and in reflecting (or concealing) contradictions within it. At the end of the Middle Ages and in early modern Europe, the relation of the wife—of the potentially disorderly woman—to her husband was especially useful for expressing the relation of all subordinates to their superiors, and this for two reasons. First, economic relations were still often perceived in the medieval way as a matter of service. Second, the nature of political rule and the newer problem of sovereignty were very much at issue. In the little world of the family, with its conspicuous tension between intimacy and power, the larger matters of political and social order could find ready symbolization.[6]

[5] De Pisan 1521, f. Ee i^v; Agrippa 1542, f. B iv^{r-v}. It should be noted that important female writers from the sixteenth to the early eighteenth century, such as Marguerite de Navarre, Madame de Lafayette, Aphra Behn, and Mary de la Rivière Manley, did not accept the "modest" view of female sexuality. Although they did not portray women as necessarily more lustful than men, they did give females a range of sexual appetites at least equal to that of males.

[6] The English characterization of the wife's killing of her husband as petty treason rather than homicide may be an early example of the kind of symbolism described here. Petty treason appeared as a crime distinct from high treason in the fourteenth century, and lasted as such until the early nineteenth century. It included the killing of a master by his servant, a husband by his wife, and a prelate by a cleric. As Blackstone presents the law, it seems to differ from earlier Germanic practice, which treated the murder of *either* spouse as an equally grave crime. The development of the concept and law of treason was closely connected with the development of the idea of sovereignty (Bellamy 1970:1–14, 225–231; Blackstone 1770, bk. 4, ch. 14). The discussion of male-female as an expression of social relationships (master-servant, sovereign-subject, and the like) does not exhaust the meanings of sexual symbolism in early modern Europe, but is the concentration point of this essay.

Thus Jean Calvin, a destroyer of ecclesiastical hierarchies, saw the subjection of the wife to the husband as a guarantee of the subjection of both of them to the Lord. Kings and political theorists saw the increasing legal subjection of wives to their husbands (and of children to their parents) as a guarantee of the obedience of both men and women to the slowly centralizing state—a training for the loyal subject of seventeenth-century France or for the dutiful citizen of seventeenth-century England. "Marriages are the seminaries of States," began the preamble to the French ordinance strengthening paternal power within the family. For John Locke, opponent of despotic rule in commonwealth and in marriage, the wife's relinquishing her right of decision to her husband as "naturally . . . the abler and stronger" was analogous to the individual's relinquishing his natural liberties of decision and action to the legislative branch of government.[7]

The female's position was used not only to symbolize hierarchical subordination, but also to symbolize violence and chaos. Bruegel's terrifying *Dulle Griet* (1564) painted during the occupation of the Netherlands by Spanish soldiers, depicts a huge armed unseeing woman, Mad Meg, as the emblem of fiery destruction, of brutal oppression and disorder. Bruegel's painting cuts in more than one way, however, and shows how female disorderliness—the female out of her place—could be assigned another value. Next to Mad Meg is a small woman in white on top of a male monster; it is Saint Margaret of Antioch tying up the devil. Nearby other armed women are beating grotesque animals from Hell.[8]

Bruegel's Margarets were by no means alone in pre-indus-

Eric Wolf (1968:287–301) considers male-female as an expression of the relationships public-domestic and instrumental-expressive. For an attempt at a very broad theory of sexual symbolism, see Ortner 1974.

[7] Calvin 1848:353–361 (1 Cor. 11:3–12); Gouge 1941–1942:246; Halkett 1970:20–24; Holmes 1967:76; Locke 1952, ch. 7, par. 82, ch. 9, pars. 128–131; Ourliac and de Malafosse 1968:66; Schochet 1969:413–441.

[8] Delevoy 1959:70–75.

trial Europe. In hierarchical and conflictive societies, which loved to reflect on the world turned upside down, the topos of the woman on top was one of the most enjoyed. Indeed, sexual inversion—that is, switches in sex roles—was a widespread form of cultural play, in literature, in art, and in festivity. Sometimes the reversal involved dressing and masking as a member of the opposite sex, the prohibitions of Deuteronomy 22, Saint Paul, Saint Jerome, canon law, and Jean Calvin notwithstanding.[9] Sometimes the reversal involved simply taking on certain roles or forms of behavior thought to be characteristic of the opposite sex. Women played men, men played women, men played women who were playing men.

The uses of these sexual inversions, and more particularly of play with the image of the unruly woman in literature, in popular festivity, and in ordinary life, will be the subject of the rest of this essay. Evidently, the primary impulse behind such wide-spread inversion in early modern Europe was not homosexuality or uncertain gender identity. Though Henri III expressed special wishes of his own when he and his male *mignons* masked as Amazons in the 1570s; though the seventeenth-century Abbé de Choisy, whose mother had dressed him as a girl through adolescence, had special reasons for using a woman's name and wearing female clothes until he was thirty-three, still most literary and festive transvestism at this time had a wider psychosexual and cultural significance.

Ritual Inversion: In the Service of Tradition or Change?

Anthropologists offer several suggestions about the functions of magical transvestism and ritual inversion of sex roles. First, sexual disguise can ward off danger from demons or malignant fairies or other powers that threaten castration or

[9] Deut. 22:5, 1 Cor. 11:14–15, Saint Jerome 1963:161–162, Robert of Flamborough 1971, bk. 5, p. 264. Calvin 1863–1880:17–19, 234; Bullough 1974:1381–1384.

defloration. Second, transvestism and sexual reversal can be part of adolescent rites of passage, either to suggest the marginality of the transitional state (as when a male initiate is likened to a menstruating woman) or to allow each sex to obtain something of the other's power (as in certain initiation and marriage customs in early Greece). Third, exchange of sex can be part of what Victor Turner has called "rituals of status reversal," as when women in certain parts of Africa usurp the clothing, weapons, or tasks of the "superior" males and behave in lewd ways. These rituals are intended to increase the chance for a good harvest or to turn aside an impending natural catastrophe. Finally, as James Peacock has pointed out, the transvestite actor, priest, or shaman can symbolize categories of cosmological or social organization. For instance, in Java the transvestite actor reinforces by his irregularity the importance of the categories high-low and male-female.

However diverse the use of sexual inversion, anthropologists generally agree that these reversals, like other rites and ceremonies of reversal, are ultimately sources of order and stability in a hierarchical society. They can clarify the structure by the process of reversing it. They can provide an expression of and a safety valve for conflicts within the system. They can correct and relieve the system when it has become authoritarian. But, so it is argued, they do not question the basic order of the society itself. They can renew the system, but they cannot change it.[10]

Historians of early modern Europe are likely to find inversions and reversals less in prescribed rites than in carnivals and festivities. Their fools are likely to escape the bounds of

[10] Gluckman 1963, Intro. ch. 3; Turner 1967, ch. 4, 1968, chs. 3–5; Bateson 1935:199; Flügel 1930:120–121; Delcourt 1956, ch. 1; Meslin 1974:301–304; James Peacock, "Symbolic Reversal and Social History: Transvestites and Clowns of Java," in this collection. See also Rodney Needham's discussion of symbolic reversal and its relation to classification in his introduction to Durkheim and Mauss 1972:xxxviii–xl.

ceremony;[11] and their store of literary sources for inversion will include not only the traditional tale of magical transformation in sex, but also a variety of stories in which men and women *choose* to change their sexual status, and a variety of comic conventions and genres, such as the picaresque, which allow much play with sexual roles. These new forms offered more occasions and ways in which topsy-turvy could be used for explicit criticism of the social order. Nevertheless, students of these festive and literary forms have ordinarily come to the same conclusion as anthropologists as to the limits of symbolic inversion: a world turned upside down can only be righted, not changed. To quote Ian Donaldson's recent study, *Comedy from Jonson to Fielding:* "The lunatic governor . . . , the incompetent judge, the mock doctor, the equivocating priest, the hen-pecked husband: such are the familiar and recurrent figures in the comedy of a society which gives a general assent to the necessity of entrusting power to its governors, judges, doctors, priests, and husbands."[12]

I would like to argue, on the contrary, that comic and festive inversion could *undermine* as well as reinforce that assent. Somewhat in contradistinction to Christine de Pisan and the gallant school of feminists, I want to argue that the image of the disorderly woman did not always function to keep women in their place. On the contrary, it was a multivalent image and could operate to widen behavioral options for women within and even outside marriage, and to sanction riot and political disobedience for both men and women in a society that allowed the lower orders few formal means of protest. Play with the concept of the unruly woman is partly a chance for temporary release from traditional and stable hierarchy; but it is *also* part and parcel of conflict over efforts to

[11] Willeford 1969:97–98.

[12] Donaldson 1970:14. McKendrick also conceives of the impact of the *mujer varonil* on Spanish theater audiences in terms of "female catharsis," male sexual fantasy, and "a temporary appeasement" of Baroque tensions (1974:320–333). See further n. 33 below.

change the basic distribution of power within the society. Furthermore, play with woman on top not only reconfirmed certain traditional ways of thinking about society, it also facilitated innovation in historical theory and in political behavior.

Sexual Inversion and the Disorderly Women in Literature

Let us begin with a review of the major types of sexual inversion that we find in literary sources—sober and comic, learned and popular—and then we will consider the disorderly woman in more detail. What kinds of license were allowed through this turnabout? First of all, we have stories of men who dress as women to save themselves from an enemy or from execution, to sneak into the opponent's military camp, or to get into a nunnery or women's quarters for purposes of seduction. In all of these cases, the disguise is not merely practical but exploits the expected physical frailty of women to prevent harm to the male or to disarm his victim. A more "honorable" trick is tried by Pyrocles in Sidney's *Arcadia* (1590), by Marston's Antonio in *The History of Antonio and Mellida* (1602), and by d'Urfé's Céladon in *L'Astrée* (1607–1619), for they dress as brave Amazons or as a Druid priestess in order to have access to the women they wish to woo. Here no more than in the first case does the inversion lead to criticism of social hierarchy. Rather Pyrocles is rebuked by his friend for "his effeminate love of a woman," for letting his "sensual weakness" rebel against his manly reason. Only with the male fool or clown do we find literary examples of male transvestism that serve to challenge order.

The stories, theater, and pictorial illustration of pre-industrial Europe offer many more examples of women trying to act like men than vice versa, and more of the time than not the sexual inversion yields criticism of established order. One set of reversals portrays women going beyond what can ordinarily be expected of a mere female, that is, they show women ruling the lower in themselves and thus deserving to be like men. We have, for instance, the tales of female saints of the early Church who lived chastely as male monks to the end of their lives, braving false charges of fathering children, raping women, and other tests along the way. Five of these transvestite ladies appear in Voragine's *Golden Legend*, which had wide circulation in manuscript and in printed editions in Latin and in the vernacular.[13]

Other uncommon women change their roles in order to defend established rule or values associated with it. Disguised as men, they prove fidelity to lovers whom they wish to marry or, as in the case of Madame Ginevra in Boccaccio's tale, prove their chastity to doubting husbands. Disguised as men, they leave Jewish fathers for Christian husbands and plead for Christian mercy over base Jewish legalism. Disguised as men, they rescue spouses from prison and family honor from stain. For example, in *The French Amazon*, one of Mademoiselle l'Héritier's reworkings of an old French tale, the heroine maintains her father's connections with the court by fighting in the place of her incompetent twin brother who had been slain. She, of course, ultimately marries the prince. Along with Spenser's Britomart, Tasso's Clorinda, and others, the French Amazon is one of a line of noble women warriors, virtuous viragos all, magnanimous, brave, and chaste.[14]

[13] Thompson 1955–1958: K310, K514, K1321, K1836, K2357.8. Delcourt 1956:84–102, Anson 1974:1–32. I am grateful to Mr. Anson for several bibliographical suggestions. The transvestite saints in Voragine's *Golden Legend* are Saint Margaret, alias Brother Pelagius (Oct. 8); Saint Pelagia, alias Pelagius (Oct. 8); Saint Theodora, alias Brother Theodore (Sept. 11); Saint Eugenia (Sept. 11); and Saint Marina, alias Brother Marinus (June 18). See also Bullough 1974:1385–1387.

[14] Thompson 1955–1958:K3.3, K1837; Aarne and Thompson 1964:33A, 890, 891A; Giovanni Boccaccio, *Decameron*, Second Day, Story 9; William Shakespeare, *The Merchant of Venice*, act 2, scenes 4–6, act 4, scene 1; L'Héritier de Villandon 1718, Avertissement and "L'Amazone Françoise"; Wright 1940:433–445; Edmund Spenser, *The Faerie Queene*, bk. 3, canto 1. For an excellent description of the virtuous virago in Spanish theatre, see McKendrick 1974, pt. 2.

To what extent could such embodiments of order serve to censure accepted hierarchy? They might reprove by their example the cowardice and wantonness of ordinary men and women. But these uncommon women used their power to support an established cause, not to unmask the truth about social relationships. By showing the good that can be done by the woman out of her place, they had the potential to inspire a few females to exceptional action and feminists to reflection about the capacities of women (we will see later whether that potential was realized), but they are unlikely symbols for moving masses of people to disobedience and resistance.

The situation is different in comic play with the disorderly woman, that is, inversion which can be expected of the female, who gives rein to the lower in herself and seeks rule over her superiors. Some portraits of her are so ferocious (such as Spenser's cruel Radagunde and other vicious viragos) that they preclude the possibility of fanciful release from or criticism of hierarchy. It is the same with those tales, considered humorous at the time, which depict a savage taming of the shrew, as in the fabliau of *La Dame escoillée*, where the domineering lady is given a counterfeit but painful "castration" by her son-in-law, and in the sixteenth-century German cartoon strip, *The Ninefold Skins of a Shrewish Woman*, which are stripped off one by one by various punishments. The legend of the medieval Pope Joan also has limited potential for mocking established order. As told by Boccaccio, it is a hybrid of the transvestite saint and the cruelly tamed shrew: Joan wins the papacy by her wits and good behavior, but her illicit power goes to her head, or rather to her womb. She becomes pregnant, gives birth during a procession and dies wretchedly in the cardinals' dungeon.[15]

There are a host of situations, however, in which the un-

[15] Spenser, *Faerie Queene*, bk. 5, cantos 4–5; Wright 1940:449–454; Brians 1972:24–36; Kunzle 1973:224–225; Boccaccio 1963:231–234.

5.1. German playing card by
Peter Floetner, ca. 1520.

ruly woman is assigned more ambiguous meanings. For our
purposes we can sort out three ways in which the multivalent
image is used. First, there is a rich treatment of women who
are happily given over to the sway of their bodily senses or
who are using every ruse they can to prevail over men.
There is the Wife of Bath, of course, who celebrates her sexual instrument and outlives her five husbands. And Rabelais'
Gargamelle—a giant of a woman, joyously and frequently
coupling, eating bushels of tripe, quaffing wine, joking ob-
scenely, giving birth in a grotesque fecal explosion, from
which her son Gargantua somersaults shouting "drink,
drink." Then the clever and powerful wife of the *Quinze joies*

5.2. Engraving by Martin Treu, ca. 1540–1543, working perhaps in Bavaria. Department of Prints and Drawings, British Museum; Albertina, Vienna.

5.3. L'Ecole des Mary. French broadsheet printed at Orléans. 1650.

5.4. Fight for the breeches.
French engraving, 1690.

de mariage—cuckolding her husband and foiling his every effort to find her out, wheedling fancy clothes out of him,
beating him up, and finally locking him in his room. Also
Grimmelshausen's Libuschka, alias Courage, one of a series
of picaresque heroines—fighting in the army in soldier's
clothes; ruling her many husbands and lovers; paying them
back a hundredfold when they take revenge or betray her;
whoring, tricking, trading to survive or get rich. In fact, the
husband-dominators are everywhere in the popular literature
(see Figs. 5.1–5.4 for examples), and are nicknamed among
the Germans Saint Cudgelman (Sankt Kolbmann) or Doktor
Siemann (she-man). The point about such portraits is that
they are funny and amoral: the women are full of life and

energy, and they win much of the time; they stay on top of their fortune with as much success as Machiavelli might have expected for the Prince of his political tract.[16]

A second comic treatment of the woman out of her place allows her a temporary period of dominion, which is ended only after she has said or done something to undermine authority or denounce its abuse. When the Silent Wife begins to talk and order her husband about in Ben Jonson's *Epicoene*, she points out that women cannot be mere statues or puppets and that what her husband calls "Amazonian" impudence in her is simply reasonable decorum.[17] When the Woman-Captain of Shadwell's comedy puts aside her masculine garb and the sword with which she has hectored her jealous and stingy old husband, she does so only after having won separate maintenance and £400 a year. The moral of the play is that husbands must not move beyond the law to tyranny. In *As You Like It*, the love-struck Rosalind, her tongue loosed by her male apparel and her "holiday humor," warns Orlando that there is a limit to the possession he will have over a wife, a limit set by her desires, her wit, and her tongue. Though she later gives herself to Orlando in marriage, her saucy counsel cannot be erased from the real history of the courtship.

The most popular comic example of the female's temporary rule, however, is Phyllis riding Aristotle (Fig. 5.5), a

[16] Chaucer, *The Canterbury Tales*, "The Wife of Bath's Prologue"; François Rabelais, *La vie très horrifique de Grand Gargantua, père de Pantagruel*, chs. 3–6; Bakhtin 1968:240–241; Rychner 1963; Harry Baxter, "The Waning of Misogyny: Changing Attitudes Reflected in *Les Quinze Joyes de Mariage*," lecture given to the Sixth Conference on Medieval Studies, Western Michigan University, Kalamazoo, Michigan, 1971; Grimmelshausen 1964; Janssen 1896–1924, vol. 12, p. 206, n.1; Kunzle 1973:225; *Mari et femme dans la France rurale*, catalogue of the exhibition at the Musée national des arts et traditions populaires, Paris, Sept. 22–Nov. 19, 1973, pp. 68–69.

[17] *Epicoene*, act 4. See Donaldson 1970, ch. 2, and Partridge 1958, ch. 7. The ambiguities in *Epicoene* were compounded by the fact that the Silent Wife in the play was a male playing a female. Professional troupes, of course, always used males for female parts in England until the Restoration and in France until the reign of Henri IV. See Wilson 1958, Lacour 1921, and Binns 1974:95–120.

5.5. Phyllis riding Aristotle. Woodcut by Hans Baldung, alias Grien, 1513.

motif recurring in stories, paintings, and household objects from the thirteenth through the seventeenth century. Aristotle admonishes his pupil Alexander for his excessive attention to a certain Phyllis, one of his new subjects in India. The beautiful Phyllis gets revenge before Alexander's eyes by coquettishly persuading the old philosopher to get down on all fours and, saddled and bridled, carry her through the garden. Here youth overthrows age, and sexual passion, dry sterile philosophy; nature surmounts reason, and the female, the male.[18]

Phyllis' ride brings us to a third way of presenting the woman on top, that is, to confer upon her directly the license

[18] Shadwell 1680; Shakespeare, *As You Like It*, act 4, scene 1. For an interesting view of Shakespeare's treatment of Katherine in *The Taming of the Shrew*, see Richmond 1971:83–101. For Phyllis riding Aristotle, see d'Andeli 1951; Schmitz 1922, pl. 66; Oettinger and Knappe 1963, pl. 66; Kunzle 1973:224.

to be social critic. Erhard Schoen's woodcuts in the early sixteenth century portray enormous women distributing fools'
caps to men; another artist shows a woman shaking male
fools from a tree (Fig. 5.6). This is what happens when
women are given the upper hand; and yet in some sense the
men deserve it. Erasmus' female Folly is, of course, the supreme example of this topos. Stultitia tells the truth about
the foibles of all classes and defends the higher folly of the
Cross, even though paradoxically she's just a foolish gabbling
woman herself.[19]

These varied images of sexual topsy-turvy—from the
transvestite male escaping reponsibility and harm to the
transvestite fool and the unruly woman unmasking the
truth—were available to city people who went to the theater
and to people who could read and afford books. They were
also familiar to the lower orders through books that were
read aloud, stories, poems, proverbs, and broadsheets.[20]

Women on Top and Transvestism at Festivals

In addition, popular festivals and customs, hard though
they are to document, show much play with switches in sex
roles and much attention to women on top. In examining this
data, we will notice that sexual inversion in popular festivity
differs from that in literature in two ways. Whereas the
purely ritual and/or magical element in sexual inversion was
present in literature to only a small degree, it assumed more
importance in the popular festivities, along with the carnivalesque functions of mocking and unmasking the truth.
Whereas sexual inversion in literary and pictorial play more
often involved the female taking on the male role or dressing

[19] *Erasmus en zijn tijd*, catalogue of the exhibition held at the Museum Boymans–
van Beuningen, Rotterdam, Oct.–Nov., 1969, nos. 151–152, also see no. 150; Willeford 1969, pl. 30, drawing by Urs Graf; Erasmus, *The Praise of Folly*. See also Dame
Folly leading apes and fools in Janson 1952:204–208, pl. 36.
[20] See, for instance, Ashton 1968:82ff; Wardroper 1970, ch. 1; Aarne and Thompson 1964:1375, 1366A; Kunzle 1973:222–223.

5.6. Woman shakes male fools from tree. Drawing by the Petrarch-Master of Augsburg ca. 1526. Art Collection, Veste Coburg.

as a man, the festive inversion more often involved the male taking on the role or garb of the woman—that is, of the unruly woman—though this asymmetry may not have existed several centuries earlier.

The ritual and/or magical functions of sexual inversion were filled in almost all cases by males disguised as grotesque cavorting females. In sections of Germany and Austria at carnival time, male runners, half of them masked as female, half as male, jumped and leaped through the streets. In France it was at St. Stephen's Day or New Year's that men dressed as wild beasts or as women and jumped and danced in public, or at least such was the case in the Middle Ages. The saturnalian Fête des Fous, which decorous doctors of theology and prelates were trying to ban from the French cathedrals in the fifteenth and sixteenth centuries, involved both young clerics and laymen, some of them disguised as females, who made wanton and loose gestures.[21] In parts of the Pyrénées at Candlemas (Feb. 2) a Bear Chase took place, involving a lustful bear and young men dressed as women and often called Rosetta. After an amorous interlude with Rosetta, the bear was killed, revived, shaved, and killed again.[22]

In England, too, in Henry VIII's time, during the reign of the Boy Bishop after Christmas, some of the male children taken from house to house were dressed as females rather than as priests or bishops. The most important English examples of the male as grotesque female, however, were Bessy and Maid Marian. In the northern counties, a Fool-Plough was dragged about the countryside, often on the first Monday after Epiphany, by men dressed in white shirts. Sword

[21] Sumberg 1941:83–84, 104–105; Leach 1949–1950, "Schemen"; Savaron 1608:10; du Tilliot 1751:8, 11–12; Sachs 1963:335–339.

[22] Van Gennep 1943–1949, pt. 3, pp. 908–918; Alford 1937:16–25. Though evidence for the Candlemas Bear Chase is fullest and clearest from the French and Spanish Pyrénées, there are suggestions that it was more widespread in the Middle Ages. In the ninth century Hincmar of Reims inveighed against "shameful plays" with bears and women dancers. Richard Bernheimer has argued for the connection between the bear hunt and the wild-man hunt, performed in several parts of Europe, and this has been confirmed by Claude Gaignebet, who relates it further to the popular folk play of Valentin and Ourson. Bruegel represented this game in an engraving and in his painting of the Battle of Carnival and Lent: a male, masked and dressed as a female, holds out a ring to the wild man. See Bernheimer 1952:52–56, Gaigneget 1972:329–331. Compare the Pyrénées Bear and Rosetta also with the Gyro or grotesque giant woman, played by young men on old Candlemas Day in the Orkney Islands (McNeill 1962:28–29).

dances were done by some of them, while old Bessy and her fur-clad Fool capered around and tried to collect from the spectators. Maid Marian presided with Robin Hood over the May games. If in this capacity she was sometimes a real female and sometimes a disguised male, when it came to the Morris Dance with Robin, the Hobby Horse, the dragon, and the rest, Marian was a man. Here again there was the chance that the maid's gestures or costume would be licentious.[23]

All interpreters of this transvestism see it, as in the African example mentioned earlier, as a fertility rite, biological or agricultural,[24] embedded into festivities that may have had other meanings as well. Did it also draw upon other features of sexual symbolism in early modern Europe, for example, the relation of the subordinate to the superior? Did it, like the transvestite Harlequin of the commedia dell' arte, suggest the blurring or reversing of social boundaries? Perhaps. When we see the roles that the woman on top was later to play, it is hard to believe that some such effect was not stimulated by these rites.

The Abbeys of Misrule

Though many festive occasions involved both male and female players, most of the organization was in the hands of male festive societies. These organizations were known as Kingdoms and, most often in France and northern Italy, as Abbeys of Misrule.[25] (In England and Scotland, we have Lords of Misrule and Abbots of Unreason, though the exact character of their bands remains to be studied.) In the coun-

[23] Strutt 1878:449–451, 310–311, 456; Barber 1951:28; Leach 1949–1950, "Fool Plough," "Morris".

[24] Leach 1949–1950, "Transvestism"; Willeford 1969:86; van Gennep 1943–1949, pt. 8, p. 910; Alford 1937:19–22; Sachs 1963:335–339.

[25] For full documentation on this material, see Davis 1971:41–75 and Thompson 1972:285–312.

tryside, the Abbeys were usually made up of unmarried youth in their teens or early twenties, while in the cities they might be composed of young men or of males of different ages, but from the same neighborhood or craft. Their activities were set to the changes of season and holiday—harvest, All Souls, the Twelve Days of Christmas, Mardi Gras, Pentecost, and so on—but also took place at marriages or whenever there was need for their carnival license to play and deride.

The Abbeys' rule extended over their own members, among whom they tried to keep peace, and also over their elders or their neighbors, whose misdeeds they would mock in noisy masked demonstrations—*charivaris, scampanate, katzenmusik, cencerrada*, and rough music, to give only a selection of European names for this behavior. Among other roles, the Abbeys expressed the community's interest in marriages and their outcome much more overtly than the cavorting Bessy or Rosetta. In the villages, they put May bushes in front of the houses of marriageable girls and smelly bushes in front of those whose morals were doubtful; they charivaried newlyweds if the woman failed to become pregnant during the first year; they used their pots, tambourines, bells, and horns to ridicule second marriages, especially when there was a gross disparity in age. Urban Abbeys often attacked the political misrule of the city fathers as well.

The unruly woman appeared in the Abbeys' play in two forms. First as officers of misrule. In rural areas, these were usually called Lords and Abbots; in the French cities, however, they took all kinds of pompous titles. Among these dignitaries were Princesses and Dames and especially Mothers: Mère Folle and her Children in Dijon, Langres, and Chalon-sur-Saône; Mère Sotte and her Children in Paris and Compiègne; and Mère d'Enfance in Bordeaux. In Wales, though I know of no female festive titles, the men who conducted the *ceffyl pren*, as the local rough music was called, blackened their faces and wore women's garb.[26] In all of this there was a double irony: the young villager who became an Abbot and the artisan who became a Prince directly adopted for their misrule a symbol of licit power. The power invoked by the man who became Mère Folle, however, was already in defiance of natural order—a dangerous and vital power, which his disguise made it safe for him to assume.

The unruly woman not only directed some of the male festive organizations; she was sometimes their butt. The village scold or domineering wife might be ducked in the pond or pulled through the streets muzzled or branked or in a creel. City people from the fifteenth century to the eighteenth were even more concerned about husband-beating, and the beaten *man* (or a neighbor playing his part) was paraded through the streets backward on an ass by noisy revelers. In England in the Midlands, the ride was known as a skimmington or a skimmety (Fig. 5.7), perhaps from the big skimming ladle sometimes used by women to beat their husbands. In northern England and Scotland, the victim or his stand-in "rode the stang," a long hobby-horse, and a like steed was used in the *ceffyl pren* in Wales. In some towns, effigies of the offending couple were promenaded. In others, the festive organization mounted floats to display the actual circumstances of the monstrous beating: the wives were shown hitting their husbands with distaffs, tripe, sticks, trenchers, and water pots, throwing stones at them, pulling their beards, or kicking them in the genitalia.[27]

With these last dramatizations, the Misrule Abbeys introduced ambiguities into the treatment of the woman on top, just as we have seen in the comic literature. The unruly

[26] Sadron 1952:222–231, du Tilliot 1751:179–182, Williams 1955:53–54, Willeford 1969:175–179.

[27] In addition to Davis 1971 and Thompson 1972, see Spargo 1944 and McNeill 1961:67.

5.7. Skimmington ride. Engraving by William Hogarth for Samuel Butler's *Hudibras*, ca. 1726.

woman on the float was shameful, outrageous; she was also vigorous and in command. The mockery turned against her martyred husband. Here the complicated play with sexual inversion operated not so much as a release from the tensions of stable hierarchical control as an expression of the struggle over change, that is, over the location of power and property within the family and without. And the message of this urban carnival was mixed: it both exhorted the hen-pecked husband to take command and invited the unruly woman to keep up the fight.

Real women in early modern Europe had less chance than men to initiate or take part in their *own* festivals of inversion. Queens were elected for special occasions, such as Twelfth Night or Harvest, but their rule was gentle and tame. Some May customs still current in early modern Europe, however, point back to a rowdier role for women. In rural Franche-Comté during May, wives could take revenge on their husbands for beating them by ducking the men or making them ride an ass; wives could dance, jump, and banquet freely without permission from their husbands; and women's courts issued mock decrees. (In nearby Dijon, by the sixteenth century Mère Folle and her Infanterie had usurped this revenge from the women; May was one month of the year when the Misrule Abbey would charivari a man who had beaten his wife.) Generally, May—Flora's month in Roman times—was thought to be a period in which women were powerful, their desires at their most immoderate. As the old saying went, a May bride would keep her husband in yoke all year round. And in fact marriages were not frequent in May.[28]

---

[28] Davis 1975:105, 114; Welsford 1935:153–154; van Gennep 1943–1949, pt. 4, pp. 1452–1472, 1693–1694; Roubin 1970:178–179; Vostet 1588:12^{r-v}; Erasmus 1558, col. 135, "Mense Maio nubunt malae"; Le Bras 1955:44. In Savoie, the women's revenge took place on Saint Agatha's Day in February, and in parts of Alsace at Pentecost. See van Gennep 1943–1949, pt. 4, p. 1694, and 1924:32. In England, in northern Wales and in the Midlands, the customs of Hock Tuesday after Easter

In Nuremberg in the sixteenth and seventeenth centuries, women may have assumed some kind of special license at carnival time. Illustrated proclamations in joking pompous language granted every female with "a wretched dissolute husband" the right to deny him his freedom and to beat him till "his asshole [was] roaring." Another decree, issued by Foeminarius, the Hereditary Steward of Quarrel and Dispute Valley, gave three years of privileges to the suffering Company of Wives so that they might rule their husbands: they could bear arms, elect their own mayor, and go out and entertain as they wished, while their spouses could buy nothing and drink no wine or beer without the wives' permission. And of course the men did all the housework and welcomed any bastards that the wives might bear.[29]

The Unruly Woman and Political and Social Change

The relationship between real marriages and May license, between real pregnancy and *Fastnacht* (Shrovetide) games returns us to the question posed earlier in this paper. What were the overall functions of these festive and literary inversions in sex roles? Clearly they *in part* filled the role attributed to them by anthropologists and historians of literature: they afforded an outlet for conflicts about authority within the system and occasions by which the authoritarian current in family, workshop, and political life could be moderated by the laughter of disorder and paradoxical play. Accordingly, they served to reinforce hierarchical structure. Indeed, even the most searching feminist critics did not challenge the sovereign authority of the father as such; the only counter-model for the patriarchal family they had come

---

gave women the license to bind and/or heave the men and release them for a ransom. Some sexual play was involved. See Hazlitt 1965, vol. 1, pp. 316–318; Thistleton-Dyer 1900:188–191; Pythian-Adams 1972:66–69.

[29] Kunzle 1973:225, 236.

to recognize by the mid-eighteenth century was the equally hierarchical one of matriarchy.[30]

Thus this study does not completely overturn the traditional theory about rites and festivities of inversion; but it does add other dimensions to it. Rather than expending itself primarily during the privileged duration of the joke, the story, the comedy, or the carnival, topsy-turvy play had much spillover into everyday "serious" life, and the effects there were sometimes disturbing and even novel.

Let us begin with historical reflection about the family. Europeans of the fifteenth to eighteenth centuries found it remarkably difficult to conceive of the institution of the family as having a "history," of changing through time. Its patriarchal form went back either to the Garden of Eden, where the woman's subjection to the man was at least a gentle one, or to the first moment in human history, when monogamous marriage set mankind off from the promiscuous horde. Political forms might follow each other in a predictable cyclical fashion; economic, religious and cultural systems might change along with them (as Vico thought), but the family stayed pretty much the same. To be sure, curious sexual customs were noted in the New World, but they were used merely to satirize European abuses or were dismissed as products of savagery or degeneration.[31] *Play with the various images of woman on top, then, kept open an alternate way of conceiving family structure.* Ultimately, when the Jesuit Lafitau found an order in the strange family patterns (matrilineal and matrilocal) that he had observed among the Iroquois and

[30] Poullain de La Barre 1675, Preface, 1676:16–22; Astell 1730:99–107. For an early example of the primitive golden age theory and male usurpation, see Agrippa 1542,f. G i^{r!v}. Also, see Turner 1968, ch. 5.

[31] Calvin 1847:172, (Gen. 3:16); Vico 1968, nos. 369, 504–507, 582–584, 671, 985–994. Vico describes changes from the Roman period in the father's authority over his sons and in the character of the wife's dowry, but shows that monogamous marriage and paternal power remained dominant throughout. On the uses of New World for Old World thought, see Hodgen 1964 and Elliott 1970, chps. 1–2.

heard about in the Caribbean, he was able to refer back to legends of the Amazons and to the Lycians, whom he had read about in Herodotus. Lafitau's new theory of "gynaecocracy," as he called the matriarchal stage, was published in 1724 in his *Moeurs des sauvages ameriquains, comparées aux moeurs des premiers temps*. It owed something to the unruly woman.[32]

Play with the exceptional woman on top, the virtuous virago, was also a resource for feminist reflection on women's capacities. Although she did not argue that men and women should change the separate offices to which God had ordained them, Christine de Pisan was nevertheless glad to use examples of ancient female conquerors, stock figures in the legends about Amazons and in the stories and proverbs about women's rule, to show that "in many women there is . . . great courage, strength and hardiness to undertake all manner of strong things and to achieve them as did . . . great men and solemn conquerors." Subsequent writers on "Women Worthies" almost always included some viragos, readily incorporating Jeanne d'Arc into the company. By the

[32] Lafitau 1724:49–90. Anticipating Bachofen's work on matriarchy a century later, Lafitau's theory of *ginécocratie* does not develop fully the notion of a matriarchal stage for all societies. He speculates that the Iroquois may have originated in Greece and the Mediterranean islands. The Amazons also play a role in Thomas Hobbes' remarkable theoretical discussion of dominion within the family. As is ususal in his period, he insists that it must be vested in one person only; but "whereas some have attributed the dominion to the men only, as being of the more excellent sex; they misreckon on it. For there is not always that difference of strength or prudence between the man and the woman, as that the right can be determined without war." In commonwealths, the conflict is settled by law, which for the most part decides for the father. But in the state of nature, the decision is made by those who generate the children. It may be made by contract. "We find in history that the Amazons contracted with the men of the neighboring countries, to whom they had recourse for issue, that the issue male should be sent back, but the female remain with themselves: so that the dominion of the females was in the mother." Where there is no contract, the dominion lies with the mother, that is, in the absence of matrimonial laws, with the only person who knows who the true parents are and who has the power to nourish the child (*The Leviathan*, pt. 2, ch. 20).

early eighteenth century, speculation about virtuous Amazons could be used not only to praise the wise rule of contemporary lawful queens (as it had been already in Elizabeth I's day), but also to hint at the possibility of a wider role of citizenship for women.[33]

Furthermore, the legendary exceptional woman out of her place enriched the fantasy of a few real women and may have emboldened them to exceptional action. Marie Delcourt has argued convincingly that Jeanne d'Arc's male garb, to which she clung obdurately to the end, was not the product of mere practical military considerations, but was inspired by the example of the transvestite saints of the *Golden Legend*. The unusual seventeenth-century mystic Antoinette Bourignon started her career by fleeing from an impending marriage in the clothes of a male hermit. Among her later visions was that of humankind originally created as androgynous, a state of whole perfection to which it would return at the resurrection of the dead. The Recusant Mary Ward, founder of an innovating unenclosed teaching order for women with no male superior but the pope, took the Jesuits as her model, but may also have received encouragement from traditions of sexual inversion. Galloping over the countryside in the vain effort to reconvert the English to Holy Mother Church, she and the members of her company struck observers as "apostolic Amazons."[34]

Two of these women ultimately went to prison; the third narrowly escaped arrest. Perhaps the virtuous virago could

[33] De Pisan 1521,ff. Ff v^v-Hh ii^r; Heywood 1624. Discussion of the Amazons by Petit (1687) and Guyon (1740) tries to find plausible arguments to account for their bravery and successful rule. Both men insist they really existed. The Cartesian Poullain de La Barre did not use them in his arguments for women entering the magistracy (1675:166ff). By the time Condorcet and Olympe de Gouges make a plea for the full citizenship of women in the early years of the French Revolution, the argument is being waged in terms of rights.

[34] Delcourt 1956:93–96; Reinach 1905, vol. 1, pp. 430, 453–456; Chambers 1882. Mademoiselle de Montpensier, one of the leaders of the Fronde and victor in the siege of Orléans, may have drawn some inspiration from Jeanne d'Arc.

be a threat to order after all. But what about the majority of unexceptional women living within their families? What could the woman on top mean to them?

Girls were brought up to believe that they ought to obey their husbands; and boys were brought up to believe they had the power of correction over their wives. In actual marriage, subjection might be moderated by the common causes of economic support, to which they both contributed, of sexual need, child-rearing, or shared religious interest. It might be reversed temporarily during the lying-in period, when the new mother could boss her husband around with impunity. And subjection might be aggravated by the husband's repeated beatings of his wife. Some women accepted these arrangements. Some women got around them by a sneaky manipulation that made their husbands fancy themselves the sole decision-makers. Still other wives rebelled, told their husbands to go to the devil, badgered them, or thrashed them. Many circumstances might produce a wife of the third type. Here I wish only to speculate that the ambiguous woman on top of the world of play made the unruly option a more conceivable one.[35]

Ordinary women might also be disorderly in public. In principle, women could pronounce on law and doctrine only if they were queens, had unusual learning, or fell into an ec-

[35] On the husband's power of correction over the wife, see Blackstone 1770, bk. 1, ch. 15, and Ourliac and de Malafosse 1968:133, 140. Evidence here comes from examination of numerous diaries, descriptions of criminal cases, and records from the Geneva Consistory. See, for instance, Nicolas Pasquier on his marriage in de Ribbe 1874, vol. 3, pp. 85–87. On wives being beaten, see Gilles de Gouberville's journal, edited by de Blangy 1892:195. On women telling off their husbands, see Archives d'Etat de Genève, Procès criminels, 1st ser., no. 1202, 2d ser., no. 1535. For women beating their husbands, in addition to the charivaris against them, see the case of 1712 in de Fréminville 1758. Alison Klairmont has described the woman's privileges during lying-in in an unpublished seminar paper at the University of California at Berkeley. Italian birth salvers (that is, trays used to bring women drinks during labor and lying-in) dating from the late fifteenth and sixteenth centuries were decorated with classical and Biblical scenes showing women dominating men (Victoria and Albert Museum, Louvre). I am grateful to Elizabeth S. Cohen and Susan Smith for this last piece of information.

static trance. Virtually never were they to take the law into their own hands. In fact, women turn up rebuking priests and pastors, being central actors in grain and bread riots in town and country, and participating in tax revolts and other rural disturbances. In England in the early seventeenth century (so Thomas Barnes has discovered) a significant percentage of the rioters against enclosures and for common rights were female, while David Jones has found them an important element in enclosure riots in Wales into the nineteenth century. In Calvinist Edinburgh in 1637, the resistance to Charles I's imposition of the Book of Common Prayer was opened by a crowd of "rascally serving women" at Saint Giles' Church, who drowned out the Dean's reading, threw stools at the Bishop of Edinburgh, and when evicted, stoned the doors and windows. The tax revolt at Montpellier in 1645 was started by women and led down the streets by a virago named La Branlaire, who shouted for death for the tax collectors that were taking the bread from their children's mouths.[36]

There are several reasons for this female involvement, such as the special concern of mothers for their children's food, but part of its background is also the complex license accorded the unruly woman. On the one hand, she was not accountable for what she did. Given over to the sway of her lower passions, she was not responsible; the responsibility lay with her husband, to whom she was subject. Indeed, this "incapacity" was embodied in varying degrees in English law and in some French customary law. In England, in almost

[36] On women in different kinds of riots, see Davis 1975:26, 92, 182–183; Thompson 1971:115–117; Hufton 1971. My colleague Thomas Barnes has kindly shown me several cases involving women tearing down enclosures, which he has examined in connection with his study of the Star Chamber. Jones 1973:33–34, 47, 66, 202–203. See also the excellent article by Patricia Higgins 1973:179–222. Spalding 1828:47–48; Gardiner 1882:105–112; LeRoy Ladurie 1966:497. J. Beauroy, "The Pre-Revolutionary Crises in Bergerac, 1770–1789," paper presented to the Western Society for the Study of French History, Flagstaff, Arizona, March 14–15, 1974, describes the important role of women in the May 1773 grain riots in Bergerac.

any felonious action by a married woman to which her husband could be shown to be privy or at which he was present, the wife could not be held entirely culpable. If indicted, she might be acquitted or receive a lesser sentence than he for the same crime. In Normandy and Brittany, the husband might have to answer for her crimes in court, and everywhere the *sexus imbecillus* might be punished less severely. The full weight of the law fell only on the ruling male. Small wonder that the husbands sometimes thought it safer to send their wives out to do the rioting alone. Small wonder that the Star Chamber grumbled in 1605 that some women who had torn down enclosure fences were "hiding behind their sex."[37]

On the other hand, sexual inversion also gave a more positive license to the unruly woman: her right as subject and as mother to rise up and tell the truth. When a great pregnant woman at the front of a crowd curses the grain-horders or cheating authorities, the irreverent Gargamelle is part of her tradition. When Katherine Zell of Strasbourg dares to write an attack on clerical celibacy in the 1520s and claims: "I do not pretend to be John the Baptist rebuking the Pharisees. I do not claim to be Nathan upbraiding David. I aspire only to be Balaam's ass, castigating his master," then Dame Folly is part of her tradition.[38]

It turns out, however, that Dame Folly could serve to vali-

[37] Margaret Ruth Kittel, "Married Women in Thirteenth-Century England: A Study in Common Law," Ph.D. diss., University of California, Berkeley, 1973, pp. 226–233. Blackstone 1770, bk. 4, ch. 2 bk. 1, ch. 15. For advice on this matter I am grateful to John M. Beattie, author of "The Criminality of Women in Eighteenth-Century England," *Journal of Social History* (8:80–116). Carol Z. Weiner discusses the ambiguities in the responsibility of married women for certain felonies and trespasses in England in the late sixteenth and early seventeenth centuries in "Is a Spinster an Unmarried Woman?" (forthcoming in the *American Journal of Legal History*). She speculates that the description of certain married women indicted for riot and other crimes in the Herfordshire Quarter Session as "spinsters" may have been a legal fiction in order to require the women to accept responsibility for their acts. On how husbands and wives jointly manipulated their diverse roles for their mutual benefit, see Castan 1971:91–107; Harvard Law School, ms. 1128, no. 334, Page vs. Page, 13 Nov. 1605 (communicated by Thomas Barnes).

[38] Bainton 1970:3.

date disobedient and riotous behavior by men too. They also could hide behind that sex. Much has been written by historians on the ideals, traditions, symbols, and solidarities which legitimated the numerous rural and urban uprisings of early modern Europe. Among these traditions was the carnival right of criticism and mockery, which sometimes tipped over into real rebellion. In 1630 in Dijon, for instance, Mère Folle and her Infanterie were part of an uprising in masquerade against royal tax officers. In fact, the donning of female clothes by men and the adopting of female titles for riots were surprisingly frequent in the early modern period. In many of these disturbances, the men were trying to protect traditional rights against change; in others, it was the rioters who were pressing for innovation. But in all cases, they were putting ritual and festive inversion to new uses.

So in Beaujolais in the 1770s, male peasants blackened their faces and dressed as women and then attacked surveyors measuring their lands for a new landlord. In the morning, when the police agents came, their wives knew nothing, and said they were "fairies" who came from the mountains from time to time.[39] In 1829–1830, the "War of the Demoiselles" took place in the Department of Ariège in the Pyrénées. The peasants dressed themselves in long white shirts, suggesting women's clothes, and wore women's hats, and defended their desperately needed rights to wood and

[39] Davis 1975:119, 307, n. 89; Henri Hours, "Les fayettes de Saint Just d'Avray. Puissance et limites de solidarité dans une communauté rurale en 1774," prepared for a forthcoming issue of the *Bulletin de l'Académie de Villefranche* (ms. kindly shown me by M. Hours). The association of these costumed figures with fairies, which is also made in a few other riots, adds another dimension to political transvestism. Fairy beliefs were still strong in rural Europe in the eighteenth century, having originated from diverse traditions, including one which associated them with the spirits of the dead. Fairies might assume male or female form, might have various sizes or shapes and dress in varied ways, but they all had a spiritual power which could be used on human beings either malevolently or benevolently. Female and fairy combine their power in these riots to help the peasants. See Briggs 1967 and Thomas 1971:606–614.

pasturage in the forests, then being threatened by a new forest code.[40]

In England we find the same thing. As early as 1450–1451 the Queen of the Fairies was abroad in Kent and Essex; in the wake of Cade's Rebellion, a troop of black-faced husbandmen, "servants of the Queen of the Fairies," broke into the Duke of Buckingham's park and took his bucks and does. In 1531, a large crowd of London supporters of Catherine of Aragon—females and males so disguised—tried to seize Anne Boleyn from a villa where she was dining alone; "nor has any great demonstration been made about this," said an observer, "because it was a thing done by women."[41] In 1629, "Captain" Alice Clark, a real female, headed a crowd of women and male weavers dressed as women in a grain riot near Maldon in Essex. They sacked a ship thought to be exporting grain to the Netherlands. Two years later, in the dairy and grazing sections of Wiltshire, bands of men rioted and leveled fences against the king's enclosure of their forests. They were led by men dressed as women, who called themselves Lady Skimmington. In May 1718, Cambridge students, at their front "a virago, or man in woman's habit, crowned with laurel," assaulted a Dissenting meeting-house. Not long afterward, laborers in Surrey were rioting in women's clothes, and at mid-century country men disguised as women tore down, to the sound of drumming and loud shouts, the hated toll booths and turnpike gates at the Glou-

[40] On the background to the economic difficulties of the peasants in the Ariège and their relation to forest use, see Chevalier 1956:500–517. Sources on the uprising include *Gazette des Tribunaux*, vol. 5, nos. 1432–1433, March 14–16, 1830, pp. 446–447, 450–451; Dubédat 1900; Clarenc 1965:293–317. A new study of this uprising by John Merriman is "The Demoiselles of the Ariège, 1829–1830," in Merriman, ed., *1830 in France* (Yale University Press, 1977).

[41] Flenley 1911:127, du Boulay 1964:254–255, Brown 1871, vol. 4, no. 701. I am very grateful to Rodney Hilton and Robert Knecht of the University of Birmingham who led me to these references. In the earlier version of this essay I could give no instances of transvestite riots before the seventeenth century.

cestershire border. In April 1812, "General Ludd's Wives,"
two male weavers dressed as women, led a crowd of
hundreds to smash steam looms and burn a factory at Stockport.[42]

In Wales and Scotland, too, there were uprisings in female
disguise. The *ceffyl pren*, with its black-faced transvestite
males, gave way in the 1830s and 1840s in west Wales to the
Rebecca riots against the turnpike tolls and other agrarian
complaints, led by one "Rebecca" and noisy men in women's
clothes. Already in 1830–1832 the striking colliers of southern Wales had terrified scabs by their ghostly midnight visits
dressed in cattle skins or women's clothes. And in 1736 in
Edinburgh, the Porteous Riots, which were sparked by a
hated English officer and oppressive customs laws and expressed resistance to the union of Scotland with England,
were carried out by men disguised as women and with a
leader known as Madge Wildfire.[43]

Finally, in Ireland, where old stories told of the ritual
killing of the King at Samhain by men dressed as animals
and as women and where funeral wakes involved fertility

[42] The grain riot near Maldon is discussed more fully by William A. Hunt in
"The Godly and the Vulgar: Religion, Rebellion, and Social Change in Essex, England, 1570–1688," Ph.D. diss., Harvard University. Kerridge 1958–1960:68–71;
Historical Manuscripts Commission 1901:237–238 (reference kindly communicated
by Lawrence Stone); Surrey Quarter Sessions, Sessions roll 241, Oct. 1721 (kindly
communicated by John M. Beattie of the University of Toronto); *Ipswich Journal*, 5
Aug. 1749 (kindly communicated by Robert Malcolmson, Queen's University,
Kingston, Ont.); Smith 1967:244–245); Public Office, London, HE 42/128, "Memo-
rial of the Inhabitants of Stockport and Vicinity." For this last reference I am grateful to Robert Glen, who discusses this episode in "The Working Classes of Stockport during the Industrial Revolution," Ph.D. diss., University of California,
Berkeley, in progress. In an article written many decades ago, Ellen A. MacArthur
said that men dressed as women formed part of a very large female demonstration in
Aug. 1643, beating on the doors of Parliament to present petitions asking for peace
with Scotland and the settlement of the Reformed Protestant religion
(1909:702–703). The recent work of Patricia Higgins (1973:190–197), however, does
not take very seriously the contemporary claim that "some Men of the Rabble in
Womens Clothes" mixed in the crowd.

[43] Williams 1955, Thompson 1971:306–307, Jones 1973:102–106, Wilson
1891:143–145, Sir Walter Scott, *The Heart of Midlothian*, ch. 7.

rites with women dressed as men, we have the most extensive example of disturbances led by men disguised as women. For about a decade, from 1760 to 1770, the Whiteboys, dressed in long white frocks and with blackened faces, set themselves up as an armed popular justice for the poor, "to restore the ancient commons and redress other grievances." They tore down enclosures, punished landowners who raised the rents, forced masters to release unwilling apprentices, and fought the gouging tithe-farmers mercilessly. Those who opposed their rule, they chastised and ridiculed. They sometimes said they acted under "sanction of being fairies," and a favorite signature on their proclamations was Sieve Oultagh (or Sadhbh Amhaltach), that is, "Ghostly Sally." Ultimately they were suppressed by the armed might of the gentlemen and magistrates, but not before they had left a legacy that the Molly Maguires and the Ribbon Societies of the nineteenth century were to pick up.[44]

The female persona was only one of several folk disguises assumed by males for riots in the seventeenth and eighteenth centuries, but it was a quite popular one and widespread. Our analysis of sexual symbolism and of the varieties of sexual inversion should help us understand why this was so. In part, the black face and female dress were a practical concealment, readily at hand in households rarely filled with fancy wardrobes and yet frightening to spectators. Equally important, however, were the mixed ways in which the female persona authorized resistance. On the one hand, the disguise freed men from full responsibility for their deeds and per-

[44] Dalton 1970:15–19; Mercier 1962:49–53; Young 1892, vol. 1, pp. 81–84, vol. 2, pp. 55–56; Lecky 1893:12–44. L. P. Curtis of Brown University and Robert Tracy of the University of California at Berkeley have given me assistance on these Irish matters. I am grateful to Brendon Ohehir of the University of California at Berkeley for his deciphering of Lecky's reading of the Whiteboy signature and for his translation of it. The Irish personal name behind the English rendering "Sally" meant "goodness" or "wealth."

haps too from fear of outrageous revenge upon their man-hood. After all, it was mere women who were acting in this disorderly way. On the other hand, the males drew upon the sexual power and energy of the unruly woman and on her license (which they had long assumed at carnival and games) to promote fertility, to defend the community's interests and standards, and to tell the truth about unjust rule.

The woman on top was a resource for domestic and public life in the fashions we have described only as long as two things were the case: first, as long as sexual symbolism had a close connection with questions of order and subordination, with the lower female sex conceived as the disorderly lustful one; second, as long as the stimulus to inversion play was a double one—traditional hierarchical structures *and* disputed changes in the distribution of power in family and political life. As we move into the industrial period, with its modern states, classes, and systems of private property and its exploitation of racial and national groups, both symbolism and stimuli were transformed. One small sign of the new order is the changing butt of domestic charivaris: by the nineteenth century, rough music in England was more likely to be directed against the wife-beater than against the hen-pecked husband, and there are signs of such a shift in America and even in France.[45]

The woman on top flourished, then, in pre-industrial

---

[45] Thompson 1971:296–304. For examples of charivaris against wife-beaters in France in the early nineteenth century, see Girault 1808:104–106, which mentions charivari *only* against men who beat their wives in May (Girault lived in Auxonne, not far from Dijon, where the May prohibition was in effect in the sixteenth century); Du Laure 1808:449, which mentions charivaris *only* against wife-beaters and against neighbors who do not go to the wife's aid; van Gennep 1943–1949, pt. 3, p. 1703. On p. 1072, van Gennep also gives examples of the older kind of charivari against the beaten husband. An example from the American colonies is found in Culter 1905:46–47. A group of men in Elizabethtown, N.J., in the 1750s called themselves Regulars and went about at night with painted faces and women's clothes, flogging men reported to have beaten their wives. I am grateful to Herbert Gutman for this reference.

Europe and during the period of transition to industrial society. Despite all our detail in this essay, we have been able to give only the outlines of her reign. Variations in sexual inversion from country to country or between Protestants and Catholics[46] have been ignored for the sake of describing a large pattern over time. Cultural play with sex roles that was intended to explore the character of sexuality itself (Where did one sex stop and the other begin?) has been ignored for the sake of concentrating on hierarchy and disorder. The timing and distribution of the transvestite riots needs to be examined and the nature of play with sex roles before the fourteenth century must be investigated (Is it not likely there was once female transvestite ritual in areas where hoeing was of great consequence? Can the unruly woman have been so much an issue when sovereignty was less at stake?). The asymmetry between male and female roles in festive life in the fifteenth through eighteenth centuries remains to be explored, as do some of the contrasts between literary and carnivalesque inversion.

What has been established are the types of symbolic reversal in sex roles in early modern Europe and their multiple connections with orderliness in thought and behavior. The holiday rule of the woman on top confirmed subjection throughout society, but it also promoted resistance to it. Maid Marian danced for a plentiful village; Rosetta disported with the doomed old bear of winter; the serving women of Saint Giles threw stools for the Reformed Kirk; Ghostly Sally led her Whiteboys in a new kind of popular justice. The woman on top renewed old systems, but also helped change them into something different.

[46] Clearly such matters as the systematic Protestant assault on festive life, the elimination of a celibate clergy, and the spiritual reinforcement of family life all had long-range implications for the matters discussed in this paper. Calvinist consistories in Geneva and Amsterdam had begun to attack wife-beating in the sixteenth and seventeenth centuries. See Davis 1975:90–91, Carter 1964:162–163.

References

Aarne, A., and Stith Thompson. 1964. *The Types of the Folktale*, 2d rev. ed. Helsinki: Suomalainen Teideakatemia.

Abensour, Léon. 1923. *La femme et le féminisme avant la Révolution*. Paris: E. Léroux.

Agrippa, Henry Cornelius, of Nettesheim. 1542. *Of the Nobilitie and Excellencie of Womankynde*. Translation from the Latin edition of 1509. London.

Alford, Violet. 1937. *Pyrenean Festivals*. London: Chatto and Windus.

d'Andeli, Henri. 1951. *Le lai d'Aristote de Henri d'Andeli*, ed. M. Delboville. Bibliothèque de la faculté de philosophie et lettres de l'Université de Liège, no. 123. Paris.

Anson, John. 1974. "Female Monks: The Transvestite Motif in Early Christian Literature." *Viator* 5:1–32.

Ashton, John, ed. 1968. *Humour, Wit, and Satire in the Seventeenth Century* [1883]. Detroit: Singing Tree Press.

Bainton, Roland. 1970. "Katherine Zell." *Medievalia et Humanistica*, n.s., 1:3.

Bakhtin, Mikhail. 1968. *Rabelais and His World*. Cambridge: M.I.T. Press.

Barber, C. L. 1951. *Shakespeare's Festive Comedy*. Princeton: Princeton University Press.

Bateson, Gregory. 1935. "Culture Contact and Schismogenesia." *Man* 35:199.

Bellamy, J. G. 1970. *The Law of Treason in England in the Later Middle Ages*. Cambridge: Cambridge University Press.

Bernheimer, Richard. 1952. *Wild Men in the Middle Ages*. Cambridge: Harvard University Press.

Binns, J. W. 1974. "Women or Transvestites on the Elizabethan Stage? An Oxford Controversy." *Sixteenth-Century Journal* 5:95–120.

Blackstone, William. 1770. *Commentaries on the Laws of England*. Oxford: Clarendon Press.

de Blangy, A., ed. 1892. *Journal de Gilles de Gouberville pour les années 1549–1552*. In *Mémoires de la Société des Antiquaires de Normandie*. Vol. 32. Rouen.

Boccaccio, Giovanni. 1963. *Concerning Famous Women*. Trans. G. G. Guarino. New Brunswick, N.J.: Rutgers University Press.

du Boulay, F. R. H., ed. 1964. *Documents Illustrative of Medieval Kentish Society*. Ashford.

Brians, Paul, ed. and trans. 1972. "The Lady Who Was Castrated." In *Bawdy Tales from the Courts of Medieval France*. New York: Harper & Row. Pp. 24–36.

Briggs, K. M. 1967. *The Fairies in Tradition and Literature*. London: Routledge & Kegan Paul.

Brissaud, Jean. 1912. *A History of French Private Law*. Boston: Little, Brown.

Brown, Rawdon, ed. 1871. *Calendar of State Papers relating to English Affairs, existing in the archives and collections of Venice*. 9 vols. London.

Bullough, Vern. 1974. "Transvestites in the Middle Ages." *American Journal of Sociology* 79:1381–94.

Calvin, Jean. 1847. *Commentaries on Genesis*. Trans. J. King. Vol. 1. Edinburgh.

———. 1848. *Commentaries on the Epistles of Paul The Apostle to the Corinthians*. Trans. J. Pringle. Vol. 1. Edinburgh.

———. 1863–1880. "Sermons sur le Deutéronome." In G. Baum, E. Cunitz, and E. Reuss, eds., *Ioannis Calvini opera quae supersunt omnia*. Vol. 28. Brunswick.

Carter, Alice Clare. 1964. *The English Reformed Church in Amsterdam in the Seventeenth Century*. Amsterdam: Scheltema & Holkema.

Castan, Nicole. 1971. "La criminalité familiale dans le ressort de Parlement de Toulouse, 1690–1730." In A. Abbiateci et al., *Crimes et criminalité en France, 17e–18e siècles*. Cahier des Annales, no. 33. Paris. 91–107.

Chambers, M. C. E. 1882. *The Life of Mary Ward, 1585–1645*. London.

Chevalier, Michel. 1956. *La vie humaine dans les Pyrénées ariégeoises*. Paris.

Clarenc, L. 1965. "Le code de 1827 et les troubles forestiers dans les Pyrénées centrales au milieu du XIXe siècle." *Annales du Midi* 77:293–317.

Clark, Alice. 1968. *The Working Life of Women in the Seventeenth Century* [1919]. London: G. Routledge & sons.

Culter, J. E. 1905. *Lynch-Law*. London.

Dalton, G. F. 1970. "The Ritual Killing of the Irish Kings." *Folklore* 81:15–19.

Davis, Natalie Z. 1971. "The Reasons of Misrule: Youth Groups and Charivaris in Sixteenth-Century France." *Past and Present* 50:41–75.

———. 1973. "City Women and Religious Change in Sixteenth-Century France." In Dorothy McGuigan, ed., *A Sampler of Women's Studies*. Ann Arbor. Pp. 22–37.

———. 1973. "The Rites of Violence: Religious Riot in Sixteenth-Century France." *Past and Present* 59:86–87.

———. 1975. *Society and Culture in Early Modern France*. Stanford: Stanford University Press.

Delcourt, Marie. 1956. *Hermaphrodite: Myths and Rites of the Bisexual Figure in Classical Antiquity*. London: Studio Books.

Delevoy, Robert. 1959. *Bruegel*. Geneva: Skira.

Donaldson, Ian. 1970. *The World Upside-Down: Comedy from Jonson to Fielding*. Oxford: Oxford University Press.

Dubédat, M. 1900. "Le procès des Demoiselles: Résistance à l'applica-

tion du code forestier dans les montagnes de l'Ariège, 1828–30."
Bulletin périodique de la Société ariégeoise des sciences, lettres et arts, vol. 7,
no. 6.

Durkheim, Emile, and Marcel Mauss. 1972. *Primitive Classification*. Translated with an introduction by Rodney Needham. Chicago: University of
Chicago Press.

Elliott, J. H. 1970. *The Old World and the New*. Cambridge: Cambridge
University Press.

Erasmus. 1558. "Mense Maio nubunt malae." In *Adagiorum Chiliades*. Col.
135. Geneva.

Fénelon, François de Salignac de la Mothe. 1966. *Fénelon on Education*.
Trans. H. C. Barnard. Cambridge: Cambridge University Press.

Flenley, Ralph, ed. 1911. *Six Town Chronicles of England*. Oxford: Oxford
University Press.

Flügel, J. C. 1930. *The Psychology of Clothes*. London: Hogarth Press.

de Fréminville, E. de la Poix. 1758. *Traité de la police générale des villes,
bourgs, paroisses et seigneuries de la campagne*. Paris.

Gaignebet, Claude. 1972. "Le combat de Carnaval et de Carême de P.
Bruegel (1559)." *Annales: Economies, Sociétés, Civilisations* 27:329–331.

Gardiner, S. R. 1882. *The Fall of the Monarchy of Charles I, 1637–1649*. Vol.
1. London: Longmans, Green.

van Gennep, Arnold. 1924. "Le culte populaire de Sainte Agathe en Savoie." *Revue d'ethnographie* 17:32.

——. 1943–1949. *Manuel du folklore français*. Vol. 1. Paris: A. Picard.

Girault, Cl. Xavier. 1808. "Étymologie des usages des principales époques
de l'année et de la vie." *Mémoires de l'Académie celtique*, vol. 2.

Gluckman, Max. 1963. *Order and Rebellion in Tribal Africa*. New York: Free
Press of Glencoe.

Gouge, William. 1941–1942. *Domesticall Duties*, quoted in William and
Mary Haller, "The Puritan Art of Love," *Huntington Library Quarterly*
5:246.

von Grimmelshausen, H. J. C. 1964. *Courage, the Adventuress, and the False
Messiah*. Trans. Hans Speier. Princeton: Princeton University Press.

Grosnet, Pierre. 1530–1531. *Les motz dorez De Cathon en francoys et en latin
. . . Proverbes, Adages, Auctoritez et ditz moraulx des Saiges*. f. F vii^r. Paris.

Guyon, Claude. 1740. *Histoire des Amazones anciennes et modernes*. Paris.

Halkett, John G. 1970. *Milton and the Idea of Matrimony*. New Haven: Yale
University Press.

Hazlitt, W. C. 1965. *Faiths and Folklore of the British Isles* [1905]. New York:
B. Blom.

Heywood, Thomas. 1624. *Gynaikeion, or Nine Bookes of Various History, con-
cerninge Women*. London.

Higgins, Patricia. 1973. "The Reactions of Women." In Brian Manning,
ed., *Politics, Religion, and the English Civil War*. London: Edward Arnold.
Pp. 179–222.

Hill, Christopher. 1966. "The Many-Headed Monster in Late Tudor and Early Stuart Political Thinking." In C. H. Carter, ed., *From the Renaissance to the Counter-Reformation: Essays in honour of Garrett Mattingly.* New York: Random House. Pp. 298–324.

Historical Manuscripts Commission. 1901. *Report on the Manuscripts of . . . the Duke of Portland.* Vol. 7. London.

Hodgen, Margaret. 1964. *Early Anthropology in the Sixteenth and Seventeenth Centuries.* Philadelphia.

Holmes, Catherine E. 1967. *L'éloquence judiciaire de 1620 à 1660.* Paris.

Hufton, Olwen. 1971. "Women in Revolution, 1789–96." *Past and Present* 73:90–108;

Janssen, Johannes. 1896–1925. *History of the German People at the Close of the Middle Ages.* Trans. A. M. Christie. Vol. 7. London: K. Paul, Trench, Trübner.

Jerome, Saint. 1963. *The Letters of Saint Jerome.* Trans. C. C. Mierow. Vol. 1. London.

Jones, David J. V. 1973. *Before Rebecca: Popular Protests in Wales, 1793–1835.* London: Allen Lane.

Jordan, Winthrop. 1968. *White over Black: American Attitudes toward the Negro, 1550–1812.* Chapel Hill: University of North Carolina Press.

Joubert, Laurent. 1578. *Erreurs populaires au fait de la médecine.* Bordeaux.

Kerridge, Eric. 1958–1960. "The Revolts in Wiltshire against Charles I." *Wiltshire Archaeological and Natural History Magazine* 57:68–71.

Kunzle, David. 1973. *The Early Comic Strip: Narrative Strips and Picture Stories in the European Broadsheet from 1450 to 1825.* Berkeley and Los Angeles: University of California Press.

Lacour, Léopold. 1921. *Les premières actrices françaises.* Paris: Librairie française.

Lafitau, J. J., S.J., 1724. *Moeurs des sauvages ameriquains, comparées aux moeurs des premiers temps.* Vol. 1. Paris: Saugraine l'aîné.

Du Laure, J. A. 1808. "Archeographe au lieu de La Tombe et ses environs." *Mémoires de l'Académie celtique,* vol. 2.

Leach, Maria, ed. 1949–1950. *Funk and Wagnalls Standard Dictionary of Folklore, Mythology, and Legend.* New York: Funk and Wagnalls.

Le Bras, Gabriel. 1955. *Etudes de sociologie religieuse.* Vol. 1. Paris: Presses universitaires.

Lecky, W. E. H. 1893. *A History of Ireland in the Eighteenth Century.* Vol. 2. New York: D. Appleton.

LeRoy Ladurie, Emmanuel. 1966. *Les paysans de Languedoc.* Paris: Mouton.

L'Héritier de Villandon, M. J. 1718. *Les caprices du destin ou Recueil d'histoires singulieres et amusantes. Arrivées de nos jours.* Paris.

Locke, John. 1952. *The Second Treatise of Government,* ed. T. P. Peardon. New York: Liberal Arts Press.

MacArthur, Ellen A. 1909. "Women Petitioners and the Long Parliament." *English Historical Review* 24:702–703.

McKendrick, Melveena. 1974. *Women and Society in the Spanish Drama of the Golden Age: A Study of the Mujer Varonil.* London, New York: Cambridge University Press.

McNeill, F. M. 1961. *The Silver Bough.* Vol. 3. Glasgow: W. Maclellan.

Mercier, Vivian. 1962. *The Irish Comic Tradition.* Oxford: Oxford University Press.

Meslin, Michel. 1974. "Réalités psychiques et valeurs religieuses dans les cultes orientaux." *Revue historique* 512:301–304.

Oettinger, K., and K.-A. Knappe. 1963. *Hans Baldung Grien und Albrecht Dürer in Nürnberg.* Nuremberg.

O'Faolain, Julia, and Lauro Martines. 1973. *Not in God's Image.* London: Temple Smith.

Ortner, Sherry B. 1974. "Is Female to Male as Nature is to Culture?" In Michelle Zimbalist Rosaldo and Louise Lamphere, eds., *Women, Culture, and Society.* Stanford: Stanford University Press. Pp. 67–87.

Ourliac, Paul, and de Malafosse, Jehan. 1968. *Histoire du droit privé.* Vol. 3. Paris: Presses universitaires.

Partridge, Edward B. 1958. *The Broken Compass.* New York: Columbia University Press.

Paulson, Ronald. 1965. *Hogarth's Graphic Works.* New Haven: Yale University Press.

Petit, Pierre, 1687. *De Amazonibus Dissertatio.* 2d ed. Amsterdam.

de Pisan, Christine. 1521. *The Boke of the Cyte of Ladyes.* Translation of *Le Tresor de la Cité des Dames* (1405). London.

Poullain de La Barre, François. 1675. *De l'excellence des hommes contre l'égalité des sexes.* Paris: Jean du Puis.

———. 1676. *De l'égalité des deux sexes.* Paris: Jean Du Puis.

Pythian-Adams, Charles. 1972. "Ceremony and the Citizen: The Communal Year at Coventry, 1450–1550." In Peter Clark and Paul Slack, eds., *Crisis and Order in English Towns.* London: Routledge and Kegan Paul.

Reinach, Salomon. 1905. *Cultes, mythes, et religions.* Paris: E. Léroux.

De Ribbe, Charles. 1874. *Les familles et la société en France avant la Révolution.* Paris.

Richmond, Hugh. 1971. *Shakespeare's Sexual Comedy.* Indianapolis: Bobbs-Merrill.

Robert of Flamborough. 1971. *Liber Penitentialis*, ed. J. F. Firth. Toronto: Pontifical Institute of Medieval Studies.

Roubin, Lucienne. 1970. *Chambrettes des Provençaux.* Paris.

de Rubys, Claude. 1574. *Les privileges franchises et immunitez octroyees par les roys . . . aux consuls . . . et habitans de la ville de Lyon.* Lyon.

Rychner, Jean, ed. 1963. *Les quinze joies de mariage.* Geneva: Droz.

Sachs, Curt. 1963. *World History of Dance.* New York: Norton.

Sadron, P. 1952. "Les associations permanentes d'acteurs en France au moyen-age." *Revue d'histoire de théâtre* 4:222–231.

Savaron, Jean. 1608. *Traitté contre les masques.* Paris.

Schmitz, Hermann. 1922. *Hans Baldung gen. Grien*. Bielefeld, Leipzig.

Schochet, Gorden. 1969. "Patriarchalism, Politics, and Mass Attitudes in Stuart England." *Historical Journal* 12:413–441.

Screech, Michael. 1958. *The Rabelaisian Marriage*. London: Arnold.

Shadwell, Thomas. 1680. *The Woman-Captain*. London: S. Carr.

Smith, A. W. 1967. "Some Folklore Elements in Movements of Social Protest." *Folklore* 77:244–245.

Spalding, John. 1828. *The History of the Troubles and Memorable Transactions in Scotland and England from 1624 to 1648*. Vol. 2 Edinburgh.

Spargo, J. W. 1944. *Juridical Folklore in England Illustrated by the Cucking-Stool*. Durham, N.C.: Duke University Press.

Strutt, Joseph. 1878. *The Sports and Pastimes of the People of England*. New ed. London: Chatto and Windus.

Sumberg, S. L. 1941. *The Nuremberg Schembert Carnival*. New York: Columbia University Press.

Sydenham, Thomas. 1681. *Epistolary Dissertation to Dr. Cole*. London.

Thistleton-Dyer, Thomas F. 1900. *British Popular Customs*. London: G. Bell.

Thomas, Keith. 1971. *Religion and the Decline of Magic*. London: Weidenfeld and Nicolson.

Thompson, E. P. 1971. "The Moral Economy of the English Crowd in the Eighteenth Century." *Past and Present* 50:115–117.

——. 1972. " 'Rough Music': Le charivari anglais." *Annales: Economies, Sociétés, Civilisations* 27:285–312.

Thompson, Stith. 1955–1958. *Motif-Index of Folk Literature*. Rev. ed. Bloomington, Ind.: Indiana University Press.

Du Tilliot, Mr. 1751. *Mémoires pour servir à l'histoire de la Fête des Foux*. Lausanne.

Timbal, P. C. 1963. "L'esprit du droit privé." *XVIIe siècle* 58–59:30–39.

Turner, Victor. 1967. *The Forest of Symbols: Aspects of Ndembu Ritual*. Ithaca, N.Y.: Cornell University Press.

——. 1968. *The Ritual Process: Structure and Anti-Structure*. Chicago: Aldine.

Veith, Ilza. 1965. *Hysteria: The History of a Disease*. Chicago: University of Chicago Press.

Vico, Giambattista, 1968. *The New Science*. Trans. T. G. Bergin and M. H. Fisch. Ithaca, N.Y.: Cornell University Press.

Vives, Juan Luis. 1524. *The Instruction of a Christian Woman*. London.

Vostet, Jean. 1588. *Almanach ou Prognostication des Laboureurs*. Paris. f. 12^{r-v}.

Wardroper, John, ed. 1970. *Jest upon Jest*. London.

Welsford, Enid. 1935. *The Fool: His Social and Literary History*. London: Faber & Faber.

Willeford, William. 1969. *The Fool and His Scepter*. Evanston: Northwestern University Press.

Williams, David. 1955. *The Rebecca Riots*. Cardiff: University of Wales Press.

Wilson, Daniel. 1891. *Memorials of Edinburgh in the Olden Time*. 2d ed. Vol. 1. Edinburgh, London.

Wilson, J. H. 1958. *All the King's Ladies: Actresses of the Restoration*. Chicago: University of Chicago Press.

Wolf, Eric. 1968. "Society and Symbols in Latin Europe and in the Islamic Near East." *Anthropological Quarterly* 42:287–301.

Wright, Celeste T. 1940. "The Amazons in Elizabethan Literature." *Studies in Philology* 37:433–445.

Young, Arthur. 1892. *Arthur Young's Tour in Ireland, 1776–1779*, ed. A. W. Hutton. Vols. 1, 2. London: G. Bell.

PART TWO

INVERSION
IN ACTION

CHAPTER 6

Ranges of Festival Behavior

ROGER D. ABRAHAMS and RICHARD BAUMAN

Celebrations involving symbolic inversion are among the least understood of cultural performances. Why should behavior that seems to fly in the face of order and propriety be tolerated, and even encouraged, in such celebrations? The problem that faces scholars is not one of unmanageable diversity in the activities themselves, for there is, in fact, an intriguing similarity among many of these performances in their exploitation, through inversion, of similar sets of symbolic oppositions—life-death, male-female, nature-culture, and so on. We would suggest, rather, that a significant part of the difficulty is conceptual, lying in the way the relationship between the celebrations and their cultural context is conventionally understood. Our concern in this article is to try to clarify, and if necessary, to reorient, some of the traditional perspectives that have been brought to bear on inversive celebrations, by comparing similar sets of festival behavior from two separate societies.

Our focus, in particular, is on carnival in St. Vincent, West Indies, and on belsnickling, a form of Christmas mumming, in the La Have Islands, Nova Scotia, both of which are characterized by a high degree of symbolic inversion—transvestitism, men dressed as animals or supernatural beings, sexual license, and other behaviors that are the opposite of what is supposed to characterize everyday life.[1]

---

[1] Vincentian carnival and La Have Island belsnickling are described more fully in Abrahams 1972 and Bauman 1972a.

Despite their association with Easter and Christmas respectively, these two sets of festival behaviors have no particular religious significance. They are, in fact, historically related activities, with roots in European masking traditions associated with various seasonal festivals. The Vincentian emphasis upon carnival reflects the influence of southern, Catholic Europe (as well as Africa), while the Christmas mumming of the La Have Islanders derives from the Protestant areas of England and Germany.

Carnival and belsnickling would seem to be type cases of what Norbeck has termed rites of reversal, "the antithesis of behavior at other times, . . . norms for special occasions which oppose norms applying at other times." According to Norbeck, "reversals are institutionalized acts opposing everyday conventions of many kinds, acts which certain individuals or whole social groups are encouraged, expected, or required to perform on specified occasions" (1970).

Norbeck has performed a useful service by bringing together much cross-cultural information on activities of this kind under the rubric of rites of reversal, and our own effort is very much in the spirit of his call for comparative study of these rites. However, there are at least two respects in which his formulation will not serve for the kind of analysis that seems to us to be called for by our material. In both the communities we have studied, it is only a segment of the community that engages in the inversive behavior to which the notion of rite of reversal draws attention, but the activities of this segment constitute part of larger events involving the entire community. Accordingly, we consider it necessary to broaden our field of view to include the entire community as it participates in these rites. This is certainly consistent with Norbeck's approach, though not explicitly discussed in his program.

The second point is more fundamental, and relates to the very concept of reversal which is at the center of Norbeck's formulation (and those of others who have dealt with such festivities from a functionalist perspective). Our quarrel is with the notion that the festival behaviors we are concerned with are "the antithesis of behavior at other times," that they "oppose norms applying at other times." To be sure, these festivals involve certain highly marked symbolic inversions of identity and aspects of behavior that characterize the everyday life of the communities and their members—men are clearly not women, animals, or supernaturals. Nevertheless, when we examined carefully who was engaged in the inversive and licentious behaviors during the festival events, and looked at their behavior at other times of the year, we found that they were often involved in and even noted for activities which had much in common with their festival behavior. Our information indicates that for St. Vincent and the La Have Islands at least, a model that views the disorder and license of festival as the antithesis of the order which is supposed to characterize the rest of the year represents an analytical distortion. The fact is that in neither place does order prevail during the rest of the year, nor is it expected to. The same people who engage in license during the festivals are the community agents of disorder during the remainder of the year. The symbolic inversions of identity and dress may not be present at other times, but the licensed contravention of ideal norms certainly is.

What we are suggesting, then, is that the inversion and license of festival must be approached in terms of the general interrelationship between order and disorder in the moral and social universe of the communities in which "rites of reversal" are conducted. If license and disorder are found to occur throughout the year, we cannot suggest that festival represents the antithesis of behavior at other times, only, perhaps, that it is the antithesis of behavior called for by the *ideal* normative system, which is a very different thing.

Once this is recognized, we can begin to account for the

skewing of the general anthropological perspective on festivals of the kind we are discussing. There is a parallel here in the failure of the social anthropologists of a generation ago to acknowledge the existence of conflict in constructing their idealized theories and accounts of social structures in stable and harmonious equilibrium. We have, of course, come a long way since then in developing models and theories that can comprehend conflict in social structures; indeed, much of the renewed interest of anthropologists in these rites stems from Max Gluckman's analyses of what he calls "rituals of rebellion" in southeast Africa (1963).

However, although these festivals are now widely viewed as symbolic expressions of conflict in the *social* structure, the old view of a stable *moral* and *normative* system, equally as idealized as the model of a stable, conflict-free social system, has persisted. We cannot help but notice the license and disorder of festival, because it is so extreme, but we have not yet begun to take adequate account of expressions of disorder and license as persistent elements in cultures, either ignoring them completely or writing them off as deviance. There is no denying the existence of ideal normative systems in communities, and the awareness of these systems on the part of the community members, but we must also attend systematically to the licensed and expected contraventions of such systems in society and culture. It becomes one of the special tasks of symbolic anthropology to analyze the symbolic classifiers and expressions of the opposition between order and disorder in communities.[2]

Christmas mumming, or belsnickling, in the La Have Islands, is an activity of the older boys and young unmarried

[2] For examples of work exploring this line of analysis see Douglas 1966, Peacock 1968, Turner 1969, Geertz 1972, Reisman 1970, Abrahams and Bauman 1971, Bricker 1973.

men of the community.[3] Most belsnickles are around eighteen to twenty-one years of age, though some are as young as fifteen or sixteen and a few as old as thirty. Belsnickling is associated with and considered most appropriate for young men in that period of their lives between the time they begin working for a living and the time they marry and leave their parents' households.

The belsnickles travel in groups averaging around twelve members, all drawn from the same community. They do not go beyond this community when they make their rounds. All but one or two in each group are disguised, the exceptions being individuals who serve their fellows as "guides," since the belsnickles are supposed to be strangers to the islands. The guides carry lanterns to light the way for the belsnickles and do the rowing when necessary, but do not enter the houses visited by the maskers en route.

The mummer's disguises are of three basic types. The first is a dissheveled and grotesque but essentially anthropomorphic figure, dressed in tattered clothes turned inside out, while the second is a more animal-like version of the foregoing, effected by painting an animal's features on the mask and wearing horns on the head and a cowbell around the neck. The third type is quite different from the other two, involving a kind of rough transvestitism: women's clothes stuffed out with padding and women's features on the mask. Those belsnickles dressed as women use "squealy" voices and exaggerated feminine movements, while the others speak with "coarse" or "rough" voices and walk hunched over with a rolling gait.

Belsnickles make their rounds after dark on Christmas eve, blowing horns and ringing bells as they go. Calling at every

[3] The description of belsnickling is written in the ethnographic present, although belsnickling has died out in the La Have Islands in the years since World War II; see Bauman 1972a.

house in the community, they request admittance by knocking at the kitchen window or door and asking, "Belsnickles allowed in?" Almost every family lets them in, with perhaps two or three exceptions, these being very old people, finicky housekeepers who do not want their floors muddied, or those whose small children are excessively frightened by the wild and grotesque figures of the maskers.

Upon entering the kitchen, the belsnickles begin to perform for their hosts, in a manner summed up in such phrases as "you'd put on a little act," "just act the jackass," "carry on a little bit," or "act the fool." Most commonly, this involves clumsy, exaggerated step dancing to the accompaniment of a mouth organ or drum, loud singing, stumbling around in a caricature of drunkenness, or, for those dressed as women, mincing around the room in an exaggerated caricature of feminine behavior. Some of the bolder belsnickles exercise a degree of mild sexual license by sitting on the knee of the woman of the house or grabbing the girls for hugs and kisses.

The belsnickles have another role to play for their hosts besides the jackass, for in addition to performing for the adults, they act as inquisitors of the children. Island children do not get to see many strangers, much less wild and grotesque figures like the belsnickles, and they fear the mummers intensely, associating them with ghosts. The belsnickles, in fact, are used as bogeymen throughout the year to threaten unruly children, and this intensifies their fears even further. During the course of their visits, the belsnickles call the children of the house forward and ask them if they have been good. When the children reply in the affirmative—what child would not?—the belsnickles reward them with candy.

The belsnickles in their own turn receive treats from the householders. Just before leaving, they ask the lady of the house for "a bit of brouse," a special term used for the belsnickle treats which all families prepare in advance for the mummers' visit. These are generally cakes, cookies, and apples, which are carried away and eaten by the whole group at the end of the evening.

Playing carnival, like belsnickling, is an activity largely for young people, but here the selective principle is not so much age as an inclination toward what the Vincentians call *rudeness* or *nonsense* behavior, characterized by drinking, noise, a good deal of physical and verbal playing, and license. Carnival groups are organized around a touring musical band, brought together by one or two leaders among the "sporty fellows" of the community, with other members of the community following along, "jumping up" to the music.

The leaders of the band are usually more elaborately costumed than the other musicians, dressing up in such traditional guises as the Devil, Wild Indian, Bold Robber, the hunchback Bruise-e-Back, a two-headed donkey, or a bull. The bandsmen may follow the same theme as the lead figure, but more often they simply blacken their faces with stove blacking, paint rude words and phrases on their white pants and T-shirts, and wear outlandish hats fashioned for the occasion. The jammers, or followers, also are costumed—common themes include sex reversal and role reversal, for example, dressing in teacher's robes with a chamber pot for a hat. Others clothe themselves in the vestments of the bush— banana trash (leaves) suits and bird's-nest hats—and leap about like animals, calling themselves Monkey Men.

Beginning at midnight on the Sunday before Lent, the carnival groups carouse down the roads and through the streets, playing their music, singing the song written for the occasion by the leader, dancing, and generally "making noise," a highly significant term in St. Vincent used to designate the most important feature of rude behavior. Drinking rum, the nonsense-maker, is a constant activity, and many of the traveling groups purposely stop before the rumshops, for the proprietors may pay in rum for their performances.

Besides the music and dancing, part of the carnival performance consists of a violent argument, well in keeping with the theme of making noise. Also, players dressed as a bull or donkey, both superphallic creatures in this culture, charge the crowd of onlookers with threats of estrangement, sexual violation, or death, at which everyone laughs while they flee their attackers. This scaring of the crowd is generally accompanied by a demand for coins, since making money is a prime objective of the carnival groups.

Unlike the belsnickles, carnival players do not restrict their carousing to their home communities, ranging through villages sometimes as far as the city of Kingstown, as much as four hours away. One of the benefits of ranging away from home is that the wanderers encounter women strange to themselves, pulling them, to their mutual delight, into the rumshops or fields. Their feet raw from jumping up, their bodies worn from carousing for more than two days without sleep, their costumes ragged from jostling and jamming and sporting in the fields, they retire to their villages and homes only when Lent begins on Ash Wednesday.

These brief descriptions should suffice to show that there are many similarities in the types and intensities of festival performance in the La Have Islands and St. Vincent. In both places, for instance, the central performers, through symbolic inversion, attack the basic categorical differences of male-female, community member–stranger, living-dead, human being–animal. In both places, noise, disruption, and sexual license are central to the festival performance. And in both places, the active performers constitute only a limited segment of the community. But there are crucial differences between the two areas, not only in the style by which the symbolic inversion is enacted, but more importantly in the place in which the performance occurs, the value assigned the performance by the community, and the relationship between the themes of order and disorder that is highlighted by the festival behavior.

One cannot understand the place of festival entertainments on St. Vincent without relating such licentious behavior to the nonsense dimension of everyday life. There is a major distinction made within Vincentian communities between behaviors appropriate in the house and yard and those appropriate on the road and at the crossroads. Yard behaviors, and household behaviors even more, must gravitate at all times toward the *sensible* and away from the *rude*. License to play is seldom given in such an environment, because play is *foolishness* and such *nonsense* attacks the sense of respectability by which the household is constantly being judged. It is in cases of this sort that the observer is forced to recognize that there are alternative modes of action and of judging behavior, alternatives which depart considerably from the norms of respectability.

By drawing upon Peter Wilson's analysis of a similar complementary set of values and norms (1969), we can see these alternative norms in terms of an alternative system of behavior and judgment, but in which one system—that of household "respectability" behaviors—is the overt basis of judgment for nearly all behavior, and the other—that of crossroad, male, reputation-seeking behaviors—is a covert set of values by which adult men usually operate when outside the household environment.

This is not the forum to spell out all the ways by which these complementary worlds coexist and interact. For our present purposes it is sufficient to point out that the world of the house and the yard may be characterized by its emphasis on family, intergenerational continuity, behaving in an orderly *cool* manner, and maintaining the house, yard, and fields in an orderly condition. This is the world of privacy for the Vincentian, a privacy which is protected by respectable behaviors. It is also the world of work, for work is associated with family (and especially mother) and respectability.

On the other hand, the crossroad world is appropriately the public arena in which friendships take precedence over family, peer-grouping over the generations, and licentious, loud, and even *rude* behavior is to be expected, indeed encouraged, especially when carried on by an attractive performer or group. This then is the public world, and significantly the world in which *play* is regarded as appropriate.

Thus, *nonsense* activity goes on regularly and is an open, if not always acknowledged, part of the Vincentian experience and dual value system. This leads to a recognition among Vincentians that there is much activity which goes on regularly and is characteristic of the community even though it is regarded as bad, as *rudeness*. Of course, such a judgment is made from the point of view of household values. What is unique is that those who act bad admit to doing so, and wear the role proudly, since a good part of masculine identity from adolescence through late middle age involves accepting this role whenever one is with one's friends. And it is expected that this will be a regular practice. Badness is thus accepted, in fact regarded highly, because licentious behavior is part of the performance complex by which men seem to feel most themselves.

This then is the context of such performances as Vincentian carnival. Playing carnival is but an extension and an intensification of crossroads and rumshop everyday play. This intensification is marked—indeed, largely accomplished—by symbolic inversion through costume and masking. The sporty fellows of the community put off their local and individual identities to emerge as the embodiment of disorder. Thus transformed, they throw themselves into the most intense and sustained nonsense of the year, in which noise, drinking, and license reign supreme. (Another name for car-

nival is bacchanal.) Carnival thus represents an extended
two-day open celebration of the nonsense motive in the community, a time when the rude and sporty segment of the
community holds the stage and the rest of the community is
compelled to acknowledge their presence. The separation
and balance between the sensible and the rude is maintained
throughout, though, for only the very sporty are attracted to
playing carnival; the participation of sensible people, if at all,
will be through observing without joining. And carnival, as
we have noted, is pre-eminently a celebration of the public
places—the street, the road, and the rumshop—where sport-
iness, rudeness, and license prevail.

If we examine belsnickling from the same perspective that
has illuminated our analysis of carnival, an interesting and
basic contrast emerges. The two festivals have many elements in common, and both represent symbolic ways of
playing out the relationship between order and disorder in
the community, but the structure of belsnickling reveals a
very different moral universe in La Have Islands culture
from that underlying Vincentian carnival.

We must begin and end with the fact that morality and
decorum in La Have Island culture are not organized in the
same kind of balanced dualistic system as in St. Vincent. To
be sure, the house, especially the kitchen, is just as much the
province of women and the cornerstone of respectability in
the La Have Islands as on St. Vincent. Island men, moreover, are far from disinterested in reputation, spending endless fall and winter evenings in the general store negotiating
their male identity and reputation through the exchange of
yarns (personal narratives) and arguments (Bauman 1972b).
The kind of reputation to which they aspire, however, is different. Island men are concerned with establishing reputation
through reference to their work, presenting themselves as
competent and accomplished fishermen, and as people with a

wide range of wisdom, knowledge, and experience. Participation in the evening sessions at the general store is markedly age-graded, with the older men, those with the most knowledge and experience, dominating the conversation. Badness, in anything approaching the Vincentian sense, is not an aspect of adult male identity; only one or two men at most in each community are known as bad, and they are feared and deplored as deviants more than admired, though their exploits can be amusing at times.

There is, however, a segment of the community with license to engage in disorderly and indecorous behavior and of whom such behavior is expected. These are the young men between the ages of fifteen or sixteen and the early twenties, in that stage between boyhood and full adulthood when they are old enough to work for a living but have not yet married and left their parents' households to establish households of their own. They are, in other words, precisely those members of the community who go belsnickling.

The islanders speak of the young men in this stage of life as "full of devilment, playing tricks," or as always "gettin' off all kinds of stuff." They are known, especially, for practical joking, playing tricks like putting a drop of molasses between the cards being used by the older men in the store, putting a nail or stick down the throat of a fish to take the edge off the knife of the man who picks it up to clean it, or stealing and hiding the dory of a suitor from another island who has come over to court a local girl. Exploits of this kind are expected of them, and are treated with amused toleration, although the immediate victim may give vent to momentary annoyance.

Against this background, the structure of the festival emerges more clearly. Here again, through the symbolic inversion of masking and costume, the members of the community who are associated with license throughout the year put off their individual identities and become the embodiment of

disorder itself. But instead of merely confronting the respectable segment of the community from their own domain in
the public areas of the island, and devoting themselves to an
intensified celebration of the motive of disorder, which they
represent, they come into direct interaction with the respectable people in the very stronghold of respectability, the
kitchen.

Ordinarily, disorder is barred from the house, but on
Christmas eve the belsnickles are allowed in, to dance out
their abstract identity in the kitchen. At first glance, the respectability of the house may appear to be compromised by
this invasion, but when we look closely at the situation it appears otherwise. First of all, the belsnickles must ask to be
allowed in; control is in the hands of the householders—they
are the hosts and the maskers are the guests. This relationship is underscored when the belsnickles ask the woman
of the house for food, thus acknowledging her place in the
household and her primacy in the kitchen. It is furthermore
noteworthy that the performance of the belsnickles, in contrast to that of the Vincentian carnival players, is not frightening to the adult audience, but rather is amusing. The belsnickles are frightening only to the children, but in this they
are themselves agents of order, for in their guise as inquisitors of the children they act as powerful agents of socialization, testing the children for proper behavior during the past
year, and exhorting them to good behavior in the year to
come.

Thus, while belsnickling allows the maskers to revel in
their antic role, and to receive a measure of acknowl-
edgement for it, in a larger sense they are acknowledging
their subordination to the household and contributing to the
socialization of children, acting themselves as agents of order.
Whereas carnival gives disorder its own day, and underscores
the dynamic balance between order and disorder in the moral

universe of the Vincentians, belsnickling acknowledges disorder, but draws upon its energy to underscore the primacy of order and respectability.

We must make clear that the festivals we have described are by no means the only events in either place in which the relationship between the themes and forces of order and disorder are played out in public.[4] However, carnival and belsnickling are the only such occasions involving symbolic inversion through masking, costume, and the personification of disorder in such abstract terms. The symbolic inversion in both places is strikingly similar, and bears further similarities to festival behaviors widely distributed around the world. The moral structure of the festivals, however, contrasts sharply between the two communities, and this has been the point of our paper.

The principal functionalist argument in the interpretation of rites of reversal is that such rites are the symbolic expression of underlying and normally suppressed conflicts within the society. Accordingly, they constitute a mechanism by which the pressures engendered by social conflict may be vented without allowing the conflict to become fully overt and threaten the survival of the society. The rites, in other words, lay bare the conflicts and allow for the expression of the hostilities they engender, but in a symbolic, encapsulated, and thus neutralized way (Wallace 1966:203–205).

Our analysis, however, calls for a different view, at least with regard to the two cases we have considered. Far from constituting events that have hostility and conflict as their organizing principle, carnival and belsnickling appear to us to draw together opposing elements in the two societies in which they occur, and to draw them together more closely and harmoniously than at any other time in the year. Most of the time in the communities we have examined, the forces or order and disorder, respectability and license, do not con-

[4] See the discussion of *tea meeting* in Abrahams and Bauman 1971.

front one another, involving as they do different people, different spheres of action, different settings, as well as different moral principles. On those occasions when these opposed segments of the comunity do come together, the result is characteristically confusion or embarrassment. In carnival and belsnickling, however, the two sets of elements, each clearly identifiable, participate together within a unified event productive of enjoyment and a sense of community. The picture, is not one of hostility, but of harmony.

Anthropologists have relied heavily on the notions of reversal and of a safety-valve mechanism in interpreting festivals of the kind we have described, viewing them as discrete and extreme events against an analytical backdrop of unitary moral systems. We have attempted to demonstrate, through analysis and comparison of two such festivals, that the above perspective is simplistic and distorted. People have a greater tolerance for disorder than anthropologists give them credit for, and analysis of festivals of symbolic inversion must take account of the place of this disorder in their lives.

References

Abrahams, Roger. 1972. "Christmas and Carnival in St. Vincent." *Western Folklore* 31:275–289.

Abrahams, Roger, and Richard Bauman. 1971. "Sense and Nonsense in St. Vincent: Speech Behavior and Decorum in a Caribbean Community." *American Anthropologist* 73:762–772.

Bauman, Richard. 1972a. "Belsnickling in a Nova Scotia Island Community." *Western Folklore* 31:229–243.

———. 1972b. "The La Have Island General Store: Sociability and Verbal Art in a Nova Scotia Community." *Journal of American Folklore* 85:330–343.

Bricker, Victoria R. 1973. *Ritual Humor in Highland Chiapas.* Austin: University of Texas Press.

Douglas, Mary. 1966. *Purity and Danger.* New York: Praeger.

Geertz, Clifford. 1972. "Deep Play: Notes on the Balinese Cockfight." *Daedalus* (Winter), pp. 1–38.

Gluckman, Max. 1963. "Rituals of Rebellion in South-East Africa." In

Order and Rebellion in Tribal Africa. London: Cohen and West. Pp. 110–136.

Norbeck, Edward. 1970. "Rites of Reversal." Paper delivered at the 1970 annual meetings of the American Anthropological Association, San Diego, Calif.

Peacock, James. 1968. *Rites of Modernization*. Chicago: University of Chicago Press.

Reisman, Karl. 1970. "Cultural and Linguistic Ambiguity in a West Indian Village." In Norman E. Whitten and John Szwed, eds., *Afro-American Anthropology*. New York: Free Press. Pp. 129–144.

Turner, Victor. 1969. *The Ritual Process*. Chicago: Aldine.

Wallace, Anthony F. C. 1966. *Religion: An Anthropological View*. New York: Random House.

Wilson, Peter. 1969. "Reputation and Respectability: Suggestions for Caribbean Ethnology." *Man* 4:70–84.

CHAPTER 7

Symbolic Reversal and Social History: Transvestites and Clowns of Java

JAMES L. PEACOCK

Two symbols of reversal are prominent in Indonesian culture: the clown and the transvestite. The clown reverses categories of rank, the transvestite categories of sex.

Among the Ngadju of southern Kalimantan (Borneo), analyzed by Schärer (1963) and Hoek (1949), are found the *basir*, men who adopt the dress and existence of women and serve as priests and shamans. Schärer interprets basir transvestism as a means of symbolically uniting the two basic divisions of Ngadju cosmology, which are associated with the division between male and female; Needham, in his work on the left and the right hand (1960), finds this interpretation compatible with his own theories of dualism.

Like the basir, the *bissu* of southern Sulawesi (Celebes) are priests who dress and live as women, or did so in the 1870s when they were described by the Dutch ethnologist Matthes (1872) and still in the 1930s when they were observed by Holt (1939:27–35) and Nooteboom (1948). The particular task of the bissu is to guard ornaments of Makassarese princes. The ornaments are said to possess sex that is of undetermined gender, hence their custodians, the bissu, must possess both male and female attributes in order that they may relate to every ornament (Chabot 1950:155). The bissu boast a special link to the creator God, Batara Guru, and they contribute to rites of fertility. At annual dances when the prince plows the year's first furrow, the bissu become possessed, enter a trance, and plunge daggers into their larynxes, allegedly without suffering consequences (Holt 1939, Nooteboom 1948).

Yet another Indonesian institution is the division of rule between a "male" and a "female" ruler, both of whom are biologically male. Still existing in the lesser Sundas (see, for example, Cunningham 1965), this pattern was also found until the mid-nineteenth century in Sumatra, among the Minangkabau. The Minangkabau distinguished between female *adat* (custom) that was concerned with the governing of matrilineally organized local descent groups, and male adat, which was concerned with Minangkabau society as a whole. The overall society was ruled by the so-called Great Lord, whose position was inherited patrilineally. Mediating between the patrilineal royal family and the matrilineal local communities was a "Girl Lord," who could be either man or woman but in either case should display feminine traits in such matters as hairstyle (de Josselin de Jong 1960).

Transvestism on Java is today associated primarily with the theater. Pigeaud (1938), the greatest authority on Javanese theater, finds in the great number and variety of forms of theatrical transvestism evidence for ancient, pre-Islamic origins of the institution. He believes that it is linked historically to dualistic cosmologies and shamanistic or priestly functions like those exemplified by the basir and bissu. One could also note a certain association between Javanese transvestism and political power. The *Pararaton* (chronicle of the Javanese Kingdom of Madjapahit) records that King Prabu Ajam of Madjapahit was playing female roles in dramas staged some seven hundred years ago (Pigeaud 1938:479), and the late President Sukarno relates in his autobiography (1965:42) that as a youth he played female parts in the *ludruk* (a popular Javanese play), stuffing his blouse with bread rolls, which he ate after the performance. But these connections to politics are oblique and scattered. Transvestism in the contemporary Javanese theater is essentially sexual and aesthetic rather than political. The male actor endeavors to present the most beautiful and erotic image of the female. The eroticism tends to spread off the stage, and many of the actors (or "actresses," as they prefer to call themselves) also work as male prostitutes, living as concubines, swishing through the marketplaces, or roving in predatory gangs in the dark alleys of such melting pots as Jakarta.

Javanese theater starring female impersonators has ranged from the elegant to the tawdry, from the court dances such as *bedaja* to the street dances such as *taledek* or *ronggeng* and the working-class plays such as the ludruk. Certain stylistic features are common to all of these more lowly forms: the slinging of a shawl alternatively around the body and out while contorting the hips, twisting the arms and hands, and singing shrilly (Wilken 1961:115). The ludruk dance (Peacock 1968:168–172) also resembles that of the *wandu* of Makassar, who used to join the bissu in the annual dance. Both the ludruk dancer and the wandu hold the fan before the face while singing, then walk in a circle wiggling the fan and rotating the upturned palm (Holt 1939:88). Stylistic similarities among all these forms (including the court dances) suggest that they must have been historically linked through diffusion or common origins.

Unlike the transvestite, the clown is peculiar to Java, at least with respect to the attributes of interest here. Known as the *panakawan*, the clown is central to all forms of Javanese theater and is regarded by many as the most significant and distinctively Javanese contribution to each layer of foreign culture that Java has assimilated, first the Hindu, then the Muslim, finally the Western. In puppet or human plays staging the Indian Mahabharata myth, the Javanese counterparts to the Hindu princes are clowns, Semar, Petruck, and Gareng, who are employed as the princes' servants. In dramatizations of the Amir Hamzah tales, the Muslim hero is provided with comic servants, Marmade and Umar Madi, or (in the region of Banjuwangi), Blendang, Blendung, and Bledes (Pigeaud 1938). And in ludruk plots, clown servants work for Westernized bureaucrats. The panakawan appear on Javanese temple reliefs dated as early as A.D. 800 (Galestin 1959) and the commonly accepted view is that these figures were indigenous to Java, grafted on, in the role of servant, to each wave of foreign mythology.

That the panakawan plays servant to the foreign master by no means deprives him of power or status. Semar is described by Kats as follows: "He gives wise advice, showing more knowledge of the affairs and plans of the Gods than does his master. He not only enters the abode of the gods but himself appears as a god. . . . He is called blood kin to Hijang Goeroe (the highest god) and equal to Kresna" (Kats 1923:40–41).

The poignancy of Semar's power is expressed in the story of his death. Semar's master, Prince Ardjuna, has been bewitched by Shiva into promising to murder Semar. Though grieving over his obligation, Ardjuna still feels compelled to proceed with the act. Semar suggests that he ease Ardjuna'a dilemma by simply burning himself. Semar builds a bonfire and stands in it, but instead of dying he turns into his godly form and defeats Shiva.

God though he is, Semar is still a clown. He is fat and grotesque, with female breasts. He speaks a gutter language rather than the refined language spoken by his master, and he injects uncouth and contemporary jokes into classical legends. As Geertz has suggested, the relationship of Semar to the prince is not unlike that between Falstaff and Prince Hal (1960:277). The same could be said of the other clowns and their masters.

The prestige of the panakawan is revealed by the role's being appropriated by the prince when certain dramas were performed in the palace; in the ludruk troupe, the clown's role is typically played by the manager. The image of Semar permeates Javanese life, appearing on ancient temple reliefs, sacred daggers, amulets (Galestin 1959), and even on the sides of pedicabs or the walls of railroad stations. Semar is featured in the fertility rites of certain villages near Cheribon (Sardjono 1947:20), and he is the subject of folk belief: for example, if his puppet representation is placed in a box of puppets, the box becomes lighter (Sardjono 1947:26). The transvestite coats himself with jewels, rich clothing, and pseudo-aristocratic roles onstage, but ironically has a low and suspect status in society. The clown, who takes the role of lowly servant in the plays, occupies a sacral status in the culture.

The clown and the transvestite differ in their mode of reversal. Using the opposition between male and female, the transvestite mixes the two. Shifting from his natural category of male (few if any of the transvestites fail to display at least the secondary biological attributes of the normal male) into the cultural one of female, he craves to possess, or be possessed by, the attributes of the opposite sex. The clown, treating the opposition between high and low status, either mocks or transcends the attributes of his master, but he never appropriates these attributes. The few scenes that I have seen where he tried to do so were regarded by the audience as abnormal. In these ludruk scenes, the servant danced to a rolling rhythm of a drum to the point that his master was hypnotized into imitating the servant's dance, at which point the two switched roles, the servant sitting pompously in a chair while the master swept the floor. The audience reacted by screaming, "Latah!" (the name of a mental disease where a low-status person, usually a female servant, compulsively imitates motions of someone else after experiencing the shock of a loud noise like that of the drum). The exchange of roles was suddenly reversed when a transvestite appeared and ordered both servant and master to assume their proper positions.

An interesting parallel, which may or may not have functional significance, can be noted between the tendency of the transvestite to possess or be possessed by his opposing attributes compared to the clown's mocking or transcending of them, and what some Indologists regard as the historic role of the two figures. The transvestites were shamans who became possessed by spirits. The clowns, whose vision of reality is wider than that of the establishment, have been known as teachers (*kijai*), after the independent intellectuals whose lonely schools have traditionally taught mystical and radical perspectives threatening the ruling hierarchies (Sardjono 1947:20). Such an interpretation would suggest an historical continuity between the contemporary transvestites and clowns and their ancient counterparts such as the presumed ancestors of the basir and bissu, or the equivalent for the clowns.

A second mode of interpretation, at least for the transvestites, is psychological. The incarceration of male prostitutes in Jakarta jails has provided at least two psychiatrists with convenient samples for psychological study. The first study, by a Dutch-trained psychiatrist in 1931, dealt with twelve male prostitutes in Glodok prison in Jakarta (Amir 1934). The second study, done by an Indonesian psychiatrist, considered twenty-five transvestites, twenty-three of whom were in prison in Jakarta (Ling 1968, Masdani 1968). The first study notes in passing that virtually all of the subjects performed in theater as well as working as prostitutes, washmaids, seamstresses, and at other female jobs, but the psychiatrist was less interested in social analysis than medical, and he devoted most of his description to his subjects' diseases of the anus and genitalia. The second psychiatrist was also interested in biology, and he performed thorough physical examination, both by inspection and laboratory tests, to

determine that in primary, secondary, and genetic characteristics the transvestites were all normal males. Nevertheless,
all but one insisted that he was a woman, and they had so
classified and conducted themselves since before puberty.
The psychiatrist explains their adopting the female role by
discovering in their life histories a dominant mother, absent
father, and too many sisters. I note in passing that transvestite life histories which I collected in the course of studying
the ludruk did not necessarily reveal an absent father. In
fact, several of the transvestites' fathers were strongly
present, became enraged by their sons' effeminacy, beat
them, cut their hair, and finally drove them away. The psychiatrist's analysis doubtless points to an important factor,
but it fails to explain all cases or to reveal why transvestism
in Java should assume its distinctive form.

Seeking at least the beginning of an explanation, I shall attempt a cultural or structural analysis of the meaning of the
transvestite, in relation to the meaning of the clown. A convenient starting point is a statement from Pigeaud:

Javanese theatrical plays are, one may say, imbued with the idea of
classification. The dramatis personae, although not altogether without some characteristics of their own, are thought of mainly as representatives of the party they belong to. Originally these parties
were neither political factions nor social classes, nor ethical divisions, good or bad, they were just partitions in the universe and in
society, both human and superhuman. In the course of time political and ethical interpretations of the classification did indeed come
to the fore, but the ancient cosmic partition must always be kept in
mind if one wants to understand the meaning of Javanese drama.
[n.d.:236–237]

Pigeaud's statement is meant to apply to the entire range of
Javanese drama. It is particularly applicable to the classical
wajang kulit (leather-puppet plays), the stories of which are
treated explicitly as cosmological systems, but the classificatory world view is evident even in the audience responses to
lowly plays such as the ludruk. One can occasionally hear a

workingclass spectator of the ludruk classify a coarse ludruk character into the sacred scheme of the wajang: "X is the color of Kresna" or "Y has the personality of Srikandi." Paraphrasing Pigeaud, one may say that not only Javanese theater but Javanese culture is "imbued with the idea of classification." I would hazard the generalization that among the Javanese, as among their neighbors the Balinese, there is traditionally more concern for classification than process, for the subsuming of objects, acts, and individuals within cosmological categories than with getting things done or forming social relationships.[1] The concern with classification instead of narrative among ludruk audiences is only one example of this pattern.

Within the Javanese drama, the transvestite and clown are especially concerned with classification, and various devices segregate them from the narrative, the *lakon* or *tjerita*. In the ludruk, a curtain is dropped before and after the appearance of the transvestite dancer to signal his seclusion from the story that runs before and after his interlude. The clowns are segregated by their stylized costumes, their use of personal names rather than story names, their failure to marry as do story characters, and by other devices (Peacock 1968:165–166). Both transvestites and clowns are, sometimes quite consciously, seen as *symbols* of something, rather than literal representations of reality, as are the comparatively naturalistic story characters. Described by one Javanese as an "illusion of feminity," the transvestite dancer does not imitate the movements of women on the street but rather imitates the stylized circular movements that were performed forty years ago by the wandu of Makassar. And the transvestite is regarded as a distillation of such feminine qualities as *luwes*, or refined softness. Even in daily life, the transvestite is not interested merely in imitating women, but in classify-

[1] For studies elucidating this generally classificatory thrust of Hinduized Balinese-Javanese culture, see Rassers 1959, Geertz 1966, and Anderson 1972.

ing himself in the category "female." To that end, the psychiatrist's male prostitutes insisted that they were women, the ludruk transvestite wears exaggeratedly feminine ornaments, and, according to the account of one of them, he makes certain that at public gatherings, where all men sit outside the house and women work inside, he is with the women. The concern among transvestites for being rigidly classified within the female half of the society is also noted by Chabot (1950:153–155) with respect to Makassar.

But if the transvestites and clowns are symbols of cosmic categories, what are these categories? Scholars such as Pigeaud assert that clown and transvestite represent sacred cosmologies derived from dualistic Javanese society of ancient times. The evidence for such assertions (as, indeed, for the existence of such a society) is patchy, and the contemporary Javanese man on the street is hardly able to spiel off the full cosmology with which transvestite and clown are associated. Nevertheless, he will provide an amazingly rich string of associations. Through such comments and through the mode of organizing the plays, the Javanese reveal a view of the clown and the transvestite (more explicitly for the former than the latter) as symbols within a complex and systematized cosmology.

Two dimensions of this cosmology turn about the opposition between male-female and low status-high status. Such attributes as colors, substances, languages, spatial divisions, and orders of existence from the animal to the spiritual are categorized in terms of these oppositions. Javanese, especially those of the Hinduized or *abangan* (syncretic, animistic) persuasion, gain pleasure and security from speculating about the structure of such a scheme, organizing their actions along its coordinates, and subsuming events within its categories.

Given their concern with cosmic order, the Javanese get a peculiar charge out of abnormal combinations that connote disorder, or perhaps paradoxically, a more ultimate order than that of the surface. They get excited at viewing peculiar combinations of male and female qualities represented by the transvestite on the stage, and they continuously remind themselves of the mix, saying repeatedly, "It is a man acting like a woman." On occasion, a spectator becomes so aroused that he endeavors to marry the transvestite, and the transvestites are reputed to possess magical power to induce such arousal. On the other hand, if the transvestite should spoil the illusion by a stiff or coarse gesture that permits maleness to show through, the audience responds with disgust, shouting that he is *tuèk*, *èlèk*, and *taèk*—old, ugly, and like excrement.

The audience gets a similar kick out of interplay between low and high, as when Semar caricatures Prince Ardjuna. The response is not simply delight that the patrician is mocked or bested; inappropriately gross triumph of a proletarian clown over an aristocratic hero is censored even by a proletarian audience because the aristocrat represents ideals common to all classes (Peacock 1968:208–210). Rather, the opposition between high and low acquires added meaning through the richness of the permutation and combination of the two categories; the clown reduces high to low, transcends the high while adhering to the low, plays a counterpoint to the high, and performs other symbolic manipulations that enliven the basic opposition in the minds of its perceivers while demonstrating its fundamental unity. Though the Javanese enjoy the clown and transvestite partly because they break taboos, release tensions, and permit the disorderly mixing of normally segregated categories, they also appreciate these figures, I would suggest, because they demonstrate the underlying unity of the cosmology, a unity which, through mysticism and other means, the Javanese have traditionally sought with fervor.

Despite the popularity and profundity of the clown and transvestite roles within traditional Javanese civilization, these symbols are regarded with suspicion and hostility by such modernizing movements as the revolutionary nationalists and the reformist Muslims.

In reformist Muslim circles, for example, among members of the movement known as Muhammadijah, such plays as the wajang kulit, ludruk, and *ketoprak*, which feature the transvestite and clown, are virtually taboo. Rare, too, are the syncretic Islamic plays such as the *wajang goleg*, which show the Amir Hamzah or Menak figures and their clown-servants. Plays are discouraged ostensibly because they express the Javanese-Hindu tradition known as *agama Djawa*, which opposes or contaminates Islam through mixing it with Hinduism, Buddhism, and animism. And the clowns strike at least some of the pious Muslims as being simply too funny, "for Islam is serious," while the transvestites violate Islamic notions concerning the segregation of male and female. Several of the ludruk transvestites stem from pious Muslim families but were driven away by their fathers, and the decline of the bissu in the courts of Makassar, as well as the exodus of the wandu from certain villages in that region, can be traced to the influence of Islam.

Some of the nationalists oppose the figures, too, though less directly and without an explicit rationale. The Marxist nationalist, Sjamsuddin, formerly director of the ludruk troupe Marhaen (but since the 1965 purge of Communism, imprisoned in East Java), launched a campaign to strip transvestites of their effeminacy, except when it was necessary on stage to serve the cause of the revolution. He forced the transvestites in his troupe to cut their hair, shackle their hips, and in some instances, to get married and father children—in short, to lead a "normal" life offstage. He also hired a psychiatrist to lecture them on their "disease." Sjamsuddin's opposition to the clowns was less deliberate than his opposition to the transvestites, but he was necessarily in competition with the lead clown and co-director of the troupe, Bawa. Sjamsuddin wrote the troupe's scenarios, and he strove to integrate the plots and heighten climax, measures that reduced the role of the clown. Sjamsuddin's rivalry with Bawa ended in 1964 when the clown was run over by the troupe bus.

Why the conflict between reform and revolution on the one hand, and transvestites and clowns on the other? Particular explanations can be found, of course, for particular instances, for example, personal antagonism between Sjamsuddin and Bawa or Muslim dogma regarding sexuality, but a general explanation is that the two sets of phenomena embody opposing world views. The symbols of reversal derive their meaning from a classificatory scheme whose categories they serve to connect at any given moment, so as to maintain an eternal, balanced unity. Reform and revolution derive meaning from a linear conception of history that imagines not static divisions but an infinite series of means harnessed to future ends. In Indonesia, the notion is caught in the term *perdjuangan*, or struggle, which is central in the ideologies of both Muslims and nationalists and is applied to both the society and the individual. When I spent several months in the Muhammadijah camps for the training of cadre leaders in 1970, I was struck by the frequency with which the trainee, narrating his life history (*riwajat hidup*) to the group, organized his account around the term perdjuangan.

Conceiving of the life history as a linear process, a struggle, a perdjuangan, reformists and revolutionaries see categories such as male and female, high and lowly, as phases within a sequence rather than fixed divisions within a static structure. They imagine the individual as capable of rising from low to high status within his lifetime, just as Muhammad rose from camel driver to prophet. Reformists see a similar progression from femaleness to maleness, at least for the male. Beginning his life in a household dominated by women (the so-called matrifocal household, in Java), the boy moves progressively into the male-dominated Muslim community,

the *ummat*. The important transition comes when he is circumcised and begins to pray at the mosque. And the reformist boy is circumcised earlier than the abangan or syncretist
boy. The reformist tendency to circumcise early admits of
varied interpretations, but one is that the reformists, perceiving the transition from female to male as an important process, endeavor to speed it up. The syncretists, perceiving
maleness and femaleness as categories existing at every stage
of the life cycle, wait until the traditional age, after puberty.
And among the syncretists the circumcision ceremony itself
is traditionally rich in symbolism signaling the presence of
both male and female elements: it is (or was) celebrated by
the performance of a shadow play, whose screen is divided
into left and right sides, probably associated with female and
male halves of the cosmos; dramas telling of the union of the
family of a bride and groom; and in some regions, male and
female groups that dance in opposition while exchanging wit-
ticisms. Such performances are absent at the reformist Muslim circumcision, where the object is simply to get the job
done and move the boy on to the next phase of his life.

What I am proposing is not that the reformist or revolutionary mode of child-rearing discourages clowning or transvestism; the fact that the pious Muslims do spawn transvestites, who flee to the ludruk or the marketplace (Chabot
1950:156), is evidence against such a psychogenetic proposition. Instead, I am suggesting that child-rearing patterns
such as early circumcision express a view of history and individual development that is logically opposed to the world
view symbolized by the transvestite and clown.[2]

To state the general principle, drawn from this one case
but probably applicable to other cases: the classificatory world

---

[2] Additional evidence of the logical association between clowns and fixed hierarchies of status is in Peacock 1968:128–129. Additional evidence associating transvestism with cosmologies postulating fixed relations between male and female categories is surveyed in van der Kroef 1956:182–195.

view, which emphasizes the subsuming of symbols within a frame, nourishes and is nourished by symbols of reversal; the instrumental world view, which emphasizes the sequential harnessing of means to an end, threatens and is threatened by such symbols. The instrumental world view would reduce all forms to mere means toward the ultimate end, but symbols of reversal call forth enchantment with the form and veneration of the cosmic categories it embodies, a fixation dangerous to the forward movement, the struggle, the perdjuangan.[3]

Whether this principle is sound or not, enunciating it should contribute to discussion of a question hardly considered by anthropological studies of such subjects as symbolic reversal and dualism:[4] how and why are these systems transformed and destroyed by the onslaught of modern society?

References

Amir, M. 1934. "De Transvestieten van Batavia." *Geneeskundig Tijdschrift van Nederlandsch Indië* 74:1081–1083.

Anderson, Benedict R. O'G. 1972. "The Idea of Power in Javanese Cul-

---

[3] Another line of interpretation is that the reformists are an "adultish" culture, hence incompatible with the "childish" character of transvestite and clown, so that they do not permit themselves the release provided by the infantile, oral, and regressive aspects of these figures (see Peacock 1968:71–73). Statistics collected by the author in Jogjakarta during 1970 show a general acceleration of the reformist Muslim, as opposed to syncretist Javanese, movement toward adulthood: earlier toilet training, earlier weaning, earlier circumcision, earlier marriage, earlier departure from home. The reformists also tend to dress children as "little men" and "little women" (as did the seventeenth-century American pilgrims in Plymouth, who resemble the reformist Muslims in certain characterological and theological patterns; see Demos 1970) and to instruct them even before they are finished with kindergarten in such rules as avoiding sexual promiscuity. Thus the reformists would be seen as a serious and adult-oriented, rather than a playful and child-oriented, subculture. This interpretation seems to me compatible with the more general one proposed in the text, but to label a tradition childish or playful without explaining the profound cosmological framework within which such a trait is subsumed is insulting as well as misleading.

[4] In the most comprehensive and authoritative compendium on dualistic classification, Needham 1974, only a single article, Brenda E. F. Beck, "The Right-Left Division of South Indian Society," concerns itself with the transformation of a dualistic system due to the impact of modernity.

ture." In Claire Holt, ed., *Culture and Politics in Indonesia*. Ithaca, N.Y., London: Cornell University Press.

Beck, Brenda. 1974. "The Right-Left Division of South Indian Society." In Needham 1974, pp. 391–426.

Chabot, Hendrik Theodorus. 1950. *Verwantschap, Stand en Sexe in Zuid Celebes*. Groningen, Djakarta: J. B. Wolters.

Cunningham, Clark. 1965. "Order and Change in an Atoni Diarchy." *Southwestern Journal of Anthropology* 21:359–382.

Demos, John. 1970. *A Little Commonwealth*. New York: Oxford University Press.

Galestin, Th. P. 1959. *Iconografie van Semar*. Leiden: E. J. Brill.

Geertz, Clifford. 1960. *Religion of Java*. New York: Free Press of Glencoe.

———. 1966. *Person, Time, and Conduct in Bali: An Essay in Cultural Analysis*. New Haven: Yale University, Southeast Asian Studies.

Hoek, Jan. 1949. "Dajakpriesters: Een bijdrage tot de analyse van de Religie de Dajaks." Diss., University of Amsterdam.

Holt, Claire. 1939. *Dance Quest in Celebes*. Paris: Archives internationales de la danse.

Jong, P. E. de Josselin de. 1960. *Minangkabau and Negeri Sembilan: Sociopolitical Structure in Indonesia*. Djakarta: Bhratara.

Kats, J. 1923. *Het Javaansch Tooneel—Wajang Poerwa*. Weltevreden: Volkslectuur.

Kroef, J. M. van der. 1956. "Transvestism and the Religious Hermaphrodite." In *Indonesia and the Modern World*. Bandung: Masa Baru.

Ling, Tan Tjiauw. 1968. "Beberapa Segi Daripada Laporan Preliminer Projek Research 'Bantiji.' " *Djiwa*, no. 2 (Apr.), pp. 45–54.

Masdani, J. 1968. "Pemeriksaan Psikologik Pada Bantji." *Djiwa*, no. 2 (Apr.), pp. 55–60.

Matthes, B. F. 1872. "Over de Bissoes of Heidensche Priesters en Priesteressen de Boeginezen." *Verhandelingen der Koninklijke Akademie van Wetenschapen* 7:1–50.

Needham, Rodney. 1960. "The Left Hand of the Mugwe: An Analytical Note on the Structure of Meru Symbolism." *Africa* 30:20–33.

Needham, Rodney, ed. 1974. *Right and Left*. Chicago: University of Chicago Press.

Nooteboom, C. 1948. "Aantekeningen over de Cultuur der Boeginezen en Makassaren." *Indonesië* 3 (Nov.):244–255.

Peacock, James. 1968. *Rites of Modernization: Symbolic and Social Aspects of Indonesian Proletarian Drama*. Chicago: University of Chicago Press.

Pigeaud, Th. 1938. *Javaanse Volksvertoningen: Bijdrage tot de Beschrijving van Land en Volk*. Batavia: Volkslectuur.

———. n.d. "The Romance of Amir Hamza in Java." In *Bingkisan Budi*. Leiden: Sijthoff. Pp. 236–237.

Rassers, W. H. 1959. *Panji, the Culture Hero: A Structural Study of Religion in Java*. The Hague: Martinus Nijhoff.

Sardjono, Koes. 1947. "De Botjah-Angon (Herdersjongen) in de Javaanse Cultuur." Diss., University of Leiden.

Schärer, Hans. 1963. *Ngaju Religion*. Trans. Rodney Needham. The Hague: Martinus Nijhoff.

Sukarno. 1965. *An Autiobiography: As Told to Cindy Adams*. New York: Bobbs-Merrill.

Wilken, G. A. 1961. *Manual for the Comparative Ethnology of the Netherlands East Indies*. Trans. S. Damas Kaan, ed. C. M. Pleyte. New Haven: Human Relations Area File Press.

CHAPTER 8

Return to Wirikuta: Ritual Reversal and Symbolic Continuity on the Peyote Hunt of the Huichol Indians

BARBARA G. MYERHOFF

> God is day and night, winter summer, war peace, satiety hunger—all opposites, this is the meaning.
>
> Heraclitus

The Peyote Hunt of the Huichol Indians

Rituals of opposition and reversal constitute a critical part of a lengthy religious ceremony, the peyote hunt, practiced by the Huichol Indians of north-central Mexico.[1] In order to understand the function of these rituals it is necessary to adumbrate the major features and purposes of the peyote hunt. Annually, small groups of Huichols, led by a shaman-priest or *mara'akáme*, return to Wirikuta to hunt the peyote. Wirikuta is a high desert several hundred miles from the Huichols' present abode in the Sierra Madre Occidentál. Mythically and in all likelihood historically, it is their original homeland, the place once inhabited by the First People, the quasi-deified ancestors. But Wirikuta is much more than a geographical location; it is *illud tempus*, the paradisical condition that existed before the creation of the world and mankind, and the condition that will prevail at the end of time.

---

[1] The Huichol Indians are a quasi-tribe of about 10,000 living in dispersed communities in north-central Mexico. They are among the least acculturated Mexican Indians and in part their resistence to outside influence is attributable to the complex and extraordinarily rich ritual and symbolic life they lead. A detailed presentation of the peyote hunt is presented in Myerhoff 1974. The fieldwork on which the present paper was based took place in 1965 and 1966.

In Wirikuta, as in the paradise envisioned in many creation myths, all is unity, a cosmic totality without barriers of any kind, without the differentations that characterize the mundane mortal world. In Wirikuta, separations are obliterated—between sexes, between leader and led, young and old, animals and man, plants and animals, and man and the deities. The social order and the natural and supernatural realms are rejoined into their original state of seamless continuity. Wirikuta is the center of the four directions where, as the Huichol describe it, "All is unity, all is one, all is ourselves."

In Wirikuta, the three major symbols of Huichol world view are likewise fused. These are the Deer, representing the Huichols' past life as nomadic hunters; the Maize, representing their present life as sedentary agriculturalists; and peyote, signifying the private, spiritual vision of each individual. To reenter Wirikuta, the peyote pilgrims must be transformed into the First People. They assume the identity of particular deities and literally hunt the peyote which grows in Wirikuta, tracking and following it in the form of deer footprints, stalking and shooting it with bow and arrow, consuming it in a climactic ceremony of total communion. Once the peyote has been hunted, consumed, and sufficient supplies have been gathered for use in the ceremonies of the coming year, the pilgrims hastily leave and return to their homes and to their mortal condition. The entire peyote hunt is very complex, consisting of many rituals and symbols; here I will only concentrate on one set of rituals, those which concern reversal and opposition, and the part they play in enabling the pilgrims to experience the sense of totality and cosmic unity that is their overarching religious goal.

Mythological and Ritual Aspects of Reversals

"In Wirikuta, we change the names of everything . . . everything is backwards." Ramón Medina Silva, the officiating mara'akáme, who led the Peyote Hunt of 1966 in which I participated, thus explained the reversals that obtain during the pilgrimage. "The mara'akáme tells [the pilgrims], 'Now we will change everything, all the meanings, because that is the way it must be with the *hikuritámete* [peyote pilgrims]. As it was in Ancient Times, so that all can be united.'"

The reversals to which he refers occur on four distinct levels: naming, interpersonal behavior, ritual behavior, and emotional states. The reversals in naming are very specific. Ideally, everything is its opposite and everything is newly named each year. But in fact, for many things there are often no clear opposites, and substitutions are made, chosen for reasons that are not always clear. Frequently the substitutions seem dictated by simple visual association—thus the head is a pot, the nose a penis, hair is cactus fiber. A great many of these substitutions recur each year and are standardized. Nevertheless, they are defined as opposites in this context and are treated as if they were spontaneous rather than patterned.

On the interpersonal-behavioral level, direct oppositions are more straightforward. One says yes when he or she means no. A person proffers a foot instead of a hand. Conversations are conducted with conversants standing back to back, and so forth. Behavior is also altered to correspond with the ritual identity of the participant. Thus the oldest man, transformed into a *nunutsi* or little child for the journey, is not permitted to gather firewood because "this work is too heavy and strenuous for one so young."

The deities are portrayed as the opposite of mortals in that the former have no physiological needs. Thus the pilgrims, as the First People, disguise, minimize, and forego their human physiological activities as much as possible. Sexual abstinence is practiced. Washing is forsworn. Eating, sleeping, and drinking are kept to an absolute minimum. Defecation and urination are said not to occur and are practiced covertly. All forms of social distinction and organization are minimized, and even the mara'akáme's leadership and direction are extremely oblique. The ordinary division of labor is suspended and altered in various ways. All forms of discord are strictly forbidden, and disruptive emotions such as jealousy and deceit, usually tolerated as part of the human condition, are completely proscribed for the pilgrims. No special treatment is afforded to children; no behavioral distinctions between the sexes are allowed. Even the separateness of the mara'akáme from his group is minimized, and his assistant immediately performs for him all rituals that the mara'akáme has just performed for the rest of the party.

In terms of ritual actions, reversals are quite clear. The cardinal directions, and up and down, are switched in behaviors which involve offering sacred water and food to the four corners and the center of the world. The fire is circled in a counterclockwise direction instead of clockwise as on normal ceremonial occasions. In Wirikuta, the mara'akáme's assistant sits to the latter's left instead of to his right.

Emotions as well as behaviors are altered on the basis of the pilgrims' transformation into deities. Since mortals would be jubilant, presumably, on returning to their pre-creation, mythical homeland, and grief-stricken on departing from it, the pilgrims weep as they reenter Wirikuta and are exultant on departing. This reflects the fact that they are deities leaving paradise, not mortals returning from it.

I should note also some of the attitudes and values toward the reversals that I observed. For example, there seems to be an aesthetic dimension since they regard some reversals as more satisfying than others. Humorous and ironic changes are a source of much laughter and delight. Thus the name of the wife of the mara'akáme was changed to "ugly *gringa*." The mara'akáme himself was the pope. The anthropologists' camper was a burro that drank much tequila. They also delight in compounding the reversals: "Ah what a pity that we have caught no peyote. Here we sit, sad, surrounded by baskets of flowers under a cold sun." Thus said one pilgrim after a successful day of gathering baskets full of peyote, while standing in the moonlight. Mistakes and humorous improvisations are also the source of new reversals. When in a careless moment Los Angeles was referred to as "home," everyone was very pleased and amused; from then on home was Los Angeles and even in sacred chants and prayers this reversal was maintained. Accidental reversals such as this are just as obligatory as the conventional ones and the new ones "dreamed" by the mara'akáme. Mistakes are corrected with good will but firmly, and everyone shares in the responsibility for keeping track of the changes, reminding each other repeatedly of the changes that have been instituted. The more changes the better, and each day, as more are established, more attention by all is required to keep things straight. Normal conversation and behavior become more difficult with each new day's accumulation of changes. Sunsets are ugly. No one is tired. Peyote is sweet. The pilgrimage is a failure. There is too much food to eat, and so forth.

The reversals were not instituted or removed by any formal rituals, although it is said that there are such. It became apparent that the reversals were in effect at the periphery of Wirikuta when someone sneezed. This was received by uproarious laughter, for, the nose had become a penis and a sneeze, accordingly, was an off-color joke. After the peyote hunt, the reversals were set aside gradually as the group moved away from Wirikuta. On returning home, the pilgrims regaled those who had remained behind with descriptions of the reversals and the confusions they had engendered.

The Functions and Symbolism of the Reversals

How should these ideas and actions concerning reversal and opposition be understood? In the Huichol context, they achieve several purposes simultaneously. Perhaps most famil-

iar and straightforward is their function in transforming the
mundane into the sacred by disguising the everyday features
of environment, society, and behavior, and in the Dur-
keimian sense "setting it apart." As Ramón Medina Silva
explained, "One changes everything . . . when [we] cross
over there to the Peyote Country . . . because it is a very
sacred thing, it is the most sacred. It is our life, as one says.
That is why nowadays one gives things other names. One
changes everything. Only when they return home, then they
call everything again what it is." Here the totality and scope
of the reversals are important—actions, names, ritual, and
everyday behaviors are altered so that participants are conscious at all times of the extraordinary nature of their under-
taking. Nothing is natural, habitual, or taken for granted.
The boundaries between the ordinary and the sacred are
sharply defined and attention to this extraordinary state of affairs cannot lag when one has to be perpetually self-conscious
and vigilant against lapses. Reversals promote the essential
attitude of the sacred, the *mysterium tremendum et fascinans*.

The transformation of mortals into deities is related to this
purpose. Again and again in theological, mythological, and
ethnographic literature one encounters the impossibility of
mortals entering a supernatural realm in their normal condition. The shaman transforms himself into a spirit in order to
perform his duties as soul guide or psychopomp. This is the
essence of the Symplegades motif in shamanism—the passage
into the other world through the crashing gates, as Eliade
(1964) points out. The "paradoxical passage" to the supernatural domain is open only to those who have been transformed from their human state into pure spirit. An apoth-
eosis is required of those who would "cross over" and achieve
the "breakthrough in planes." The peyote hunt opens Wirikuta to all proper pilgrims, but they, like the shaman, cannot
enter in mortal form. To enter Wirikuta, the Huichol
peyote-seekers do not merely impersonate the deities by as-

suming their names and garb. Ritually and symbolically, they *become* supernatural, disguising the mortal coil, abrogating human functions and forms.

This "backwardness" operates on two levels: as the deities, they are the obverse of mortals; as deities, they are going back, going backwards, and signifying this by doing everything backwards. Backwardness is found frequently in connection with supernatural states, and with the denial of humanity. Lugbara witches are inverted beings who walk on their heads (Middleton 1960). And in Genesis we find that "the inhabitants of paradise stand on their heads and walk on their hands; as do all the dead" (Graves and Patai 1966:73, citing Gen. 24:65). The examples could be expanded indefinitely. Eliade suggests this widespread association of backwardness and the supernatural when he comments, "Consequently to do away with this state of [humanity] even if only provisionally, is equivalent to reestablishing the primordial condition of man, in other words, to banish time, to go backwards, to recover the 'paradisial' *illud tempus*" (1960:72).

A third function of these reversals is their provision of mnemonic, or aid to the imagination and memory, for conception and action. For a time the peyote pilgrims in the Huichol religion live in the supernatural. They go beyond invoking and discussing it, for Wirikuta exists in ritual as well as mythical terms. Ritual, unlike myth, requires action. Ritual is a dramatization. Pilgrims must not only imagine the unimaginable, they must behave within it. It is through its action dimension that ritual makes religious values "really real," and fuses the "lived-in" and the "dreamed-of order," as Geertz puts it. Full staging is necessary. The unfathomable—*illud tempus*, the primordial state before time—is the setting. Props, costumes, etiquette, vocabulary, emotions—all must be conceived and specified. The theme of opposition provides the details that are needed to make the drama credible and convincing; the metaphor of backwardness makes for a concretization and amplification of the ineffable. Again Eliade's writings offer an insight along these lines. He points out that the theme of *coincidentia oppositorum* is an "eschatological symbol par excellence, which denotes that Time and History have come to an end—in the lion lying down with the lamb" (1962:121). It is in the Garden of Eden that "opposites lie down together," it is there that conflicts and divisions are ultimately abolished and man's original innocence and wholeness are regained.

Separation, transformation, and concretization then are three purposes achieved by the reversals in Wirikuta. There is a fourth, perhaps the most important and common function of rituals of this nature. That is the capacity of reversals to invoke continuity through emphasis on opposition. How this operates in the Huichol case was explained in very precise terms by Ramón Medina Silva in a text he dictated about the 1966 peyote hunt five years later. He was elaborating on the beauties of Wirikuta and for the first time indicated that it was the state that would prevail at the end of time as well as that which characterized the beginning. When the world ends, the First People would return. "All will be in unity, all will be one, all will be as you have seen it there, in Wirikuta." The present world, it became clear, was but a shallow and misleading interlude, a transient period characterized by difference and separations, bracketed by an enduring condition of totality and continuity.

When the world ends it will be like when the names of things are changed during the Peyote Hunt. All will be different, the opposite of what it is now. Now there are two eyes in the heavens, the Sun and the Moon. Then, the Moon will open his eye and become brighter. The sun will become dimmer. There will be no more difference between them. Then, no more men and no more women. No more child and no more adult. All will change places. Even the mara'akáme will no longer be separate. That is why there must always be a *nunutsi* when we go to Wirikuta. Because the old man and the tiny baby, they are the same.

[Personal communication, Los Angeles, 1971]

Polarity reaffirms continuity. The baby and the adult ultimately are joined, ends of a single continuum. Watts states it as follows: "What exactly is polarity? It is something much more than simple duality or opposition. For to say that opposites are polar is to say much more than that they are joined . . . , that they are the terms, ends, or extremities of a single whole. Polar opposites are therefore inseparable opposites, like the poles of the earth or of a magnet, or the ends of a stick or the faces of a coin" (1970:45).

Surely the vision of an original condition of unity, before the world and mankind began, is one of the most common themes in religions of every nature and place. Again to draw on Eliade, "Among the 'primitive' peoples, just as among the Saints and the Christian theologians, mystic ecstasy is a return to Paradise, expressed by the overcoming of Time and History . . . , and [represents] a recovery of the primordial state of Man" (1960:72).

The theme of nostalgia for lost paradise recurs so often as to be counted by some as panhuman. Theories attribute this yearning to various causes: a lingering memory of the undifferentiated state in the womb, the unfilled wish for a happy childhood, a fantasy of premortal blessedness and purity, a form of what the Jungians call uroboric incest, a fatal desire for nonbeing, and so forth (see Neumann 1954). Many theologians have viewed this vision of cosmic oneness as the essence of the mystical experience and of religious ecstasy. The particulars vary from one religion to the next but the ingredients are stable: paradise is that which existed before the beginning of time, before life and death, before light and darkness. Here animals and man lived in a state of easy companionship, speaking the same language, untroubled by

thirst, hunger, pain, weariness, loneliness, struggle, or appetite. Humans knew neither discord nor distinction among
themselves—they were sexless, without self-awareness, and
indeed undifferentiated from the very gods. Then an irreversible and cataclysmic sundering took place and instead of
wholeness there was separation, the separation that was Creation. Henceforth, the human organism was no longer indistinguishable from the cosmos. The primordial splitting left
mankind as we know it now, forever haunted by remem-
brance of and attraction for an original condition of wholeness.

The reversals, then, express the most lamentable features
of the human condition by emphasizing the loss of the paradisical state of oneness. Humans are fragmented, incomplete,
and isolated from the deities; they are vulnerable and literally
mortal, which is to say helpless before the ravages of pain,
time, and death. At the same time, the reversals remind
mankind of the primordial wholeness that will again prevail
when paradise is regained. Here is the theme expressed in a
cultural form familiar to most of us, the Gospel according to
Thomas:

> They said to Him: Shall we then, being children
> enter the Kingdom? Jesus said to them:
> When you make the two one, and
> when you make the inner as the outer
> and the outer as the inner and the above
> as the below, and when
> you make the male and the female into a single one,
> so that the male will not be male and
> the female [not] be female, when you make
> eyes in the place of an eye, a hand
> in the place of a hand, and a foot in the place
> of a foot, an image in the place of an image,
> then shall you enter [the Kingdom].
> [Logia 23–35, cited in Guillaumont et al. 1959:17–19]

Conclusions

The theme of reversal, in all its permutations and combinations—opposition (complementary and binary), inversion, and dualism—has always been of great interest to anthropologists, mythographers, theologians, psychologists, linguists, and artists. The subject seems inexhaustible. In anthropology alone, we continue to unravel additional layers of meaning, to discover more and more functions fulfilled by reversals in various contexts. Recent studies especially have shown how reversals can be used to make statements about the social order—to affirm it, attack it, suspend it, redefine it, oppose it, buttress it, emphasize one part of it at the cost of another, and so forth. We see a magnificently fruitful image put to diverse purposes, capable of an overwhelming range of expression. Obviously there is no question of looking for the true or correct meaning in the use of reversals. We are dealing with a symbolic referent that has new meanings in every new context and within a single context embraces multiple and contradictory meanings simultaneously. In Wirikuta, the reversals accomplish many purposes and contain a major paradox. They emphasize the difference between Wirikuta and the mundane life, and the differentiated nature of the human condition. Also they stress the nondifferentiated nature of Wirikuta. The reversals thus portray differentiation and continuity at the same time. Both are true, separation and oneness, though this is contradictory and paradoxical. But this should come as no surprise, for paradox is the very quick of ritual. In ritual, as in the Garden, opposites are made to lie down together.

Appendix: How the Names Are Changed
on the Peyote Journey

Text dictated by Ramón Medina Silva, mara'akáme of San Sebastián, Mexico, to explain the reversals used on the peyote hunt.

Well, let's see now. I shall speak about how we do things when we go and seek the peyote, how we change the names of everything. How we call the things we see and do by another name for all those days. Until we return. Because all must be done as it must be done. As it was laid down in the beginning. How it was when the mara'akáme who is Tatewarí[2] led all those great ones to Wirikuta. When they crossed over there, to the peyote country. Because that is a very sacred thing, it is the most sacred. It is our life, as one says. That is why nowadays one gives things other names. One changes everything. Only when they return home, then they call everything again that it is.

When everything is ready, when all the symbols which we take with us, the gourd bowls, the yarn discs, the arrows, everything has been made, when all have prayed together we set out. Then we must change everything, all the meanings. For instance: a pot which is black and round, it is called a head. It is the mara'akáme who directs everything. He is the one who listens in his dream, with his power and his knowledge. He speaks to Tatewarí, he speaks to Kauyumari.[3] Kauyumari tells him everything, how it must be. Then he says to his companions, if he is the leader of the journey to the peyote, look, this thing is this way, and this is how it must be done. He tells them, look, now we will change everything, all the meanings, because that is the way it must be with the *hikuritámete* (peyote pilgrims). As it was in ancient times, so that all can be united. As it was long ago, before the time of my grandfather, even before the time of his grandfather. So the mara'akáme has to see to everything, so that as much as possible all the words are changed. Only when one comes home, then everything can be changed back again to the way it was.

"Look," the mara'akáme says to them, "it is when you say 'good morning,' you mean 'good evening,' everything is backwards. You

[2] Huichol name for the deity with whom the shaman has a special affinity, roughly translatable as Our Grandfather Fire.

[3] Kauyumari is a trickster hero, quasi-deified and roughly translatable as Sacred Deer Person.

say 'goodbye, I am leaving you,' but you are really coming. You do not shake hands, you shake feet. You hold out your right foot to be shaken by the foot of your companion. You say 'good afternoon,' yet it is only morning."

So the mara'akáme tells them, as he has dreamed it. He dreams it differently each time. Every year they change the names of things differently because every year the mara'akáme dreams new names. Even if it is the same mara'akáme who leads the journey, he still changes the names each time differently.

And he watches who makes mistakes because there must be no error. One must use the names the mara'akáme has dreamed. Because if one makes an error it is not right. That is how it is. It is a beautiful thing because it is right. Daily, daily, the mara'akáme goes explaining everything to them so that they do not make mistakes. The mara'akáme says to a companion, "Look, why does that man over there watch us, why does he stare at us?" And then he says, "Look, what is it he has to stare at us?" "His eyes," says his companion. "No," the mara'akáme answers, "they are not his eyes, they are tomatoes." That is how he goes explaining how everything should be called.

When one makes cigarettes for the journey, one uses the dried husks of maize for the wrappings. And the tobacco, it is called the droppings of ants. Tortillas one calls bread. Beans one calls fruit from a tree. Maize is wheat. Water is tequila. Instead of saying, "Let us go and get water to drink," you say, "Ah, let us take tequila to eat." *Atole* [maize broth], that is brains. Sandals are cactus. Fingers are sticks. Hair, that is cactus fiber. The moon, that is a cold sun.

On all the trails on which we travel to the peyote country, as we see different things we make this change. That is because the peyote is very sacred, very sacred. That is why it is reversed. Therefore, when we see a dog, it is a cat, or it is a coyote. Ordinarily, when we see a dog, it is just a dog, but when we walk for the peyote it is a cat or a coyote or even something else, as the mara'akáme dreams it. When we see a burro, it is not a burro, it is a cow, or a horse. And when we see a horse, it is something else. When we see a dove or a small bird of some kind, is it a small bird? No, the mara'akáme says, it is an eagle, it is a hawk. Or a piglet, it is not a piglet, it is an armadillo. When we hunt the deer, which is very sacred, it is not a deer, on this journey. It is a lamb, or a cat. And the nets for catching deer? They are called sewing thread.

When we say come, it means go away. When we say "shh, quiet," it means to shout, and when we whistle or call to the front we are really calling to a person behind us. We speak in this direction here. That one over there turns because he already knows how it is, how everything is reversed. To say, "Let us stay here," means to go, "let us go," and when we say "sit down," we mean, "stand up." It is also so when we have crossed over, when we are in the country of the peyote. Even the peyote is called by another name, as the mara'akáme dreamed. Then the peyote is flower or something else.

It is so with Tatewarí, with Tayaupa.[4] The mara'akáme, we call him Tatewarí. He is Tatewarí, he who leads us. But there in Wirikuta, one says something else. One calls him "the red one." And Tayaupa, he is "the shining one." So all is changed. Our companion who is old, he is called the child. Our companion who is young, he is the old one. When we want to speak of the machete, we say "hook." When one speaks of wood, one really means fish. Begging your pardon, instead of saying "to eat," we say "to defecate." And, begging your pardon, "I am going to urinate" means "I am going to drink water." When speaking of blowing one's nose, one says "give me the honey." "He is deaf" means "how well he hears." So everything is changed, everything is different or backwards.

The mara'akáme goes explaining how everything should be said, everything, many times, or his companions would forget and make errors. In the late afternoon, when all are gathered around Tatewarí, we all pray there, and the mara'akáme tells how it should be. So for instance he says, "Do not speak of this one or that one as serious. Say he is a jaguar. You see an old woman and her face is all wrinkled, coming from afar, do not say, 'Ah, there is a man,' say 'Ah, here comes a wooden image.' You say, 'Here comes the image of Santo Cristo.' Or if it is a woman coming, say 'Ah, here comes the image of Guadalupe.' "

Women, you call flowers. For the woman's skirts, you say, "bush," and for her blouse you say "palm roots." And a man's clothing, that too is changed. His clothing, you call his fur. His hat, that is a mushroom. Or it is his sandal. Begging your pardon, but what we carry down here, the testicles, they are called avocados. And the penis, that is his nose. That is how it is.

When we come back with the peyote, the peyote which has been

4 Our Father Sun.

hunted, they make a ceremony and everything is changed back again. And those who are at home, when one returns they grab one and ask, "What is it you called things? How is it that now you call the hands hands but when you left you called them feet?" Well, it is because they have changed the names back again. And they all want to know what they called things. One tells them, and there is laughter. That is how it is. Because it must be as it was said in the beginning, in ancient times.   [Adapted from Myerhoff 1974]

References

Eliade, Mircea. 1960. "The Yearning for Paradise in Primitive Tradition." In H. A. Murray, ed., *Myth and Mythmaking*. New York: Braziller. Pp. 61–75.

———. 1962. *The Two and the One*. New York: Harper Torchbooks.

———. 1964. *Shamanism: Archaic Techniques of Ecstasy*. Trans. W. R. Trask. Bollingen Series LXXVI. New York: Pantheon.

Furst, Peter T. 1972. "To Find Our Life: Peyote among the Huichol Indians of Mexico." In P. T. Furst, ed., *Flesh of the Gods: The Ritual Uses of Hallucinogens*. New York: Praeger. Pp. 136–184.

Furst, Peter T., and Barbara G. Myerhoff. 1966. "Myth as History: The Jimson Weed Cycle of the Huichols of Mexico." *Antropologica* 17:3–39.

Graves, Robert, and Raphael Patai. 1966. *Hebrew Myths: The Book of Genesis*. New York: McGraw-Hill.

Guillaumont, A., et al., trans. 1959. *The Gospel According to Thomas*. New York: Harper.

Middleton, John. 1960. *Lugbara Religion: Ritual and Authority among an East African People*. London: Oxford University Press.

Myerhoff, Barbara G. 1970. "The Deer-Maize-Peyote Symbol Complex among the Huichol Indians of Mexico." *Anthropological Quarterly* 43:64–78.

———. 1972. "The Revolution as a Trip: Symbol and Paradox." In P. G. Altbach and R. S. Laufer, eds., *The New Pilgrims*. New York: McKay. Pp. 251–266.

———. 1974. *Peyote Hunt: The Sacred Journey of the Huichol Indians*. Ithaca, N.Y.: Cornell University Press.

Neumann, Erich. 1954. *The Origins and History of Consciousness*. New York: Bollingen.

Watts, Alan W. 1970. *The Two Hands of God: The Myths of Polarity*. New York: Collier.

CHAPTER 9

The Rhetoric of Control:
Ilongots Viewed as Natural
Bandits and Wild Indians

RENATO I. ROSALDO, JR.

What happens to language when the state and its agents confront peoples who remain beyond conventional social role and class positions—beyond the state's jurisdiction? What happens when those who are "civilized" and "controlled" attempt to incorporate peoples perceived as "wild" and "savage." My investigations indicate that civilized society is most likely to infer the social character of indigenous peoples from those acts that impede commerce and that are completely at variance with civilized social norms (and hence especially likely to be defined as criminal). In addition, it seems that inferences about social character lead to deductions about the habitat of indigenous peoples. It would seem plausible that a certain correlation exists between social character and natural habitat, but such correspondences should never be assumed, and it is a good deal less obvious that both derive primarily from acts that challenge civilized society. Nor is it so readily apparent that the acts, the character, and the habitat of indigenous peoples should be defined by referring to the usually antithetical ideal statements about the conduct, character, and habitat of members of civilized society. Yet this is what I have found to be the case, at least in this one instance.[1]

[1] My two-year period (1967–1969) of field research among the Ilongots of Northern Luzon, Philippines, was financed by a National Science Foundation predoctoral fellowship and NSF research grant GS-1509. Other relevant accounts of Illongot so-

Representatives of Western civilization in Northern Luzon, Philippines, have over the past four hundred years or so developed an increasingly rational and explicit language for speaking about their repeated attempts to attain political and administrative control over the Ilongots, a non-Christian hill people. These attempts, I should add, are still today largely unsuccessful. The agents of control and colonization have been various and diverse; ranging from the first military expeditions to the days of the mission outposts, from the American Bureau of Non-Christian Tribes to the present government in the Philippines. Yet close analysis reveals that (despite differences of period and agency) an underlying similarity of principles has shaped the rhetoric of control, of containment, and of the impetus toward colonization.

My concern is familiar in anthropology, though anthropologists usually view Europeans through the eyes of indigenous peoples rather than the reverse. According to Middleton, for instance, the Lugbara conceive of Europeans as "literally inverted" people who walk upside down and embody social values the opposite of their own. In general those who are socially or historically distant are seen by the Lugbara as sharing the attributes of "physical inversion, cannibalism, incest, living outside the bounds of society" (1960:236). Middleton's thesis has been elaborated by Leach (1964) who used English and Kachin examples to show how language categorizes both social and physical distance into corresponding zones, ranging in graduated steps from "close" through "ambiguous" to "far." While my sense of problem has been shaped by the work of Middleton and Leach, I have chosen to invert the normal anthropological stance: rather than elucidate the natives' vision of Europeans, I shall instead peer

---

ciety may be found in M. Rosaldo 1972, 1973; M. Rosaldo and Atkinson 1975; and R. Rosaldo 1970, 1975, 1976. I am indebted to Jane Atkinson, Shelton Davis, Bridget O'Laughlin, Sherry Ortner, Yosal Rogat, Michelle Rosaldo, and Victor Turner for comments on this paper.

over the shoulders of the agents of the state, from the colonial era to the present, as they look upon indigenous peoples.

In particular, the colonizing agents view the indigenous peoples as dangerously mobile and as a threat to the larger society attempting to bring them under control.[2] In exploring this problem I have relied to a large extent on the work of Kenneth Burke and his notion of "key ratios" (1962). For instance, one might ask whether there is any correlation between the *act* (taking a head) and the *agent* (Ilongot social character as criminal); or between the *agent* (criminal character) and the *scene* (overgrown habitat, nomadic way of life). Lest there be any confusion, in these two ratios only the *act* is an accurate portrayal and it has provided the base from which both *agent* and *scene* have been deduced (with little correspondence in fact to anything Ilongot). In addition, most of the terms used to describe the Ilongots are "polar" (Burke 1961b:23); that is, they imply an opposite, such as "criminal" versus "lawful," and "filthy" versus "clean." For the most part, terms such as "criminal" are associated with the Ilongots and their savage natural state while terms such as "lawful" are associated with civilization and its agents. Finally, I believe that the dominant motive of agents of the state is control. As Burke has described it, "to control a bad situation, you seek either to eradicate the evil or to channelize the evil" (1961a:236). In this particular case, what constitutes "control" in the rhetoric of the colonizers wavers between the rare extremist outburst advocating genocidal extermination of the Ilongots and the more persistant and relatively humane proposals for pacification and incorporation

---

[2] Many treatments of the frontier situation have stressed the effect of the frontier on the development of national character. What most readily comes to mind here is the thesis of Frederick Jackson Turner (see Taylor 1956, Wyman and Kroeber 1965) with its notion of democracy arising from the exigencies of the frontier situation. Without making such comparisons explicit here, my intention is that this study be read in the context of other comparable frontier confrontations between "civilized" peoples and those they regard as "barbaric" or "savage."

into the larger body politic through education and improved communications.

From the time of the first military expeditions late in the sixteenth century the frontier situation was accurately recognized as a confrontation with peoples who were alien, exotic, and wholly other. Members of these early expeditions either used the sword ("control" in this case being a euphemism for eradication) or attempted to discover exotic, perhaps indigenous formulas for making peace with the alien nations in their path. In one such meeting the Spanish captain, Pedro de Sid, was "bled with them in order to make the peace sure" (Blair and Robertson 1904:290). In other instances not only indigenous peoples but Spanish soldiers as well acted on Frazer's principal of sympathetic magic—the notion that "like produces like"; they threw eggs on the ground and "said together that just as those eggs had been broken, so they would be broken should they not fulfill their promises" (p. 283). Alternatively, they extinguished candles, so that "just as that candle expired and was consumed so would he who broke his promise be slain and perish" (p. 290).

It is worth noting in passing that the Ilongots today make amends for past beheadings in accordance with the same principle, but they employ salt rather than eggs or candles, and the notion is that just as salt dissolves in water so may they perish if they fail to keep the peace. Curiously enough, as Joseph Greenberg has pointed out to me, certain ancient Aramaic inscriptions are comparable in form; for instance, one curse runs as follows: "Just as this wax is burned, so may Matî'el be burned by fire! Just as [this] bow and these arrows are broken, so may 'Inurta and Hadad break the bow of Matî'el, and the bow of his nobles! And just as a man of wax is blinded, so may Matî'el be blinded! Just as this calf is cut in two, so may Matî'el be cut in two, and may his nobles be cut in two" (Fitzmyer 1967:15). Whether such a symbolic device in the swearing of an oath is Spanish or indigenous in its immediate origins, it clearly represents an attempt to deal with alien peoples in their own terms, or at any rate in terms comprehensible to them. However, these early expeditions were limited in their impact; they were exploratory, fleeting, and temporary, little more than a quick reconnaissance and return.

By the eighteenth and nineteenth centuries the more serious task of conversion, pacification, and control was undertaken by agents of the mission outpost, involving the patient and often humane labors of friars—Augustinian, Dominican, and Franciscan—along with the various garrisons providing military support (Bolton 1917, Gibson 1967, Scott 1974). The task of the friars went beyond that of providing catechism and religious indoctrination and included training the people in European agricultural techniques, such as using a plow behind draft animals. Here, the Spanish set out to make the indigenous peoples sedentary and to subject them to control and instruction, both civil and religious. The towns set up by the friars were ordered on the grid plan, and their very existence was in fact threatened by the headhunting incursions of the Ilongots that remained unconverted and beyond their reach in the hills. Numerous reports speak of people, that is to say, infidels, that descended from the hills and raided, killed, and burned in the newly founded towns of the valleys (see, for example, Malumbres 1919:31). As a result of such raiding, new converts, perhaps out of sheer preference or perhaps because they felt too vulnerable in the towns, became apostates and fled to the hills to join their Ilongot brethren. The threat to the mission towns, then, was very real. More to the point, the friars imputed a distinct character to the Ilongots based almost solely on these acts. What I am questioning is the extent to which isolated acts—even if violent and extreme—can be taken as representative.

A Dominican of the late nineteenth century, Campa, reporting on his visit to certain Ilongot settlements, declared that "the infidel, in general, is an unredeemed criminal, an enemy of his peers and destructive of the fabric of society: he robs without scruples; he murders at will whenever he wishes; he prevents the free travel from town to town and from province to province" (1891:632). Thus, since the Ilongots were "uncivilized," and since their lack of civilization threatened town and roadway, they became categorized (along with all other infidels) as brigands and butchers. This elaboration built on a grain of truth. Ilongots did in fact raid and take heads. However, to be strictly accurate, they did not rob. Butchers they may have been; brigands they never were. In short, since civilized society perceived head-taking as the most heinous criminal act (as contrasted, say, with the retaliatory massacres by soldiers), it defined Ilongots as grossly criminal and attributed lesser criminal acts that must spring from a basically criminal character. From the mission viewpoint, the task was to induce Ilongots to settle in towns where they would come to know, and more importantly, comply with, "the obligations of natural law, social law, civil law and above all religious law, the law that encompasses all the rest" (Campa 1891:637). The Spanish friar, then, viewed the Ilongots as people living in a deplorable state of nature, caught up in a web of evil-doing without access to knowledge of the laws for ordering their political and moral lives.

At this point, it is worth briefly digressing to compare and contrast the friar's vision of "natural bandits" with those whom Hobsbawm (1965, 1971) has called "social bandits." A figure like Robin Hood, for example, was a social bandit who, as the cliché had it, robbed from the rich and gave to the poor; such figures often arise "where the state is remote, ineffective and weak" (1971:44). While the legitimate authorities may view them as criminals, members of peasant societies often consider the social bandit as a "champion, the righter of wrongs, the bringer of justice and social equity" (1971:35). In their origins social bandits are often peasants

and they continue to depend on the peasantry for their survival: in symbolic terms, they stand for local aspirations of
freedom and justice. However, the notion of the alliance of
peasant societies, which are under the control of the state,
with social bandits, men who have moved out of their own
society to an elevated place where they can be admired as
champions, bears little relation to the reality of Ilongot society. Ilongots live in the hills, beyond the control of the state,
in a place where raiding is considered normal; rather than
being a physically and socially separate group, set apart from
the rest of their society, Ilongots who take heads are normal
members of their society, distinctive only in their sex and
age—they are men from their teens to adult maturity.

In large part, the missionary enterprise entailed remaking
the landscape by constructing towns and roads. Not surprisingly, the description of the habitat of the Ilongots largely
derived from the character of the Ilongots. The notion that
the situation or the environment shapes the person, or the
more sophisticated notion that ultimately the mode and organization of production determines social relations, is familiar
to us. However, in the narrative of the Dominican friar
Campa, the correspondence between social character and
natural habitat is clearly assumed, and in addition the characterization of the habitat is derived from notions of social
character rather than the reverse. In his eyewitness report
the friar said that Ilongot "gardens were miserable, filled
with undergrowth and untended" (1891:612). Yet my observations led to the very opposite conclusion. I admired the
neatness, the regularity and symmetry of the gardens, especially around the time of planting. The seed is evenly spaced
and as the young rice sprouts an elegant grid pattern emerges
on the freshly cleared gardens. How could an admirer of the
grid plan in Spanish towns fail even to notice the spatial organization of Ilongot gardens? To begin with, the Dominican

friar visited the Ilongot settlements shortly after the rice had been harvested and before the gardens had been recleaned; the fields were indeed overgrown. But were basic cultural preconceptions also at work?

A friar should have been able to recognize a harvested field and he should have known that the untended growth was only a phase and not an enduring characteristic of the gardens. He advanced a further argument: the "houses corresponded perfectly with the gardens" (p. 612). They were "silent, unkept, miserable" (p. 613). He then went on to characterize the people as "impertinent" and "filthy" and attributed their character to the "moral atmosphere in which they were raised" (pp. 614–615). Through a series of correspondences, moving from garden to house to people, the Dominican friar piled evidence on top of evidence (actually rather messily) to demonstrate that Ilongots lived in a condition of moral disorder and evil. Thereby he justified his enterprise of introducing a lawful order that consisted of his religion and his civilization.

With the twentieth century and the United States occupation the rhetoric of control shifted somewhat and was clearly the product of a centralized administrative system rather than relatively isolated and autonomous mission outposts. Perhaps this is nowhere more evident than in the following, written for the *National Geographic* by the Secretary of the Interior at the time:

In this regard there are wide differences between the several tribes. The Negritos are not far above the anthropoid apes, and the Ilongots and the Mangyans have advanced but little beyond the Negritos. The Bontoc Igorots are filthy, and while Governor Pack, of the Mountain Province, insists that the Benguet Igorots are just naturally dirty rather than filthy, I venture to disagree with him. The Ifugaos are comparatively clean. The Kalingas are more so. The Tinguians are one of the cleanliest peoples in the world.

[Worcester 1913:1251]

It is clear here and elsewhere that an overarching administrative system was at work, and that one of its major concerns was to classify indigenous Philippine peoples within a framework at once comprehensive and hierarchically ordered in terms of a people's capacity for schooling, as evidenced by the physical manifestation of cleanliness.[3]

Like the Spanish missionaries, the earliest American officials urged remaking the landscape as a step toward control, saying, to begin with, that "sketch maps will aid very much, also information as to the accessibility of these wilder peoples" (Barrows 1914). The constabulary branch of the American enterprise was eager to move from the drawing board to the actual implementation of these ideas, including the introduction of plow agriculture and the construction of roads. Turnbull, a lieutenant in the Philippine constabulary, wrote, "Later trails can be made to connect with the outside, and gradually all will become friendly" (1909:13), the notion apparently being that as the landscape changed so would the character of the inhabitants (and I think they were correct).

The agents of contact and civilization were no longer religious but secular; the bells calling people to descend and settle in valley towns were moved from the Spanish mission to the American schoolhouse. It should be stressed, however, that the role of the mission and the schoolhouse appears relatively humane when one considers the alternatives of the day. For instance, an American employed by the Bureau of Education called on a provincial governor, and "in answer to my inquiry as to how we could induce the Ilongots to come

[3] It is worth noting that the Philippine film version of *West Side Story* portrayed the tragic love story of an Ifugao "princess" and a wealthy man from Manila. The two lovers met at Harvard and shuttled by helicopter between the modern elegance of Makati and the photogenic rice terraces of Banawe. Throughout, a pastoral version of the innocent beauty of Ifugao society was blended with its dialectically related version of Ifugaos as bloodthirsty savages brandishing head-axes. This fusion of opposites was similar to early American visions of Indians (see Bellah 1975:6–9). However, up until the 1970s the colonists' pictures of Ilongots have stressed the bloodthirsty imagery to the virtual exclusion of the "noble savage."

down from the hills and live in settlements he said he thought it would be better to drive them still further back into the hills" (Miller 1914). And a lieutenant in the constabulary reported that "formerly it was customary to kill the Ilongots on sight; they were hunted like mad dogs" (Turnbull 1929:469).

As the occasional colonial official spoke of eradication, Ilongots continued to ambush and decapitate travelers, thereby impeding commerce and threatening inhabitants of towns (see, for example, Miller 1914), and their reputation was considerably blackened after they murdered an anthropologist, William Jones. Then, as a member of the constabulary put it, the Ilongots were "rated the worst of our wild non-Christians" (Turnbull 1929:337). Yet remarkable continuities in the rhetoric of control persisted, and the remaking of the landscape and the imposition of roads and schoolhouses still remained the essential task (see, for example, Worcester 1913:1243).

One finds a particularly clear example of the relative alteration in but basic underlying continuity of rhetoric in the census-taker's distinction between "wild" and "tame" Ilongots. And Lope K. Santos (1919:5–6), on the whole an especially well-informed government official, claimed there were basically two kinds of Ilongot settlements: loyal and rebellious; that is, peaceful and organized versus headhunting and nomadic. Again, as with the Dominican friar, he was factually mistaken. Ilongots were hunters and dry rice agriculturalists. They did move their houses and settlements from time to time, sometimes for reasons of subsistence, at other times to flee from the law. In the strictest terms they were neither sedentary nor nomadic. Yet this distinction of wild and tame, nomadic and sedentary, persists to this day. "Civilization" still equates a nomadic mode of subsistence with headhunting, banditry, and the outlaw elements threatening civil order. That is, it perceives and denominates with a heavily moral antinomy. It derives the first part of the antinomy from what is known and civilized while it bases the second part on the imperfectly known or completely unknown. Consistently, from the days of Spanish missions to the present, the more civilized Ilongots have been said to be loyal in character rather than disloyal or rebellious. Extrapolating from particular acts through social character to natural habitat with no basis in fact, the loyal Ilongots are said to inhabit organized and sedentary settlements while the rebellious Ilongots are said to live in a disorganized and nomadic manner.

My account of the historical origins and persistence of certain stereotypes of Ilongot character and culture may suggest that this particular case is a peculiarly exotic aberration from the usually enlightened civilizing enterprise. If anything, however, the Ilongot case is more the rule than the exception. I wish at this point neither to cast blame nor to impute motives; instead, my purpose is to suggest a means to uncover and attempt to locate the sources of ideological distortion in a number of characterizations of indigenous peoples with reputations comparable to the notoriety that Ilongots have achieved. To make this point let one example stand for many. A recent work by an American intellectual historian starts with the same preconceptions and ends with the same error made by my other sources. As Louis Hartz explains: "The character of the North American tribes, in contrast to the more advanced Indian civilizations to the south, obviously had much to do with the matter. Locke is not to be blamed for the nomadic character of the Iroquois" (1964:94). Thus he justifies and exonerates his nation's past by saying that in large part the difference between Hispanic and American colonization is related to the difference between "sedentary" Aztecs and "nomadic" Iroquois.

To bring this account up to date I should like to review the journalistic explosion in the rhetoric of control that took place in late 1959 and early 1960. At that time a member of the Philippine constabulary murdered an Ilongot father and son, and Ilongots in turn retaliated by beheading forty-four Christians, creating panic in the towns of the valleys and receiving headline coverage in the Manila press. Some of the reports urged eradication (control in the sense of a final solution). One local mayor urged the bombing and extermination of the Ilongot people, saying, "the only good Ilongots are dead Ilongots" (*Chronicle Magazine*, January 10, 1960). There was a rough relation between administrative level and rhetoric of containment: high officials in Manila by and large urged moderation, claiming that "the Ilongots know nothing of the laws, so we who know the laws should implement them with due care" (*Manila Times*, December 30, 1959). The notion here was an elaboration, in a liberal and extenuating direction, of the earlier claim that Ilongots were criminals, for the assertion in 1959 became that they were outside the law because of ignorance and hence their actions were not so culpable. Depending in part, then, on distance from the Ilongots and level of position in the administrative hierarchy, officials took stances ranging from simple eradication to more long-term education as a means of meeting the crisis.

The second of these solutions was given rather lengthy treatment in the press. The idea seems to have been to bring the Ilongot region under control of the central government, to promote peace while providing Ilongots with the benefits of schooling and civilization. These proposals often involved plans for changing the landscape in programmatic and costly ways, including the settlement of titles and land rights, the creation of farm and forest preserves, and the construction of numerous roads and schoolhouses. A corollary of this notion of control was the attribution of a peculiar motive to the Ilongots; that they were fighting a grim guerrilla war to defend their territory. As one newsman reported, "Ilongots are determined, even at the expense of their lives, to hold their lands" (*Daily Mirror*, April 19, 1958). This interpretation of the Ilongots, as consisting of bands of terrorists descending on towns in the valleys in a determined, if perhaps doomed, effort to protect their rightful homeland, was curious in light of the fact that to the best of my knowledge the Ilongot raiders never have had what we would call political intentions. The Christian allegation would seem an accurate assessment of the consequences but not of the motives of Ilongot head-taking.

Apparently, even over an extended period of time, little of the baggage of the past is lost. Thus one recent explanation of Ilongot raiding blamed their exotic and savage mating customs. This explanation derived from a tale that circulated widely in the valleys, dating from at least the latter part of the nineteenth century, and perhaps related to the fact that it was unmarried young men who exemplified the grace and agility that was associated with head-taking. One current version of the tale goes roughly as follows: When the firetree blossoms during April, May, and June, the Ilongot mating season is in full swing and unmarried young men are overcome with an urge to go on the warpath in search of Christian heads, either to present to the prospective bride or to her august father.[4] As one reporter phrased the tale: "It is during the summer months when Ilongots observe their mating season. It is part of the Ilongot's marriage ritual to present a Christian head to his prospective bride" (*Chronicle*, June 8, 1963). This version singled out unmarried young men as especially culpable, but presupposed that the entire social order was totally alien and grossly bestial.

The Christian tale was probably fabricated from a partially accurate observation. Broadly, those who are most mobile

[4] One recalls medieval explanations of the Jewish need for the blood of gentiles. Of course, in this case, unlike with the Ilongots, both the practice and the explanation are imaginary.

are most likely to become members of raiding parties. This is taken for granted because it is so much a matter of common sense, for in fact the highly mobile unmarried young men of Ilongot society do mainly constitute the headhunters. Young men of this age may weep with desire in anticipation of taking a head, and Ilongots (not unlike Erik Erikson) generally say that the social persons of youths are not well defined—as their songs express it, they are like fog or the even more distant clouds. Ilongot normative conceptions of the person generally place a high value on a particular kind of youthful style and grace in body movement. Young manhood is a cultural ideal emulated by young and old alike.

But how could a formula for peace be phrased in terms that would be comprehensible to such an alien people? A number were put forward. In 1957, for instance, the Governor of Nueva Vizcaya, perhaps inspired and prompted by the lore of the American frontier, ascended to the hills where he met with "chieftains" from the so-called Maddela and Kasibu tribes and together they "smoked the peace pipe" (*Manila Times*, June 21, 1957).[5] Later, in 1963, amid a great fanfare, with reporters, local dignitaries, and the Commissioner on National Integration all present, an Ilongot-Christian peace treaty was signed and "the signatories sealed their pact by drinking rice wine mixed with blood" (*Philippine Herald*, July 8, 1963). With the return to the ritual of blood brotherhood of the late sixteenth-century, and the somewhat

[5] As Fred Eggan has reminded me, one need not look to dime novels as the sole source of ideas about the American West: many American officials at the turn of the century had known the "wild West" from first-hand experience. For instance, David Prescott Barrows passed through Tucson in 1902 as he traveled from Manila to Washington to recruit ethnographers for the Bureau of Non-Christian Tribes. He described Tucson as "tough" and "wide-open" and he met a man who had been involved in the famous feud between the Earps and Clantons (1962:73). The language of the American "wild West" was probably introduced into the Philippine context through the direct experience of Barrows and others; later manifestations of "peace pipes," "blood brotherhood," and Ilongot "braves," may derive from the prior historical experience in combination with newspapers, movies, and television.

perplexing use of blood by civilized society as a peacemaking medium, this account of a particular frontier and its concomitant rhetoric of the colonizers, ever seeking control and containment, might seem to have come full circle. Yet the pioneering process of colonization is not reversible, and the present-day ritual of blood brotherhood followed in the wake of threatened air raids and the gradual but inexorable incursions of buzz saws and bulldozers.

To recapitulate, my argument has been that two rhetorical devices were central in fabricating the verbal portraits that colonists drew of Ilongot character and culture. First, colonists constructed their characterizations of Ilongots through the mechanism of symbolic inversion (Middleton 1960:236). If, for example, civilized people were said to be sedentary, then Ilongots were to be regarded as nomadic; the civilized thesis generated its savage antithesis. Like ethnocentric and racist perspectives on "the other," the colonists' formula—as symbolically potent as it was distorted—was to take a characteristic regarded as morally ideal in their own society and verbally endow the Ilongots with its opposite. Through a principle of inversion that, following Erikson, might be termed negative identification, members of civilized society found in themselves the sources for particular attributions of Ilongot *acts*, *agents*, and *scenes*. Second, the colonists employed the rhetorical technique of generalization, basing their series of hypothetical deductions on a kernel of truth. The kernel of truth in these characterizations was what Burke (1962) called an act (taking a head); the rhetorical device for making further deductions was through a striving for consistency among certain key ratios, particularly the ratios of act (taking a head) to agent (criminal character), and agent (criminal character) to scene (overgrown habitat, nomadic way of life).

What emerged from my interpretative venture beyond

symbolic inversions, taken pair by pair in isolation as if to be stacked in two columns, was a perception of the transition zone, lying between *act* and *agent*, where the colonists' more or less accurate cultural perceptions were shredded by the intrusive distortions of ideological statements. In so proceeding I followed Geertz (1964) in his proposal for the study of ideologies as cultural systems and attempted a close reading of the meanings embedded in a particular set of ideological texts. In this context, symbolic inversions became more a crucial point of entry than a final resting grounds for my interpretation of the colonists' ideological formations.

The colonists' ideological formations, as is probably clear by now, contrasted with other symbolic processes relating to status inversion within a social hierarchy, particularly those characteristic of festive occasions. In certain festivities, for instance, the slave may play at being the master for a day, and he may look forward to another turn of the annual cycle when once again he temporarily becomes master for a day. Such instances of symbolic inversion, moving to and fro in an indefinitely repeated rhythm, may appear as timeless as the oscillation of a finely crafted pendulum. At the opposite end of the continuum from the more festive symbolic language of the temporary social inversions of class, status, and even sex, the colonists and Ilongots, willy-nilly, were enmeshed in an irreversible historical process. The shape of this progressive historical movement was set during the Spanish era, from the earliest fleeting encounters to the days when the friars remade the landscape with their chapels, towns, and plowed fields. Events continued to develop on a similar course from the time when Americans entered under the secular canopy of their relatively rationalized bureaucracy to the present and ever-increasing incursions of settlers and loggers. At once pushing back the frontier and pulling the Ilongots toward political containment, this lengthy process of transformation constitutes the frame within which the colonists have constructed their symbolic sketches of Ilongot character and culture.

References

Barrows, David P. 1914. "Letter of November 5, 1901, to Gov. Jacob F. Kreps, San Isidro, Nueva Ecija, P.I." In H. Otley Beyer, ed., *The Itneg-Kalinga Peoples*. Vol. 2, paper no. 59. Peabody Museum, Harvard.

———. 1962. "Memoirs of David Prescott Barrows, 1873–1954." Bancroft Library, University of California, Berkeley.

Bellah, Robert N. 1975. *The Broken Covenant: American Civil Religion in Time of Trial*. New York: Seabury.

Blair, E. H., and J. A. Robertson. 1904. *The Philippine Islands, 1493–1898*. Vol. 14. Cleveland: Arthur H. Clark.

Bolton, H. E. 1917. "The Mission as a Frontier Institution in the Spanish-American Colonies." *American Historical Review* 23:42–61.

Burke, Kenneth. 1961a. *Attitudes toward History*. Boston: Beacon.

———. 1961b. *The Rhetoric of Religion*. Boston: Beacon.

———. 1962. *A Grammar of Motives*. Berkeley: University of California Press.

Campa, Fr. Buenaventura. 1891. "Una visita a las rancherías de Ilongotes." *El correo Sino-Anamita* 25:563–646.

Fitzmyer, Joseph A., S.J. 1967. *The Aramaic Inscriptions of Sefire*. Rome: Pontifical Biblical Institute.

Geertz, Clifford. 1964. "Ideology as a Cultural System." In David Apter, ed., *Ideology and Discontent*. New York: Free Press of Glencoe. Pp. 47–56.

Gibson, Charles. 1967. *Spain in America*. New York: Harper Torchbooks.

Hartz, Louis. 1964. *The Founding of New Societies*. New York: Harcourt, Brace and World.

Hobsbawm, Eric. 1965. *Primitive Rebels*. New York: Norton.

———. 1971. *Bandits*. New York: Dell.

Leach, Edmund. 1964. "Anthropological Aspects of Language: Animal Categories and Verbal Abuse." In Eric H. Lenneberg, ed., *New Directions in the Study of Language*. Cambridge: M.I.T. Press. Pp. 23–63.

Malumbres, Julian, O.P. 1919. *Historia de Nueva Vizcaya y Provincia Montañosa*. Manila: Imprenta del Colegio de Santo Tomás.

Middleton, John. 1960. *Lugbara Religion*. London: Oxford University Press.

Miller, Merton L. 1914. "Letter of June 25, 1906, to Dean C. Worcester, Secretary of the Interior." In H. Otley Beyer, ed., *The Itneg-Kalinga Peoples*. Vol. 2, paper no. 60. Peabody Museum, Harvard.

Rosaldo, Michelle Z. 1972. "Metaphor and Folk Classification." *Southwestern Journal of Anthropology* 28:83–99.

——. 1973. "I Have Nothing to Hide: The Language of Ilongot Oratory." *Language in Society* 2:193–223.

Rosaldo, Michelle Z., and Jane Monnig Atkinson. 1975. "Man the Hunter and Woman: Metaphors for the Sexes in Ilongot Magical Spells." In Roy Willis, ed., *The Interpretation of Symbolism*. London: Malaby. Pp. 43–75.

Rosaldo, Renato I., Jr. 1970. "Ilongot Kin Terms: A Bilateral System of Northern Luzon, Philippines." In *Proceedings of VIIIth International Congress of Anthropological and Ethnological Sciences, 1968*. Tokyo: Science Council of Japan. Pp. 81–84.

——. 1975. "Where Precision Lies: 'The Hill People Once Lived On a Hill.' " In Roy Willis, ed., *The Interpretation of Symbolism*. London: Malaby. Pp. 1–22.

——. 1976. "The Story of Tukbaw: 'They Listen as He Orates.' " In Frank E. Reynolds and Donald Capps, eds., *The Biographical Process: Studies in the History and Psychology of Religion*. The Hague: Mouton. Pp. 121–151.

Santos, Lope K. 1919. "Memorandum especial sobre los Ilongotes de Nueva Vizcaya." Typescript. National Library, Filipiniana Division, Manila.

Scott, William Henry. 1974. *The Discovery of the Igorots: Spanish Contacts with the Pagans of Northern Luzon*. Quezon City, Philippines: New Day.

Taylor, George Rogers. 1956. *The Turner Thesis concerning the Role of the Frontier in American History*. Boston: Heath.

Turnbull, Wilfrid. 1909. "Report of an Inspection Trip through the Ilongot Rancherias and Country on and near the Cagayan River." Typescript. Philippine Studies Library, Department of Anthropology, University of Chicago.

——. 1929. "Among the Ilongots Twenty Years Ago." *Philippine Magazine* 26:262–263, 307–310, 337–338, 374–379, 416–417, 460–470.

Worcester, Dean C. 1913. "The Non-Christian Peoples of the Philippine Islands, with an Account of What Has Been Done for Them under American Rule." *National Geographic* 24:1157–1256.

Wyman, Walker, and Clifton B. Kroeber. 1965. *The Frontier in Perspective*. Madison: University of Wisconsin Press.

CHAPTER 10

Deviance as Success: The Double Inversion of Stigmatized Roles

BRUCE JACKSON

Il boit, mais il était fait pour l'opium: on se trompe aussi de vice; beaucoup d'hommes ne recontrent pas celui qui les sauverait. Dommage, car il est loin d'être sans valeur.

André Malraux, *La condition humaine*

This article in part derives from a conversation I had one afternoon several years ago with a person I thought was an habitual burglar.[1] We had been talking about his criminal career and I realized early in the conversation that his working criminal career was very short, but his convict career was depressingly long, that he evinced far more animation when talking about his convict role than when talking about his criminal role, and that he perceived his criminal acts as discrete and his convict role as continuous, even though the latter was gapped temporally (he'd stayed out several years a couple of times) and geographically (he'd done time in California, Texas, Kansas, and other states). The last time he'd been free he stole a bright red jeep, held up a finance company with the jeep double-parked directly in front of the finance company's large and clear plate-glass window, then drove two blocks away where he again double-parked, this time in front of a bar. The robber then went inside and set the cashbox and his pistol on the bar and ordered drinks for the house. He was arrested a few minutes later. When he told me the story he cursed his luck and omitted most of the

---

[1] An expanded version of this article, with comments by Theodore Mills and Howard S. Becker, forms part of a larger discussion of violence and deviance in my forthcoming book, *Killing Order: The Legitimization of Extreme Behavior* (McGraw-Hill).

details. Others later filled me in on the twice double-parked jeep and the drinks-for-the-house gambit; my friend simply said he'd had the misfortune to be picked up right after a clever daylight robbery.

But he was always very good at escaping from prison: he'd escaped from two state prisons in California, one federal institution, and several others. Shortly after the last time I saw him he escaped from a Texas prison, stole a car, and took off along the nearby interstate highway and headed toward Dallas—a couple of hundred miles north. The only problem was, the car he stole was a state car, and all Texas state cars—as he must have known—have large block numbers painted on their roofs. The state police helicopters spotted him in minutes.

It was clear to me—and to him too—that he was basically happy as a convict, though he hated prison, and basically unhappy in the free world, though he very much liked its options. He didn't keep coming back to prison because he couldn't keep from stealing, but rather because he didn't know how to live anyplace else.

Sometime later, when I was doing a study of prison sex roles, I recognized a similar pattern with a number of informants. It seemed clear that many of those occupying the role of "punk" (insertee, in present sociological jargon)[2] *needed* the prison community. Their words didn't say that directly, and most wouldn't agree to it if asked, but many got themselves into prison for the most trivial reasons, and many violated parole in the most absurd ways. The same applied, though to a far less significant extent, to some of the men occupying the "stud" (insertor) role. The only sex role actors who seemed consistently outside this pattern were those who had been acting-out homosexuals in the outside world, "free-world queens" in the prison argot.

[2] See the interviews about, and my comments on, prison sex in Jackson 1972:353–412.

The queens seemed to hate prison, but they managed and coped. According to other inmates, prison was for them "the promised land," for they were needed there in ways they were not needed outside, and, in the prison value system, it was common to hear them described with some respect by men who in the free world held homosexuals in contempt. The logic was, "At least they're man enough to admit what they are." The punks were lowest on the status ladder, and the other inmates generally assumed that the punks allowed themselves to be used sexually because they were "weak," because they wanted protection or extra food. Most studs maintained that they were homosexual in prison only because of the absence of women, that they used punks in preference to masturbation. The particularly aggressive studs were often described by other inmates as "punks out for revenge," in other words, individuals who presumably had been punks in reformatories and were now getting even. In conversation, most of the punks and studs said they filled those roles only because they "had to." Almost none admitted homosexual behavior in the free world—the queens did that, not they— and only a few admitted knowing any homosexuals outside of prison.

I finally understood this: many—not all, but many—of those argot-role actors, especially punks and some of the studs, would very much like to be homosexual outside, but they just *didn't know how*. Because of their ethnic or geocultural backgrounds or situations, they never learned—and they were now too old to learn—how to be competent homosexuals. They could not ever admit that to themselves, surely; if one suggested it to them, one risked violence. So they were discharged from the institutions, went back to "normal" but transitory and apparently unsatisfactory relationships with women (the unsatisfactory part of the relationships rarely, in their accounts, had to do with specifically sexual matters; rather they had to do with problems the women presented—dishonesty, adultery, and so on), lived a "normal" life, then were busted again, and again sent back to prison, where they immediately assumed the sex roles they had occupied previously.

For them—and I must stress they comprise only some of the argot-role actors—prison was the only place they had a moral structure that permitted them to be acting-out homosexuals, a place where there was a grand body of folk culture that legitimized their behavior. There was some stigma, but it was quite another kind: for the social agencies dealing with these men, the problem was criminal—theft, burglary, forgery, and the like. But in fact these individuals used the criminal behavior only as a vehicle for admission to a place where their real deviance could for them be legitimately enacted.

The prison dealt with them in terms of the wrong stigma, which is why they kept coming back and back again. The only way their cycle might have been stopped would have been for them to be located on a comfortable heterosexual track or for them to be taught how to be competent homosexuals. For all of them, these ambiguous prison sex-role actors, the stigma of convict was far less troublesome than the problem of homosexuality, and by adopting the convict stigma they were enabled to act out the homosexual roles without any of the attendant stigma they would have suffered (and self-applied) in the free world. Even the punks, so much disrespected and disliked in prison, had clear and accepted roles in prison. These were roles the actors could often claim were thrust upon them—either by necessity or by force—rather than being roles of choice.

The problem with a stigma, as Erving Goffman several times points out in his book on the subject (1963), is that it becomes a focus for identity; most of the other characteristics of the individual are subsumed to it. A dwarf who is a skilled brain surgeon and concert pianist is certain to be forever regarded as a dwarf who happens to have those skills, not as a surgeon or pianist who happens to be notably smaller than everyone else. A deviance stigma produces what Everett C. Hughes calls a "master status" (1945), a status that overrrides all others and provides a continuing focus for identification, however unfair or inappropriate.

But that focus may, and often does, work in just the opposite direction: those who, for whatever reason, *need* such a status, may take it on more or less voluntarily, more or less consciously, and they may rest in it. The stigma may block perception of another stigma far more awful or terrifying or difficult to negotiate (in which case the assumption works exactly as "screen memories"), but it is the stigmatized and deviant role that is in fact selected and enacted and informed.

For Goffman, it is the stigma that spoils identity (p. 4), and his subtitle—*Notes on the Management of Spoiled Identity*—properly indicates his concern with how people negotiate the stigma itself. He describes how it is perceived by "normals" and how the stigmatized persons negotiate their own and others' perception of the stigma. My concern here is quite the opposite: I am interested in persons who *adopt* a stigmatized role as an accommodation, and I am suggesting that many individuals label *themselves* deviants and that the affirmation of stigma is what ratifies identity in a manageable way.

I have for some time been concerned with techniques used to rationalize or legitimize extraordinary violence, such as using nonhuman names for the "enemy" (gook, slope, kike, nigger, savage, and so forth), thereby removing him from the area of moral concern; or by ritualizing the event (by having a priest be an integral actor in criminal execution, for example), thereby removing the event from the area of moral responsibility; or by chemically altering one's own state (by excessive consumption of alcohol before beating up one's children, for example), thereby removing oneself from moral responsibility.

These legitimizations involve a process of making a non-person of the one who is to be harmed or of making a non-person of the one doing the harm ("I was crazy . . ." "I was drunk . . ." "I was tripping . . ." "The state has determined . . ." "It was only a gook . . ."). This process becomes problematic only when the device of other-making or depersonalization is only partial or fails, and the other is still partially like or among us, in which case the violence becomes something like eating a pet duck—legitimate in theory, but terrifically distasteful.

A similar process goes on (consciously or unconsciously) among many who choose deviant careers. The only difference is, in the deviance situation the person who is made the *other* (what, as my colleague Theodore Mills points out, Melanie Klein calls the "not-me") is oneself, and that otherness is selected because it offers a kind of identity not available in the boundaries of "straight" or "square" society. Many modes of deviance—which to us in the square world almost always represent some significant failure of energy, will, character, or morality—actually represent a careful management of strengths, and the process is not at all unlike the normal process of occupational selection. People select the deviance that is most appropriate to them, or at least try to.

The quotation from *La condition humaine* with which I prefaced this paper expresses that notion most concisely. Old Gisors, the retired sociology professor, is talking with his son, Kyo, about Baron de Clappique, the frenetic hustler who has just left the room. Gisors, himself an opium addict, discusses Clappique's alcoholism and suggests that it's the wrong vice, that Clappique would suffer far less if he found one better suited to his needs. Gisors' problem is an inability to act: he is the frozen intellectual, so immobilized by theory that he is capable only of considering options. His opium addiction gives a form or name to his impotence (just as the prison situation gives a form and tolerable name to the role actors I discussed in the first section of this essay), and he ascribes Clappique's constant disequilibrium to the latter's inability to find the drug or vice that would fit his own psychic configuration, that would explain himself to himself.

It is impossible to adopt fully a deviant life-style and identity without also assuming the symbol pattern associated with them. Since both the style and the identity are negatively perceived and frequently negatively sanctioned by the larger society, we have a symbolic inversion given full articulation: instead of taking on the role of transvestite or the mode of amorality only for a transient ceremony—as described in several other papers in this volume—the individual adopts it as a basic life-style, for only with that life-style can some degree of comfort be achieved or can suffering be substantially reduced, and only with exclusion or exile from the larger society may the perceived disorder be made orderly.

Howard S. Becker has written about deviance as more a function of a labeling process than an inherent quality of an actor—the deviant person is one who has been labeled as such by others. This identification, Becker writes, engenders a master status:

The question is raised: "What kind of person would break such an important rule?" And the answer is given: "One who is different from the rest of us, who cannot or will not act as a moral human being and therefore might break other important rules." The deviant identification becomes the controlling one.

Treating a person as though he were generally rather than specifically deviant produces a self-fulfilling prophecy. It sets in motion several mechanisms which conspire to shape the person in the image people have of him. In the first place, one tends to be cut off, after being identified as deviant, from participation in more conventional groups, even though the specific consequences of the particular deviant activity might never of themselves have caused the isolation had there not also been the public knowledge and reaction to it. [1963:33–34]

But once the labeling process occurs with any frequency, the deviance acquires a public form, and specific behavior is deviant whether or not one goes through a formal labeling process. People usually know when they are acting in those behaviors, just as they know when they are acting in most other roles that have acquired a public label and a public definition. Some behaviors are of course ambiguous and some are of course not recognized as such by the actor, but even if he has never been arrested, a middle-aged man who "hustles" young men in public restrooms knows he is deviant, as does a young man who sticks a needle in his arm four times a day and pumps heroin into his veins.

The form is there and it has a name. As much as a social agency can affix it to any actor or any agent, any actor or any agent has the option of affixing it to himself. If society doesn't confer the label, an individual can assume it. Becker notes that the group has an identity and offers worked-out justifications for the deviant behavior, which is why deviant individuals may join such groups (p. 38). But conversely, what is important for us is that the group offers a ready-made identity that one can assume totally.

The inversion here is twofold: one part is the assumption of the deviant role, and the other has to do with the role actor's relation to it. We usually assume that the latter is negative and loathsome, but frequently exactly the opposite is the case. What seems to be happening is that *the deviance makes tolerable, or explains acceptably, something awful for the actor.* That process of making tolerable or explaining acceptably may simply consist of giving a name to what was nameless or a form to what seemed formless. Heroin becomes the reason, speed becomes the reason, the prison situation is the reason. . . . But since even masochists seek comfort, the problem is finding what is most comfortable; much deviance selection is in fact comfort-seeking behavior.

A critical step is the enunciation and annunciation of

stigma: "I am this other." This is not the same as Melanie Klein's dichotomized "me" and "not-me," for the statement "I am this other" is one of identification of the self when no such identification was previously possible or adequate, not a setting off of someone else or something else. The enunciation and annunciation "normalize" the actor's otherness, make him a member of a stigmatized group, hence someone now *based*, rather than a problematic member of a larger society in which he is a stigmatized other (perhaps secretly stigmatized, but that is no less real for anyone who perceives his own stigma—*he* knows it is there). There is a shift from a shame-guilt status in which the individual must cope with the consequences of his "problem," to an occupational status in which the individual copes with the needs of his stigma, and identifies and is concerned with problem-solving rather than truth-hiding.

Once inside the deviant structure, as many observers have pointed out, one is deviant only in regard to normals (who are now "those squares" or some equivalent); that is perhaps only partial comfort, but it is comfort nevertheless. That one is a convict causes no shame within the prison community (though other things may); it is only outside, with squares, that the historical role may become a problem. Many exconvicts without firm social or family supports seek out other exconvicts for association, not because they have something in common to "talk about," but rather because the things that are present but *unspoken* with squares are nonexistent with other exconvicts.

There are two discrete aspects to this process:

1) Some selection of deviant community membership is deliberate and serves to focus a constellation of personality problems that previously lacked focus. The stigma attendant upon deviant-group membership is less onerous than were the constellation of problems, and in fact that stigma seems to explain if not actually legitimize them.

2) Some selection of deviant community membership functions exactly as the screen memory functions in excluding from consciousness memory of an event too painful to negotiate directly. Just as the victim of an awful assault may remember only the exact and trivial details of an insignificant event that occurred some while before it all happened, the deviant in this mode says, "*This* is my problem," and for him, acting in terms of that assertion is far less anguishing than confronting another alignment or constellation with identical contributing elements. He selects the most comfortable master status: "dope fiend" is more comfortable than "useless" or "impotent"; "speed freak" is more comfortable than "purposeless"; "convict" is more comfortable than "catamite." The first status in each of these sets is socialized, which means it has the social and moral support that comes with membership in any group, the legitimizing power of culture; the latter status of each pair is solitary and isolated from the general community. Part of the function of asserting a deviant role is disasserting other roles: "I am this thing, so I am not that other one." All sorts of translations are possible, depending on what is selected, and all sorts of roles are excluded: "I've never hurt a woman, child, cripple; I've never shot dope, been a drunk, robbed the blind; I've never snitched on a pal; I've never done it for money . . ."

Becker has adequately described the labeling of actors as deviants, but my concern here is with the individuals whose private situations are such that they select for themselves deviant patterns and communities which name and explain their site and locus. Many actors use nominally negative social slots to maximize their options and reduce suffering in the most fruitful and tolerable ways. Their inversion, as I noted above, is twofold: in the *fact* of being deviant (that is, being in the deviant role rather than no role at all), and in the *selection* of what we usually consider an eschewed role. I think of the following: heroin addicts who lament how dope acquisition takes all their time and how heroin addiction destroys their sexual drive; speedfreaks who complain about not being able to do anything useful because amphetamine lets them do trivial things for hours on end (such as picking the lint out of a rug by hand) as if these things were important; prison catamites who complain about being sexually used and scorned; prison pederasts who complain about prison catamites; prostitutes who hate social sex because their workaday trade poisons their attitude toward heterosexual intercourse.

After a lot of time doing fieldwork I learned what most people in the Life knew all along: many of those junkies had a lousy sex life before heroin or at least had consistently unsatisfactory relationships with the people with whom they had those sexual affairs; that a lot of the speed freaks were barely functional anyway and began taking speed in the hope of functioning better; that a lot of prison catamites and pederasts seemed to work very hard getting back into prison; that a lot of the prostitutes hated intercourse even when it was done for free and with a friend.

Not all; none of this applied to all. Not all; but enough so that I wondered about people who adopt a form of deviance that makes tolerable or explains acceptably something awful in themselves. I described above the situation of convicts who would like to be homosexual in the free world but simply do not know how, and who therefore get themselves thrown into prison again and again. There are amphetamine addicts who use the great busywork drug as a rationale for dysfunction. There are alcoholics who thus acquire a vehicle for the rage they must otherwise suppress and with which they cannot quite live. And there are addicts who find addiction less disturbing than the psychosexual hang-ups that have no explanation without dope, and who find the pattern of drug acquisition and use so full of success that it matches nothing in a previous career of failure.

John William Rawlin, of the Delinquency Study Center of Southern Illinois University, reported to me an addiction pattern in the St. Louis area in the mid-1960s that I found puzzling for some time. According to Rawlin, heroin became very hard to get at that time. The normal traffic pattern of New York to Chicago to St. Louis produced a very dilute product anyway, and when the New York concentrations in that period decreased, the quality of dope declined all along the market route. St. Louis junkies were mostly buying nickel bags of mannite, milk sugar, or hydroquinone. One would expect they would either abandon their habits (since pharmacologically most of them were nearly clean anyway, however much of the supposed junk they injected) or start robbing drugstores. Neither happened. Instead, many of the former heroin addicts began shooting methamphetamine hydrocholoride (which they called "splash" and "spliven"; elsewhere it is called "crystal"). St. Louis narcotics squad detectives told me Rawlin was correct, and said they didn't understand it at all. The pharmacological effects of opiates and amphetamines are polar: opiates numb, close, shrink; amphetamines sharpen senses, stimulate movement, make time comfortable. Opiates produce quietude, amphetamines produce busyness. Opiate overdose produces coma, amphetamine overdose produces toxic psychosis that often manifests itself in severe paranoia and violence.

But the St. Louis junkies didn't seem to care: they went to the same shooting galleries to shoot up, scored from the same connections, and bought the magic white powder (methamphetamine instead of heroin) in the same little glassine envelopes they knew so well. The addicts maintained the heroin subculture on a methamphetamine metabolism; obviously the subculture had had powerful and spectacular magic working for it.

From the security and legitimacy of the square world, we perceive the descent into junk, into heroin addiction, as a

shutting off; the decision to nod in the corner, as the penultimate cop-out (the ultimate is suicide, and much addiction is
a courting of that). But this is an oversimplification. A junkie
spends only a small portion of his day nodding; most of his
time is spent having little, but significant, successes: he must
hustle money by stealing, by turning tricks, by peddling
something stolen previously, by passing a check, by tapping
a till, etc., and he sometimes must do this under the pressure
of oncoming withdrawal. He must score for some dope,
sometimes with the withdrawal symptoms already manifest-
ing themselves; he must find a dealer, find a safe place for a
transaction, and enact the transaction. He must find a place
to cook up his dope, a place where some other junkie won't
take it away from him and where a passing policeman won't
take him away from it, a place safe enough that he can nod
off—if the dope is decent—for a little while. He must, four
or so hours later, begin the process all over again.

Little successes every day. Dozens of them. Failures are
immediate, success is absolute. Most street junkies have a career of failures—failure in school, in jobs, in marriage. But
junk, however it is regarded by the anti-junk world, is not
simply the ultimate failure. Quite the contrary: it is a contin-
ual reaffirmation of the fact and efficacy of success.

Little wonder then that the St. Louis addicts were unwilling to abandon their world of success, that they were willing
to substitute another chemical even though it was a pharmacological opposite; little wonder that so many junkies are
so hard to cure, that so many spend two to five years in
prison, are released, spend a frustrating week or two on the
streets, and then go find a connection who can make them
smile again.

I wondered about the applicability of all this to the soldier
addicts returning from Vietnam, but recent federal reports
seem to support my theory. Most of these addicts—who
were getting a grade of dope of better quality than any

United States mainland addicts except physicians—kicked the habit on their own, most of them very soon after their return to the U.S.[3] If chemical effects were the dominant mechanism of opiate addiction, this group should have been the most difficult to cure. The apparent ease with which they seem to have kicked indicates the relative insignificance of chemical dependence outside a social situation that makes the chemical dependence useful. For these soldiers, kicking heroin, the best heroin around, was easy once they were out of the war situation. The government claims that only about 3000 serious addicts remain of the Vietnam group; even if this is off by a factor of three, the abandonment is extraordinary and can be explained only by a lack of subcultural supports and a change in intrapersonal needs.

I am not attempting here an ontogenetic explanation of deviance or deviation. This essay does not try to establish why a certain person should become deviant in the first place, nor does it try to describe the personal or social pathologies operating. One of my concerns, however, is to view deviance in a manner other than the traditional pathological model. My focus is on adaptive behavior: given a set of circumstances, what might an individual do with them? My essay picks up the scenario of the role actor *after* he is fully developed as a character and at the point where he is seeking or has already discovered the proper play to act within.

[3] This pattern was reported to me by T. D. Hutto, former Arkansas Commissioner of Corrections. I think it deserves serious study because it is the first time since the passage of the Harrison Act over fifty years ago that a large addict population has given up drugs because of a simple change in situation. Back in 1916, all those "old lady addicts" the government worried about so much quietly gave up their laudanum compounds; they never did go howling through the streets in search of a fix. That the New York heroin was much weaker than the Vietnamese heroin isn't enough to explain the mass abandonment of addiction: there are a lot of drugstores and doctor's offices. Since the majority of line infantrymen were from the same socioeconomic groups as the majority of stateside addicts, the abandonment is even more significant.

When I use the words "choice" and "choose" I don't always mean that the individual sat down and rationally selected a pattern of action. I use choice in the Sartrean sense: every yes or no, every decision one makes, has a normative component; every decision is itself an act, every act reflects a decision. One is responsible for one's acts if only because one may eventually be called to account for them—for punishment *or* reward. That accounting may be internal or external, but the process is there; it is there even when one escapes it, for we all know when we've gotten away with something. Things matter, acts matter, decisions matter. The sum of one's choices, the sum of one's acts, define position, role, pattern, locus. These little choices generate larger ones, those smaller resolutions produce larger definitions.

When I say that some deviants select the form and style and scenario most suited to them, the one most likely to permit some success or shield some intolerable perception or pain or relieve some general suffering, I don't mean to imply that they're happy about it. Some may be, but many are not. I don't know many really happy heroin addicts; after a long hook the drug gives little pleasure and the work is very hard. But given their situation in life at that point, it may be that addiction offers less unpleasantness than any other options open, for the forces working for it are so strong that ignoring them will give more pain than acquiescing. That applies equally to job selection in the square world, where the job for which one is most suited by temperament may not be the job for which one is most suited by training, and it often happens that at a particular time some compromise is necessary to find work at all; one may not be particularly happy in the work, but one is less unhappy than one might be doing something else, or doing nothing at all. Few persons are fortunate enough to have temperament and training coincide perfectly with general opportunity; the question is how satisfactory a compromise one can manage and what the ultimate costs of that compromise are.

We usually make certain assumptions about those we label as deviant. One is that they act out of weakness, in distinction from the successful people of the world, who act out of strength. They are what they are because they failed into it; the successful—us—are what they are because they've worked to get there, be there, live there.

But is the process really so different? In a way, many of those deviants also act out of strength: they select, from the range of behaviors and roles apparently open to them, a set they can do. And they don't kill themselves. The savagery with which they sometimes pursue those behaviors and roles reveals a ragged resistance that suggests an irreducible pride of self, sense of self, demand to live.

"Healthy" people act as much from their weakness as their strength—it's only that they find the appropriate place to locate that weakness, and place it so it doesn't appear as weakness at all (and we should regard this notion of "weakness" as an illegitimate category for discussing behavior—we should talk only of appropriate and inappropriate, adequate and inadequate, successful and unsuccessful). Ira Cohen says, "You take somebody who's compulsive and suspicious and he's a meticulous good researcher. Or take somebody who's narcissistic enough and he's a good stand-up comedian—*if* he's narcissistic enough. If he isn't, he gets in trouble—like Lenny Bruce."[4]

The losers of this world, those we label as losers, we say have chosen out of weakness: we see their choices as reflecting inadequacy or impotence or inability to achieve. And we like to think that we, on the other hand, choose out of freedom and from vast possibility, that our choice is out of

---

[4] In conversation.

strength rather than weakness. The difference between them and us has to be very great, we need that difference and so many of our labels depend on it: sanity, socialization, success. We claim lucidity, and we need to deny it to them. But the process of occupation selection is in fact exactly the same.

Order, we know well enough, always seems preferable to chaos. That is because within order, however uncomfortable one's position, one at least knows what the position is, while chaos, by definition, admits of no easy or constant definitions about anything. The labels convict, addict, homosexual, alcoholic all have attendant stigma, but the taint is often preferable to the chaotic disorder of a life without the label. Some of those labels define socialized roles, they need complex cooperation of others, but all of them, once recognized as a role, define a locus.

There is a need for study of what happens in this peculiar world somewhere between game and theater: almost a scripted drama with clear and unambiguous roles, roles that have prerogatives and limits. The advantage of having everyone cast in a role isn't only that the role defines oneself, but that it limits everyone else.

But this isn't a game. The enactment of these patterns lacks one essential element of game or theater: adequate closure. Time runs out on a game, curtains ring down on the players. These outsiders, like us, go on and on. There is no point at which the teams go off to some private place to shed their bulky uniforms and don street clothes, no place where the actors go to wash off the grease and paint, no point at which the audience packs up and goes home. There is no audience for this play, and other than death, the third act rarely seems to end. That's because this is, ultimately, real life, and real life is, however much our simplifying theorizings suggest otherwise, neither game nor play.

I think of William Faulkner talking about Joe Christmas: "He didn't know who he was, and so he was nothing. He deliberately evicted himself from the human race because he didn't know which he was. That was his tragedy, that to me was the tragic, central idea of the story—that he didn't know what he was, and there was no way possible in life for him to find out. Which to me is the most tragic condition a man could find himself in—not to know what he is and to know that he will never know" (Gwynn and Blotner 1959:72). I have suggested in this essay that some of our outsiders have found something that gives their outsiderness a name, and that naming permits them to survive.

References

Becker, Howard S. 1963. *Outsiders: Studies in the Sociology of Deviance*. New York: Free Press.

Goffman, Erving. 1963. *Stigma: Notes on the Management of Spoiled Identity*. Englewood Cliffs, N.J.: Prentice-Hall.

Gwynn, Frederick L., and Joseph L. Blotner, eds. 1959. *Faulkner in the University*. New York: Vintage.

Hughes, Everett C. 1945. "Dilemmas and Contradictions of Status." *American Journal of Sociology* 1:353–359.

Jackson, Bruce. 1972. *In the Life: Versions of the Criminal Experience*. New York: Holt, Rinehart & Winston.

Comments and Conclusions

VICTOR TURNER

It is a striking feature of this collection that most of its articles relate to what might be called the leisure-time or free-time entertainments of nontribal, industrial, or at least post-agrarian societies—festivals; mumming and masking in Canada and the West Indies; literary genres and figures of Western culture; and popular dramas in Indonesia at a time when some of their traditional personae, transvestites, and clowns were coming under attack from modernizing unilinear ideologies. To bring out the contrast between symbolic inversions in the types of societies, on the one hand, with which Rosaldo and Myerhoff deal, and with which I am most familiar—the so-called tribal societies, including agrarian societies already within the scope of historical documentation; and, on the other hand, all the societies influenced by the industrial revolution (including the industrializing Third World societies, and societies which, though they are dominantly agrarian, nevertheless represent the playgrounds or granaries of metropolitan industrial and post-industrial societies), I am going to discuss the concepts *work*, *play*, and *leisure* and how placing a different explanatory stress on each of them can influence symbolic manipulation sets, including the subset of inversions.

Clearly in societies of the band, horde, tribal, and simpler agrarian types of the past, there was a commonly shared cosmological or theological world view, and ritual was at once work and play, or work and play were intricately intercalibrated within ritual. The very term "liturgy" early became established as public service to the gods, and is derived from the Greek *leos* or *laos*, the people, and *ergon*, work. The Tikopia ritual cycle is called by them the "work of the gods." The work of the Cluniac monks was singing the office in choir. I have heard Ndembu tell me that someone "worked" (*ku-zata*) at being a diviner or ritual specialist. The point is that such crucial forms of symbolic action as ritual were participated in by almost everyone and were regarded no less as "work" than hunting, cultivating, maintaining social control, and political action. As Durkheim describes it, "religion is, in these societies, *de la vie sérieuse*," it belongs to the serious sphere of existence. Undoubtedly, there are main episodes where play, games, sport, joking, gambling, and so on penetrate tribal ritual, that is, these episodes have a *ludic* aspect, massively documented in the ethnographic literature. But the fact is that such play is obligatory, part of the serious life, and is directed, like the solemn "work of the gods," to the ultimate goals of promoting fertility, curing illness, averting plague, maintaining or restoring the cosmological order, and transforming people, essentially through initiation, by the orderly and efficacious manipulation of sacred, serious, *work*-manlike symbols. When we examine symbolic inversion in this context we see that it is a process which holds good for the whole community or for those segments of it which perform a representative role in each specific ritual of the total ritual round. Ultimately everyone will have played a symbolically inverted role, sometimes several, as a matter of obligation, not optation or consent. The total social process undergone by the whole community is conceived of as an alternation of dominantly profane and dominantly sacred phases, the latter stressing symbolic and the former technical action—though each informs the other, being polarities of the same life, a point Barbara Myerhoff makes in her essay. In these "tribal" societies, inversion is often a general marker or index of the fact that the mainstream social process has entered a new stage—is now a time of mobilization, not dispersion; of recollection of tradition, not response to practical immediate experience; of shared affects, not divided interests; and so on. This general symbolic inversion may be signaled by such devices as the use of an archaic or a secret language in the ritual setting, the provision of a place apart from profane life at a time when profane tasks are not usually undertaken, and so forth. Religious specialists may wear the garb or mimic the behavior of the opposite sex to demonstrate that the phase through which the whole community is passing, either directly or mediately, is antithetical to that which directly preceded it. Then there are symbolic inversions that apply specifically to the social roles and statuses of those who are the main ritual subjects, the candidates, neophytes, or novices. In African girls' puberty rites there are episodes where novices act and dress as men, partly in mockery, partly in sincere imitation, while in boys' initiations candidates play female roles. Chiefs at installation rites are treated as slaves; in other community-wide planting or first-fruits rituals, statuses are inverted and the low play at being lords. Several articles in this book discuss the way in which rituals and festivals portray symbolically the relationship between order and disorder, cosmos and chaos, what ought to be and what unfortunately often is. Something of this universal human opposition between order and disorder is part of the generic, markerlike symbolic inversions I am pointing to here.

Liminal symbols—symbols found in the second stage of van Gennep's tripartite model: separation, limen or margin, and reincorporation—often possess inversional properties, but more characteristically they display those of abrogation of a ritual subject's sociocultural past. Many rites elaborately construct emblems of cosmological structures that are then solemnly destroyed.

The novice and his or her seclusion-setting are symbolically equated with dying, death, invisibility, darkness, decomposition, eclipse, the dark of the moon, uniformity, humus, compost, and the like, followed by symbols of rebirth, new dawn, vegetative growth, naming anew, new dress, and so on. Liminal symbols tend to be ambiguous, equivocal, neutral, ambisexual rather than be classificatory reversals. This is because liminality is conceived of as a season of silent, secret growth, a mediatory movement between what was and what will be where the social process goes inward and underground for a time that is not profane time.

Qualitatively different from these serious work-play rituals of total societies are the symbolic products, the genres of leisure in the complex, large-scale industrialized societies (Dumazedier 1968). Both radical and conservative social theorists have pointed out that leisure is the artifact of industrialized, rationalized, bureaucratized, large-scale social systems with arbitrary rather than natural delimitation of work—here it is not a case of the ecological cycle determining cultural and especially productive rhythms. On the contrary, work is now organized by industry so as to be separated from "free time," which includes sleeping, resting, and feeding time as well as "leisure" properly so called. When the concept of leisure is found in rural societies it is when agricultural labor is tending toward an industrial mode of organization and rural life is becoming permeated by the urban values of industrialization—this holds true for the Third World today as well as for the rural hinterlands of long-established industrial societies.

Leisure time has two types of freedom, "freedom from" and "freedom to," to advert to Isaiah Berlin's well-known distinction. Leisure represents freedom from a whole mass of institutional obligations prescribed by the basic forms of social, and particularly technological and bureaucratic, organization. It represents for each individual freedom from the forced, chronologically regulated rhythms of factory and office and a chance to recuperate and enjoy natural, biological rhythm again. Leisure is also freedom to enter, even to generate, new symbolic worlds of entertainment, sport, games, and diversions of all kinds. It is freedom to transcend structural limitations, freedom to play with ideas, with fantasies, with words, as in the case of a William Blake or a Samuel Beckett (so brilliantly discussed here by Diane Christian and Dina Sherzer respectively), and with social relationships. Far more than in tribal ritual, the ludic is stressed. In complex societies there are many more options: games of skill, strength, and chance can serve as models for future behavior or represent the symbolic equivalent of work experiences—now viewed as release from work's necessities and as something one chooses to do. Sports like football, games like chess, recreations like mountaineering can be hard and exacting and governed by rules and routines even more stringent than those of the work situation, but, since they are optional, they are part of an individual's freedom, of one's growing self-mastery, and hence are imbued more thoroughly with pleasure than those many types of industrial work in which men are alienated from the fruits and results of their labor. And, as Bruce Jackson suggested, even deviant role-playing in such a society carries this optional sense of play. Leisure can release potentially creative powers, individual or communal, either to criticize or buttress the dominant values of culture. Leisure can make for self-transcendence; it also gives us a vantage point from which to take stock of the conditions of the work-domain, which may seem strangely to resemble a prison.

At this point I can refocus my attempts to extend the van Gennepian concept of liminality from the serious, sacred work context of tribal and early agrarian societies to the symbolic genres such as carnival, festival, folk drama and "high" cultural drama, popular and "serious" literature, the rural foklore of industrial societies, and so on. Several articles in this collection have impressed on me that the real homology between symbolic genres in, on the one hand, archaic or technologically simple societies, and, on the other, industrial and postindustrial societies was not between adult rituals in the former case and leisure-time entertainments and carnivals in the latter. It was between children's games or interludes of masked dancing or entertainment within ritual in "tribal" societies, on the one hand, and adult sports, games, plays, entertainments, and so forth in the leisure of industrial societies.

It is true that I have in *The Ritual Process* (1969) stressed the potentially subversive character of liminality in tribal initiations, when, in the betwixt-and-between states, social-structure categories are forced to relax their grip on thought and behavior, but this potentiality never did have any hope of realization outside a ritual sphere hedged in by strong taboos. However, in complex, industrial societies, characterized by a high degree of social and economic division of labor, the models and paradigms presented in dramas, poems, folk tales, carnivals, literature, and so on do have a chance of influencing those who exercise power over the work structure of society and of modifying that structure (as expressed in Natalie Zemon Davis' paper); they may even revolutionize it, when the originally ludic models are taken up by and help to mobilize the dispossessed and disadvantaged, who, by virtue of their numbers, organization, and motivation, have very real power resources in political arenas.

The inversions characteristic of industrial leisure do not have the comprehensive, pan-societal, obligatory qualities of tribal and agrarian ritual and are not rooted in a commonly shared, relatively systematic, world view. Rather are they piecemeal, sporadic, and concerned with the setting of one segment of society, one product of the division of labor, against another. Furthermore, the inversions respond more sensitively to contemporary circumstances; they emerge from history more than from atemporal structures of society, thought, and belief. Davis' paper shows how male and female transvestism became symbolic indicators of shifts in the power structure, and badges of militancy in peasant and anticolonial struggles.

Nevertheless, the symbolic genres of industrial leisure are analogous, if not homologous, to rituals (particularly their liminal phases) in tribal societies. That is, they are similar in function, if not in structure. They are, to complex, changing, class-stratified, multi-occupational, contract-dominated, technologically sophisticated and dynamic societies, what religious rituals are to simple, slowly changing, clan-, lineage-, or kindred-structured social systems with few specialized occupations—societies that are status-based, technologically stagnant, and vulnerable to climatic changes and natural disasters. In other words, they play with the factors of culture, assemble them in random, grotesque, improbable, surprising combinations, just as tribesmen do when they make masks, disguise as monsters, combine many disparate ritual symbols, or invert or parody profane reality. But they do this in a far more complicated way, multiplying genres of artistic and popular entertainments, and within each allowing authors, dramatists, painters, sculptors, musicians, folksingers, and others lavish scope to generate not only weird forms but also models highly critical of the status quo. Although their style is much more ludic, less culturally constrained and less subordinated to "the ritual process" than in tribal and agrarian societies, it nevertheless very often has a serious intent. Barbara Babcock's paper superbly illustrates much of what I have been saying in the extreme case of the picaro. Again and again our authors in this book show us how these industrial leisure genres, by symbolic inversion and other devices, as Barbara Myerhoff has said, make statements about the *workaday* social order—"to affirm it, attack it, suspend it, redefine it, oppose it, buttress it, emphasize one part of it at the cost of another."

Two papers, those by Roger Abrahams and Richard Bauman on "Ranges of Festival Behavior" and James Peacock on "Symbolic Reversal and Social History," illustrate my argument admirably. The societies described, St. Vincent, West Indies, La Have Islands, Nova Scotia, and the islands of Indonesia (the East Indies), are all within the orbit of complex industrial societies, and the symbolic inversions described— and in the case of Peacock's Javanese, abrogated under modernization pressures making for unilinear developments—do not have the all-encompassing, pan-societal character of inversions occurring in tribal initiations or agrarian-cycle rituals. They are piecemeal and optional. Thus, in the belsnickling of the La Have Islands, only young married men and older boys of the community control the activity; we are not told what percentage of these in a given community take part and how representative they are, though I would guess that they are regarded, in fact, as "voices of the whole people" in this mumming, masking, or costuming situation. But optionality characterizes the the whole belsnickling process. Belsnickles cannot force their way in but must ask to be allowed entrance. Some householders refuse. I cannot imagine a situation in which Ndembu, Luvale, Chokwe, or Luchazi masked dancers from circumcision camps would be refused entry to villages, at the phase in which they emerge from circumcision seclusion camps to dance in villages and threaten women and children. Nor do they ask permission to enter; they storm in! Belsnickles have "to ask for" treats from householders. Ndembu *makishi* demand food and gifts as a right. Optation pervades the one, obligation the other. One is all play and choice, an entertainment; the other is a matter of dread, it is demanding, serious, obligatory (though indeed fear provokes nervous laughter, particularly among the women).

In St. Vincent only certain types of personalities are attracted to the carnival as performers, "the rude and sporty segment of the community," who are rude and sporty whenever they have the opportunity so to be, all the year long, and hence can most aptly personify "disorder" versus "order" at the carnival. Here again, optation is dominant—people do not have to act invertedly; some people, but not all people, choose to act invertedly at carnival, which unlike a tribal ritual can be attended or avoided, performed or merely watched, at will—for it is a genre of leisure enjoyment, not an obligatory ritual, it is play not work.

Abrahams and Bauman tellingly made the point that differences between St. Vincent and La Have have respectively Catholic and Protestant roots: "Whereas carnival [in St. Vincent] gives disorder its own day, and underscores the dynamic balance between order and disorder in the moral universe of the Vincentians, belsnickling [in La Have] acknowledges disorder, but draws upon its energy to underscore the primacy of order and respectability." The Vincentians perform at "the crossroads," the belsnickles "in the house." The former see cosmos and chaos like the wheat and the tares, as being at odds in the public life until Judgment Day; the latter see the possibility of the domestication of chaos within the hearth and breast, in each person's life.

Yet both these mumming and masking situations are probably transitional types between the sacred-work and secular-leisure extremes. St. Vincent has medieval Catholic and African tribal foundations for its carnival, and La Have has the "old time religion" type of Protestantism (though with echoes of Catholic and pre-Christian ritual pasts behind that). In other words, there is still more than a hint of the serious-sacred–pan-communal "work of God" function of symbolic inversion in these maskings, as well as the ludic, optional, piecemeal, leisure-time–genre aspect characteristic of societies after the industrial revolution. Something of the numinous awe and moral power of liturgical action based on cosmological consensus still adheres to these performances. Abrahams and Bauman, however, make a valid point, which firmly places Vincentian carnivals in the modern-leisure genre, when they stress that it is the "bad, unruly, 'macho' type men" who choose to perform carnival inversions indicative of disorder, people who are disorderly in many situations. In tribal ritual, even the normally orderly would be obliged to be disorderly in key rituals, regardless of their temperament; the sphere of the optional is much reduced.

Peacock's paper admirably underlines this issue of cultural dynamics, the change from an order framed, classified, moved, and motivated by rituals based in a coherent cosmology, to a culture that contains the debris of formerly dominant religious and ideological systems, and is itself changing rapidly under the influence and pressure of various Western industrial forces and paradigms, both economic and ideological. He selects the invertive images of clown and transvestite, the one concerned with the vertical problem of high and low status, the other with the horizontal (or perhaps diagonal) one of male and female, to shed light on change. He makes the assumption that behind the complex religious field of Javanese and Bornean culture, which is composed of Hindu, Muslim, and other values and symbols, there is a set of common cosmological principles, one of which is that there is an ultimate balance between sharply classified principles such as male and female, high and low status (as with Yin and Yang in China). All social classification of living humans means existential deprivation for those classified, and the resulting loss and frustration are compensated for by symbols of reversal, such as *ludruk* transvestism and clowning. Such symbols give to those human beings who lose out on the plane of cosmological design, symbolic identifications that subjectively restore to them their lost attributes or advantages. Men who are symbolic women in the ludruk world of leisure-genres compensate men in the audience for the classificatory loss of their own feminine component; people who as clowns put down princes restore to the members of the audience their lost self-respect as occupants of lower-class statuses. There is implicit here a cosmological order of equilibrated forces. As Peacock suggests, in this "classificatory world view, which emphasizes the subsuming of symbols within a frame" that both nourishes and is nourished by symbols of reversal, the invertive clown and transvestite have a function. On the other hand, when Islamic reformists and nationalist (sometimes Marxist) revolutionaries impose their notions of struggle toward a "goal" (a struggle between religions or classes or to produce wealth through work) upon such a cultured milieu, among their targets are the very forms of symbolic inversion that have such a therapeutic and adjustive value in the older world view. The new, modernizing, instrumental world view, as Peacock says, threatens and is threatened by inverted symbols. Such symbols still have the agrarian quality of cyclical, repetitive, ecosystems, the Yin-Yang quality of antithetical seasons and opposite biological sexes, which, once clearly defined, can be clearly reversed to cancel out the sins and errors of men who fail to correspond with the ideal delineations. Kill the inversions and you kill the undesirable world-view axioms that resist what you believe to be progress.

Briefly, "liminality" should be primarily applied only to ritual proper in tribal and agrarian societies or to those special sectors of complex, industrial societies that are still communitarian enough over a long run of time to have or generate true rituals with a *rite de passage* initiation structure. Leemon's densely documented book on fraternity rushing as a *rite de passage* (1972) exemplifies this and so does Partridge's recent study of the urban hippie ghetto (1973). When liminality is applied to cultural phenomena of leisure in industrial or postindustrial societies, we must clearly realize that its use is metaphorical, carried over from its primary sphere to another. As such it might have an exploratory function, but it might block further analysis by confusing quite distinct orders of processes and phenomena. Thus symbolic inversion has different properties and meanings in tribal ritual from those it possesses in the complex, experimental milieu of industrial societies, where it may be found in a wide spectrum of critical, reformist, or subversive forms in many genres, ranging from charivaris and folk dramas to Expressionist art, the underground cinema, picaresque novels, and the de-constructive manipulations of language by Samuel Beckett. Perhaps we could use "liminoid" for the modern symbolic inversions and expressions of disorder, and reserve "liminal" for the ritual, myth-telling contexts of less complex societies.

Symbolic inversions and transformations may possess, in addition to cognitive functions, an existential quality related to what I have called "communitas," and perhaps to Georges Gurvitch's "communion." This is a relation between human individuals outside normative social structure, perhaps sometimes a metasocial relation, but which in any case assumes that human beings are concrete, historical, idiosyncratic individuals, and not in their basic humanity segmented into roles and statuses and divided by particularistic group loyalties. One aspect of symbolic inversion may be to break people out of their culturally defined, even biologically ascribed, roles, by making them play precisely the opposite roles. Psychologists who employ the sociodrama method as a therapeutic technique claim that by assigning to patients the roles of those with whom they are in conflict, a whole conflict-ridden group can reach a deep level of mutual understanding. Perhaps ritual or dramatic symbolic inversion may operate in a similar way, breaking down the barriers of age, sex, status, class, family, clan, and so on to teach the meaning of the generic humanity; so that each person becomes the joker in the pack, the card who can be all cards, the method actor.

Natalie Zemon Davis' paper, "Women on Top: Symbolic Sexual Inversion and Political Disorder in Early Modern Europe," is a brilliant example of how historians and anthropologists are beginning to create a new field, what Evans-Pritchard suggested might be called "anthropological history" or "historical anthropology," the use of anthropologically derived concepts and methods to illuminate historical data and vice versa. Of course, the concept of symbolic inversion cries out for historical treatment—there must be an antecedent "something" to be inverted, a temporal relation. And since cultural symbols imply the crystallization of large-scale processes going on for a long time, historians can tell us much about such processes, including those of inversion. I have seen some of Davis' technical papers and can only wonder at the miraculous way in which she has simplified and compressed her rich and complex data while losing nothing of its significance. She is concerned, as are other contributors, such as Abrahams, Baumann, Peacock, and Kunzle, with the "order-disorder" antithesis and its representation by symbols of inversion. Here the "structurally inferior" sex, woman, becomes a "master-mistress" symbol (to echo James Joyce in the Night Town liminal episode of *Ulysses*) of disorder. Davis is dealing with a period of history that is itself transitional (metaphorically liminal) between agrarian and industrial socioeconomic orders in Europe. Hence she is able to trace a development in the "festive treatment of males and females" of the theme of "topsy-turvy play," putting woman on top, misrule, leveling, and disorder triumphing over hierarchical patriarchal order; she can trace its development from its "function" of "reinforcing everyday order" to a new creative or revolutionary role in nascent industrial society, that of "promoting resistance" to the previously established order. Symbolic femaleness is donned later as a revolutionary mask by men, the Lady Skimmingtons, Molly Maguires, and Madge Wildfires, underdog rebels in drag.

There is another possible aspect: I have suggested in *The Ritual Process* that in male-dominated politico-legal systems, social links through women, and by abstraction, femininity itself, tend to become associated with communitas, as opposed to formal hierarchical structures. Often, when structures begin to break down in periods of major socioeconomic change, communitas emerges from its small enclaves into public space. In male-dominated societies communitas may wear a skirt or appear as nature, Mother Nature, versus culture, Father Culture. This can be further discussed in terms of what I have called the "power of the weak," in its connection with the metaphorically liminal process of revolution. One example, the subject of an interesting article by Eric Wolf (1958), is the Dark Virgin of Guadalupe in Mexico, the miraculous painting at Tepeyac, supposedly conferred on an Aztec commoner by the Virgin Mary ten years after Cortés had conquered his people. From 1531 to 1810 the Virgin's Shrine at Tepeyac was the focus of a cultus that drew on pilgrimage by Indios, Mestizos, European and American Creoles, and Spaniards alike—a symbol of Spanish New Spain. But after Miguel Hidalgo made a banner of Our Lady of Guadalupe the standard of an armed revolt against Spain mainly supported by Indios and Mestizos, the Dark Virgin acquired a more insurgent and indigenously Mexican character, reinforced by the fact that the Spanish viceroy employed as his and the Spaniards' patroness the Virgin of Los Remedios, a small statue reputed to have been brought to Mexico originally by one of the conquistadores. Here the "familiar form" of Guadalupe remained but its meaning had become contrary—the peasants were no longer acquiescent, passive devotees of a cult representing the colony; they were now ardent devotees of a cult connected with insurgent nationalism.

The political focus would become even sharper during the Zapatista revolution, when Don Emiliano's followers wore the Guadalupe icon on their warlike sombreros. Religion, revolution, and nationalism were combined in one multivocal symbol. And we see the connection with Natalie Zemon Davis' insight that in some early modern carnival and charivari contexts women and things feminine can become invertive symbols of criticism and revolt. Just as St. Margaret rides on top of a male dragon in Bruegel, so does Our Lady of Guadalupe, a young Indian virgin, dominate successive systems of masculine political control. It was the War of Independence, no doubt, which changed the meaning of Guadalupe, but Hidalgo's sudden inspiration of snatching her banner from a rural church at the beginning of his rampage may have been a deep response to pre-existing changes in Mexican attitudes to the symbol. In any case, the creative liminality of the revolutionary "moment of madness" (as my political scientist colleague Ari Zolberg calls this kind of phenomenon in ironic admiration) made Guadalupe a true symbol of insurgent indigenousness, Creole as much as Indian and Mestizo.

Barbara Myerhoff's paper, "Return to Wirikuta," is a beautiful exposition of liminality (in its primary sense) in a tribal religion, where the peyote pilgrimage is part of the "work of the gods." Here the liminal world of Wirikuta is indeed an elaborate construct of reversals, inversions, and opposites of profane reality, serving the four purposes of separation, transformation, concretization, and the invocation of continuity through emphasis on opposition. Words and nonverbal symbols alike cannot communicate the fathomless lucidity of peyote-generated insight. All one can do is to invert all that has been classified or can be classified and laugh, as gods, at the folly of mortals.

Myerhoff's paper dwells on the atemporal, or rather, the

illud tempus, the creative time of beginnings, after which "things fall apart." This is apparently, but only apparently, in contrast to Davis' injunction to anthropologists "to examine symbolic inversion which is not limited only to the bounds of ritual time and space, and to consider its repercussions over a long period of time." In point of fact, as Myerhoff makes clear, the Huichol know a good deal about modern industrial Mexico, whose cities they visit to sell their glowing, symbolic, wool-and-cotton "God eyes" woven under the influence of peyote. But as their absorption of "campers," "Los Angeles," and so on into their "reversed speech" at Wirikuta exemplifies, they transform history into timelessness. They are one of the consciously and defensively autochthonous groups, like the Karamojong of Uganda, who see "civilization" and opt for their own traditional culture. But this very act of opting out is part of the history of an industrializing society. Note too the curious convergence with modern American rural communards, who, like the Huichol, reject the modern industrial social system, but unlike them, have an ancient literate culture to fall back on which is already full of liminal inversions—perhaps the Huichols' encounter with the Spaniards was the first model for their later attitudes toward all strangers. One wonders, though, whether their ritual life, if it continues, may not become very rigid as a result of consciously opposing it to the modern world. People can get locked in inversion and fail to get out again.

Renato Rosaldo's paper, "The Rhetoric of Control," deals with symbolic inversion at the level of ethnic stereotypes. It is John Middleton's "Myth and the Field of Social Relations" (ch. 5, sec. 1, of *Lugbara Religion*) in reverse. Among the Lugbara, a conquered colonial people, there is a system of categories of social space and time which places social beings, that is, decent Lugbara, in the center, beings with both social and inverted attributes further away in space and time, and "inverted beings" beyond the horizon and beyond social relations. Sorcerers fall in the middle category, and have both social and inverted attributes. The first Europeans fell, along with incestuous cannibals and other mythical beasts, into the category of inverted beings, and were regarded as asocial and amoral. When the first district commissioner arrived, he fell, along with Lugbara sorcerers, into the middle category! In the Lugbara case, inverted beings are associated with myth, social beings with genealogies and history.

In Rosaldo's paper, the Ilongot, an unconquered people, are seen by the colonizing agents rather as the Europeans were seen by the Lugbara—as asocial, amoral, and outside the system of political authority. They are classified as mythical inverted beings: the Ilongot is "an unredeemed criminal, an enemy of his peers and destructive of the fabric of society: he robs without scruples; he murders at will whenever he wishes," etc.

It is remarkable that, by Rosaldo's account, many Ilongot remain fairly independent, as they have done for centuries, during which the classification of them as "alien" and "grossly bestial" has prevailed. Today, of course, the "buzz saws and bulldozers" may finally reduce them to tamed helots, but what is interesting to me is that "the representatives of Western civilization" made no really serious attempt to subdue them completely. It may be that classificatory systems have their own compulsive logic—someone, somewhere, has to occupy the category of inverted beings. For Turnbull it seems to be the Ik; for Uganda governments, both white and black, it has for long been the Karamojong, though there is some ambivalence here—the Karamojong, like the Suk and the Masai, are at the same time regarded as "splendid savages," "nature's gentlemen." This corresponds to the ambiguity of ordered, cultural man's attitude to disorder and nature—which may either be seen as pure and pristine, a source of truth, "oh let it be left, long live the wild and the wilderness yet," or as a rank chaos continually threatening tidy categories, a source of pollution and danger.

I do detect a note of the "noble savage" view in the press reports Rosaldo cites about the governor of Nueva Vizcaya "smoking the peace pipe" with Maddela and Kasibu "chieftains," and Ilongots and Christians sealing a peace treaty by drinking rice wine mixed with blood. Shades, indeed, of the Old West! I would imagine, too, that it might have been to the Ilongots' advantage to perform occasional acts to maintain the colonizers' stereotype of them as "inverted" beings, "wild savages." That way, they could have slowed down the process which would reclassify them as peons by reinforcing the romantic need for inverted beings beyond the horizon, be they gods, ghosts, devils, or Dawn Beings.

The general theory of symbolic inversion can be further exemplified by the work done by Sutton-Smith (1972, 1975), in a fascinating study of children's play "viewed as a two-fold adaptive process having to do with the maintenance of personal equilibrium and the generation of novelty." In discussing children's games he analyzes "their opposing poles of order (imitation, ritual, games, contests) and disorder (mimicry, vertigo, steadfastness). The orderly pole always exists in antithesis to some disequilibrating force of the natural or cultural type or some internal psychological disorder. The play activity is an attempt to bring order out of that other chaos, or other disequilibration. However, even the order in these games often breaks down into disorder, and that inadvertence may sometimes itself give rise to enjoyment. [And here he gives as example the well-known European game of ring-a-ring-a-roses.] At the other end of the dimension, it is disorder itself which is directly enjoyed, and yet paradoxically organized to prolong that possibility" (1972:9).

Much of what he has to say about play is directly applicable to the study of symbolic genres in the leisure culture of industrial societies, notably, the notion that "taking power over circumstances (in play) also functions on behalf of the generation of variability." In the metaphorical liminality of art, literature, drama, and festival, all kinds of variations on normative themes are devised, some of them stressing invertive symbolism and reversed behavior. Sutton-Smith borrows a term from me, "anti-structure," and applies it to a number of play phenomena with penetrating effect: "The normative structure [and I would add the "work" dimension of organized society] represents the working equilibrium, the anti-structure represents the latent system of potential alternatives from which novelty will arise when contingencies in the normative system require it. We might more correctly call this second system the *proto-structural* system because it is the precursor of innovative normative forms. It is the source of new culture" (1972:18–19).

I suggest that the term "metastructural" might be applied here also, for such a system develops a language for talking about normative structures. One can see, on the analogy of Gödel's theorem, an infinite regress of liminal situations, each of which devises a metastructural way of "establishing" the rules of its predecessor, similar to the infinite regress of paradox discussed by Babcock in the Introduction.

Sutton-Smith concludes that "we may be disorderly in games [and I would add in rituals, charivaris, and dramas] either because we have an overdose of order *or* because we have something to *learn* through being disorderly" (1972:21). This fits in well with what I said about the difference between inversion in tribal or agrarian rituals, which are regarded as work and which are binding and tend to be stereotyped, and inversion in the leisure time, games, plays, and literatures of complex industrial societies, which greedily produce and store variant models for thought and behavior, for use in the endless variety of historical circumstances. I do not have a static, conservative view of anti-structure, liminality, and the liminoid, nor do I consider them auxiliary functions of the larger structure. In my earlier essay "Betwixt and Between" (1964), in several passages in *The Ritual Process* (1969), and in my book *Dramas, Fields, and Metaphors* (1974), I stress the innovative potentials of all "liminal" or "liminoid" situations. For example, in chapter 6 of *Dramas, Fields, and Metaphors*, originally presented in 1967 at Dartmouth College as a paper for a conference on myth and ritual convoked by James Fernandez and Hans Penner, I wrote: "It is the analysis of culture into factors and their free recombination in any and every possible pattern, however weird, that is most characteristic of liminality, viewed cross-culturally, rather than the establishment of implicit syntax-like rules" (as a colleague argued) or the development of an "internal structure of logical relations of opposition and mediation" (1974:255). The limitation of possible combinations of factors by convention would indicate to me the growing intrusion of structure (that is, normative structure) into this potentially free and experimental region of culture.

References

Dumazedier, Joffre. 1968. "Leisure." In *International Encyclopedia of the Social Sciences*.

Leemon, Thomas A. 1972. *The Rites of Passage in a Student Culture*. New York: Teachers College Press.

Middleton, John. 1960. *Lugbara Religion*. London: Oxford University Press.

Partridge, William L. 1973. *The Hippie Ghetto*. New York: Holt, Rinehart & Winston.

Sutton-Smith, Brian. 1972. "Games of Order and Disorder." Paper presented to Symposium on Forms of Symbolic Inversion, American Anthropological Association, Toronto.

———. 1975. "Play as Variability Training or the Useless Made Useful." *School Review* 83:197–214.

Turner, Victor. 1964. "Betwixt and Between." *Proceedings of the American*

Ethnographic Society, ed. June Helm. Seattle: University of Washington Press.

———. 1969. *The Ritual Process.* Chicago: Aldine.

———. 1974. *Dramas, Fields, and Metaphors.* Ithaca: Cornell University Press.

Wolf, Eric R. 1958. "The Virgin of Guadalupe: Mexican National Symbol." *Journal of American Folklore* 71:34–39.

Index

Library of Congress Cataloging in Publication Data
(For library cataloging purposes only)

Forms of Symbolic Inversion Symposium, Toronto, 1972.
  The reversible world.

  (Symbol, myth, and ritual series)
  Symposium held at the 1972 meetings of the American
Anthropological Association.
  Includes bibliographies and index.
    1. Symbolic   inversion—Congresses.   2. Symbolism   in   literature—Con-
gresses.   3. Ethnology—Congresses.   I. Babcock, Barbara A., 1943–   II. Amer-
ican Anthropological Association.   III. Title.
  GN462.5.F67   1972   301.2'1   77-3113
  ISBN 0-8014-1112-2